FROM SELF-CARE TO WE-CARE

From Self-Care to We-Care

The New Science
of Mindful Boundaries
and Caring from an
Undivided Heart

JORDAN QUAGLIA

SHAMBHALA

Shambhala Publications, Inc.
2129 13th Street
Boulder, Colorado 80302
www.shambhala.com
© 2025 by Jordan Quaglia

Cover design: Lauren Michelle Smith
Interior design: Amanda Weiss

9 8 7 6 5 4 3 2 1

First Edition
Printed in the United States of America

Shambhala Publications makes every effort to print on acid-free, recycled paper.

Shambhala Publications is distributed worldwide by Penguin Random House, Inc., and its subsidiaries.

Library of Congress Cataloging-in-Publication Data

NAMES: Quaglia, Jordan, author.
TITLE: From self-care to we-care: the new science of mindful boundaries and caring from an undivided heart/Jordan Quaglia.
DESCRIPTION: First edition. | Boulder, Colorado: Shambhala Publications, [2025] | Includes bibliographical references and index.
IDENTIFIERS: LCCN 2024034133 | ISBN 9781645473473 (trade paperback)
SUBJECTS: LCSH: Compassion. | Well-being. | Boundaries (Psychology) | Self-care, Health.
CLASSIFICATION: LCC BJ1475 .Q83 2025 | DDC 158.1/3—dc23/eng/20241112
LC record available at https://lccn.loc.gov/2024034133

The authorized representative in the EU for product safety and compliance is eucomply OÜ, Pärnu mnt 139b-14, 11317 Tallinn, Estonia, hello@eucompliancepartner.com.

Contents

Foreword

Each of us is deeply connected to the people in our lives who matter most to us, from the inner identities we have as individuals to the small circle of beloved family and friends that defines our close social ties. We often find it relatively easy to offer kindness and compassion to these people, even in a challenging world. Yet we are also part of something more extensive. We are capable of connecting within a larger network of individuals and groups—with whom we share values, beliefs, and belonging—and then outward to an even wider embrace of our membership as a fundamental part of all of nature. Unfortunately, these widening circles of connection may get lost in modern times as we listen to an all-too-common message in many contemporary cultures that who we are is simply an individual: an identity as a disconnected self or an isolated, differentiated "solo-self" alone in the world. With this mindset of individualism, not only is our experience of belonging constrained but our search for meaning can become a desperate, lonely attempt to focus on the "me" of that solo-self view. The risk of believing this myth of the solo-self is a life of disconnection, one that encourages an excessive focus on self-related endeavors like "self-care," "self-compassion," and "self-development."

In contrast, if we open our minds to the ancient invitations of Indigenous cultures and contemplative traditions from thousands of years of our human history, and then combine these wise reminders with modern scientific explorations from fields such as anthropology and neuroscience, we become alerted to the risk of seeing our identities—the essence of our experience of being alive—as nothing but the isolated constructions in our minds. There is so much purpose we miss when we limit ourselves to this perspective.

In this powerful book, Jordan Quaglia provides a carefully curated survey of scientific studies and inspiring stories about how we can live into the notion of what he calls *we-care*. In our culture there is an oft-expressed sentiment that it is important to move "from me to we," but unfortunately this sentiment is often understood as a kind of "letting go of me and moving only to we." What is so exciting about Quaglia's notion of *we-care* is that it leaves room for being both a *me* within the individual body as well as a *we* within our relational connections. We-care presents a model of caring that includes both the individual-focused process of *self-care* as well as the important process of caring for other individuals—*other-care*. We-care focuses our kindness and compassion on the well-being of *all* people, both inside these bodies we were born into and the bodies of "other" individuals. In this crucial way, the title of this helpful book, *From Self-Care to We-Care,* does *not* have that same limitation of moving "from me to we." Instead, it implies a move from an isolated *me* to an integrated *me with we,* an identity construct I term *MWe.* It is with this integrated shift in identity that we can name our caring *we-care.*

Within, Quaglia's skillful presentation of we-care and beautiful illustrations of its application give us both an internal way of naming an approach to our behavior and a fresh perspective on our inner mindset as a relational way of being in the world. *We-care* is both a new term and an important contribution to our understanding of how we can embrace the individual nature of who we are—the subjective, felt sense of our lives as the inner identities we have—as well as the relational connections that link us all as human beings: each of us part of one human family and a fundamental part of all of nature. As individuals, we are *inter*connected to each other in the ties between us as unique, separate entities; as fundamental aspects of the interwoven nature of all living beings, we are *intra*connected.

As you read through this important exploration of how we can approach the challenging times we are in by more effectively bringing care into the world, it may be helpful to envision how becoming aware brings us the opportunity for choice. *From Self-Care to We-Care* can expand your consciousness by clearly illuminating a choice you can make: with ancient wisdom and modern science backing you up and guiding your way forward, you can choose to see your identity as broader than the brain and bigger than the body you were born into. When we have the courage to care, to intentionally place energy into an effort to improve life, we can choose to widen our identity lens to see beyond the lie of the separate self that modern culture has often told us, directly or indirectly. Yes, we have a body and can exercise that body— stretch it, feed it well, protect it, and enjoy it. We can take breaks and balance out how we focus our work and play. We can nurture and care for our relationships and find personal meaning in life. These are all important aspects of self-care, but we-care doesn't stop there. We can *also* realize that who we are is more than these bodies alone—and so caring "for others" is really caring for a larger sense of self, an integrated identity as MWe, which both empirical research and wisdom traditions suggest is a way to promote health within our own bodies and minds and within the world at large. As we enact other-care practices of reaching out to those in need and the natural world and being open to the suffering of people and the planet, we can learn to connect with this suffering without overidentifying with it. By maintaining this balance of differentiation (honoring and caring for our own inner lives) and linkage (recognizing our relationality and caring for others)—what Quaglia refers to as agency and communion—we become more effective in our care and maintain our effective focus and actions while avoiding depletion and burnout. This process of linking without losing differentiation is called *integration*, and it plays a crucial role in empowering ourselves toward compassionate action.

In this inspiring and useful guide, we are brilliantly advised to avoid the either/or thinking of personal versus other, of me versus we, of us versus them. Instead, integration dissolves these false dichotomies as we realize that we can be *both* a me and a we. With this integration comes a greater appreciation for the relational field, a sense of what the inspiring Zen teacher Thich Nhat Hanh termed *interbeing*. Or, as it is so eloquently expressed in the meaning of the African word *ubuntu*: "I am because we are."

The power of we-care is its integrative nature that encourages us to fully inhabit a kind and compassionate life that emphasizes me, you, and us. We-care gives us the mindset of embracing the integrated nature of our identity as MWe and empowers us to bring the harmony of integrative caring into the world that so desperately needs us to show up and be fully present. Bringing kindness and care into the world in a sustainable way requires this differentiation and linkage. With gratitude for this deep and timely inspiration, we can thank our courageous and insightful guide for this illuminating and empowering gift.

—*Daniel J. Siegel, MD*

Reading Guide

This book is written to be flexible and user-friendly for a wide range of readers. While I recommend starting with the introduction and continuing through from beginning to end, feel free to skip around based on your interests and needs. Each chapter is largely self-contained and covers a specific topic, allowing you to engage with the sections that are most relevant to you at any given time. You can use the table of contents to navigate to the chapters and practices that interest you the most.

FROM SELF-CARE TO WE-CARE

Hidden Choices

All flourishing is mutual.
—ROBIN WALL KIMMERER,
*Braiding Sweetgrass: Indigenous Wisdom, Scientific
Knowledge, and the Teachings of Plants*

In a psychology laboratory at the University of Kansas, a study participant named Iris faced a daunting choice. She had just lucked out in a random drawing between her and another participant, Elaine. The prize? Being spared from a series of painful electric shocks, soon to be administered as part of a research experiment on "stressful conditions." But after Iris sat and watched Elaine squirm with discomfort from the first few shocks, something happened that dramatically escalated the situation. Elaine spoke up, confessing that as a child she had been thrown off a horse onto an electric fence. Given this disclosure of prior shock trauma, the experimenter pulled Iris aside to present her with a gut-wrenching decision: either continue to observe Elaine be painfully shocked or volunteer to take her place and suffer the shocks herself.

In case this rings any bells about electric shocks and psychology, note that this was not the famed Milgram shock experiment in which participants were asked to deliver shocks to others as a test of their obedience to authority. Instead, this seminal study involving our hypothetical participant, Iris, was designed by Daniel Batson and his colleagues in 1981 to test the limits of people's altruistic motivations—pushing them to the brink of self-sacrifice.[1] As perhaps you've guessed by now, the shocks were not real; the other participant named Elaine was an actor, and the situation had all been meticulously designed to force a difficult decision: *Care for another at the expense of yourself or care for yourself at the expense of another?*

Before I get to what the study's participants chose, it seems worthwhile to reflect on what you might choose as an unsuspecting participant: Would you stay in the role of observer or volunteer to be shocked yourself? Prioritize your own well-being or selflessly care for another? Beyond what you might choose, how would your choice make you feel? If you choose to remain an observer, how might it feel to watch another get shocked repeatedly? And if you choose to take their place, might there be a part of you that regrets putting your own well-being on the line?

Through careful design and rigorous analysis of participant choices across two studies, Batson and his colleagues discovered a consistent pattern: individuals were more inclined to take Elaine's place when they *felt* greater care for her. This tendency persisted even under conditions that made it easy for participants to escape the situation and not witness Elaine endure more shocks. For instance, when participants experienced lower feelings of care and escape was easy, only 18 percent of them chose to swap places with Elaine. By contrast, when caring feelings were higher and escape remained easy, 91 percent of participants swapped places, volunteering to be shocked themselves in lieu of allowing Elaine's continued suffering. The overall pattern of findings, reinforced by numerous subsequent studies, supports the view that true altruism exists—that is, there are times when actions are primarily aimed at alleviating another's distress rather than one's own.[2]

Of Two Hearts

Looking back on Batson's study, now several decades later, there are a few takeaways I find worth contemplating, apart from any specific theories or findings. One that particularly stands out is how the study's design sets up a familiar social dilemma, albeit in an exaggerated way. Outside the laboratory in daily life, we do sometimes face situations that appear to present us with only two options, each trading off between our own or another's well-being in an either/ or manner. For instance, stay in a bad romantic relationship *or* say goodbye to the partner pleading with us to stay; attend our friend's destination wedding *or* use the time off for a much-needed family trip; move to a new city for an exciting opportunity *or* stay closer to aging parents who could soon need assistance. These situations can make us feel not just of two minds, but of two hearts.

Most of the time, however, life is not so clear-cut and binary as to demand we choose caring *either* for ourselves *or* others alone. For example, research has shown repeatedly that kindness often benefits both the giver and receiver—hence why Batson and others have spent decades devising clever experiments simply to demonstrate that altruism, kindness, and prosocial behavior can, at times, occur without any material benefit to the giver. But despite this increasingly nuanced evidence, the tendency to think in either/ or terms about the nature of our social lives and care persists. People often fail to acknowledge mutual benefits even when they are clearly present,[3] and millions of people report experiences such as feeling guilty for self-care, struggling to set boundaries, or suffering burnout from always putting others first. These are just a few of the symptoms of a tendency to divide our care in an either/or manner, not unlike choosing to let others be shocked versus getting shocked ourselves.

This persistent tendency toward either/or thinking in our care— what I call the *either/or mindset*—has far-reaching consequences that come to seem rather strange when we take a closer look. For instance, we tend to use the same word, *self-care*, to describe needless activities like an impulsive shopping spree right alongside truly healthy ones like exercise and sleeping well. Or if we see someone caring for others, such as a business executive volunteering at a high-profile charity event, we might dismiss the significance of this caring act simply because it could bring about personal benefits for their reputation.

Some people push themselves to the brink trying to be *selfless*, driven by impossible standards that backfire right when they are needed most. Still others will burden their loved ones with selfish demands, failing to realize that they stand to benefit more when those same individuals are well-resourced and able to give freely. These examples represent only some of the ways in which our social lives and care become divided.

The following questions lie at the heart of this book:

- Why do we fall into these either/or patterns in our views and practices of care, and what are the consequences?

- Is there a less divided approach to caring for ourselves and others?

Throughout the chapters ahead, we will explore these questions through various lenses—scientific, cultural, experiential, and real-world application. We will see how the tendency to divide our social worlds gets reflected in how we think and speak about our lives, biasing our actions in conscious and subconscious ways. And we will consider how this tendency matters, with negative implications for our own and others' well-being. As confirmed by scientific evidence, this divided approach contributes to many kinds of personal and social problems, including unhealthy relationships, loneliness, empathy-based guilt, empathic distress, self-sabotage, boundary issues, and burnout. Zooming out, we will also see how divided views about care are embedded in and reinforced by many of our relationships, organizations, cultural practices, and institutions.

On the other side of this ubiquity lies an opportunity. Given how common our tendency is to divide our world and care, there is enormous potential for transforming our lives through a different approach. I call this more expansive approach *we-care*.

What Is We-Care?

We-care means what it sounds like—caring for a *we*. This stands in contrast to caring for oneself as an individual (self-care) or for one or more others (other-care) on their own, introducing a new category or subset of care altogether. This new category of we-care encompasses and emphasizes instances in which self-care and other-care overlap and interrelate.

We-care integrates exciting new scientific findings and models, applied tools, and practices for how to maximize care for ourselves and others as part of a greater whole. At its core, we-care is about fostering a sense of interconnectedness, moving away from individualistic interpretations of self-care, and embracing a more social and collaborative approach to care. A we-care view does not deny that our interests may sometimes be incompatible with those of others. But it is grounded in the scientific understanding that, more often than people typically think, caring for ourselves enables us to care for others more effectively, and caring for others often results in more care for ourselves. We-care goes further still, revealing to us how self-care can itself be an expression of our care for others and vice versa. By adopting this new view and approach, we can break free from the limitations of an either/or mindset and find new, creative ways to care. Moreover, since we-care sits at the nexus of us and others, the personal benefits from this kind of transformation ripple far beyond us, enriching our relationships and strengthening the intricate web of connections that forms society.

By integrating self-care with care for others, the practice of we-care embraces our social nature and reflects it back to us. This reveals that care is more than just personal activities or social support. Whether directed toward ourselves or others, care is a social force that fosters healthy reciprocity, weaves and restores the social fabric, and may even guide us toward our highest potential as human beings. In recognizing this profound richness and complexity of care, we uncover new pathways—previously *hidden choices*—toward a more balanced and ultimately unified approach to care throughout our lives.

The Plasticity of Care

My own journey to we-care began long before I had a name for it. More than a decade ago, I was enrolled in a master's program, focused on starting a career of caring for others by training to be a therapist. During college, psychotherapy had been immensely supportive for me, helping me to find meaning in and ultimately recover from a long period of debilitating panic attacks. I was drawn to the idea of learning to provide the same support for others. Yet, some time into the program, I realized the actual work of seeing clients intimidated me. I was especially concerned by what seemed an unworkable tendency of mine to absorb and internalize the negative mindsets and emotions of clients—something I feared might trigger my own panic attacks again. A few instances of taking on too much from others seemed to confirm my fear, and, eventually, I decided I was not cut out to be a therapist.

Over the program's remaining semesters, I gradually pulled away from a career in therapy and instead started assisting with research in two psychology and neuroscience laboratories. I found solace in the detailed, meticulous work within the confines of each lab, a contrast to the emotional intensity of training to support clients in crisis. To be fair to myself, my transition was not merely about avoiding a career as a therapist—I also found myself believing in my unique potential to have a bigger positive impact through research, teaching, and writing about topics linked to therapy. Upon completing the master's degree, this newfound direction led me to an experimental psychology doctoral program, immersing me further in the elaborate worlds of social psychology, contemplative science, and cognitive neuroscience.

I was particularly struck by the concept of *neuroplasticity*, the brain's remarkable ability to reorganize and change with experience. My experience of recovering from panic attacks had made me a believer in the tremendous potential we all have for psychological healing and growth. Yet the concept of neuroplasticity challenged me to look deeper through its suggestion that the right methods and conditions could facilitate more profound transformations—not only through lessening suffering but also through allowing us to guide changes and promote positive qualities aligned with our goals and values. This potential for *self-guided neuroplasticity* made me wonder: Could the principles of neuroplasticity, proven effective in other learning contexts, also be applied to transform our social lives? Was it possible for a person to modify things like their sense of empathy, boundaries, or intrinsic drive for self-care? The idea of creating lasting changes to important qualities such as these made me wonder if it might even be possible to address the difficulties that had dissuaded me from a career as a therapist.

This line of questioning, which I pursued throughout my doctoral program, reinvigorated my passion for the applied side of psychology. By the time I accepted a faculty position at Naropa University and began directing my own psychology and neuroscience research lab, I was eager to marry new scientific insights with a renewed involvement in its applications. I was therefore thrilled when, in my first year, my colleagues Dr. Judith Simmer-Brown and Charlotte Rotterdam approached me about a new compassion training program they and others from throughout the university had been developing. I eagerly signed on as a student for their upcoming pilot program, immersing myself in the practices and devouring the nascent scientific literature on compassion training. This new focus revealed pieces of an emerging puzzle—one that seemed capable of fully bridging my scientific goals with the part of me that initially pursued being a therapist. It was the part of me that yearned to directly support people's mental health, to nurture their personal growth, and to catalyze transformational changes. Now, this motivation seemed less individual and more universal. If I could piece it together, I knew this new puzzle could unlock insights relevant to the goal of fostering the well-being of therapists, their clients, those suffering from more severe forms of mental distress, and perhaps many others throughout society. This potential for a broader impact gave me a clearer sense of purpose and a surge of inspiration, reminding me of the heart at the center of my science.

Many of the missing puzzle pieces, which I will share with you in the pages ahead, relate to the fundamental plasticity of our *care tool kit*—the core set of capacities needed not only to care for ourselves and others but also to dynamically balance our self-care and other-care. Critically, I discovered these puzzle pieces not in one place but from a blend of emerging scientific literature, experiential practices, and applied perspectives. The unique explanatory power of this blend has continued to be central to how I think about the puzzle of care, bolstering my belief in the importance of combining different ways of knowing to understand we-care. A clear intellectual understanding of we-care is important, but it's only one aspect of what is needed to realize it as an enduring experience. Consequently, you will find this book filled not only with what I consider to be the most important scientific discoveries on care but also with numerous actionable insights, tools for self-exploration, and practices for familiarizing yourself with its view and elements.

Although I felt greater clarity with every new piece of the puzzle, even after years of research and experimentation, I knew a critical piece was still missing. I could tell because, no matter how I tried to fit the different puzzle pieces together, the end result seemed to add to the complexity of my understanding rather than simplifying it. Determined to find the missing piece that would finally bring everything together, I joined the teaching team for the new compassion training program, signed on as the research director for the university's Compassion Initiative, and redirected the central focus of my lab toward the science of care and compassion. Then one day, as I was preparing for class, I had an insight about care that seemed to rotate all of my other thoughts about it. I now found myself looking at care from an entirely new angle. And I could see that the missing puzzle piece I had been seeking was right in front of me all along.

This was the missing piece: Our collective quest to understand and promote care has so often been placed in a self/other framework that we have been inadvertently undermining the essence of care. This framing is literally the case in terms such as *self-care* and *self-compassion*, and it's also true more broadly in the dichotomous nature of discourses on care. At its core, all care, *including what gets called self-care*, is inherently social. Therefore, care that strengthens the social fabric of our lives is likewise good for us individually. With that in mind, I now see care as fundamentally undivided. Care is care. And it's possible not just to *think* of care this way but to actually *unlearn the habit* of approaching our care in terms of self-care or care for others. Ultimately, *self* and *other* are not opposing factors in the calculus of care; they're variables in an equation that can yield far more elegant solutions.

We can further elucidate this key insight, the missing puzzle piece, through the metaphor of breathing. Just as we draw distinctions between self-care and caring for others, we commonly divide the breath into inbreath and outbreath. When we choose, we can steer the flow of our breathing, changing its rhythm and patterns in a variety of ways. We hold our breath when we need to. We sigh. With awareness and practice, we can unlearn old habits of breathing and establish new, healthier ones. The flow of air is even critical to how we speak and express what's in our hearts. And yet, despite all of this variety and nuance in how our breath moves, cycles, and transforms—it's all breathing. The inbreath and outbreath are two complementary components of one continuous process. Together, they serve the same underlying purpose of maintaining a delicate physiological balance within our blood. Inhaling oxygenates the cells. Exhaling removes carbon dioxide. Combined, they ensure our cells stay energized. As one undivided system, breathing sustains our life. And, just like the inbreath and outbreath, self-care and care for others can be *considered separately* but are never truly in opposition to each other, nor are they activities that make much sense when approached in total isolation from each other.

In the pages ahead, we will examine this critical insight and its numerous implications. We will outline the pitfalls of the predominant approach and discover how we-care avoids them. It is possible for us to reclaim care's true essence.

The Transformative Power of We-Care

Imagine the next time you encounter a difficult social situation— someone rudely cuts ahead of you in line at the grocery store, a loved one confronts you with a burst of unexpected anger, you open your email to find an accusatory message about a mistake you made at work, or an old friend reappears in your life, asking for a favor that feels too big. Regardless of the details, imagine knowing deep down you've got what it takes to handle it. You can say no when you need to, set clear boundaries, and navigate tough conversations with relative ease. Sure, you may still experience some discomfort, frustration, and worry at times—but beneath it all, there is a sense of inner peace that remains undisturbed.

What's more, when you want to deepen your connection with others, you also know how to create genuine, meaningful relationships. You know how to listen nonjudgmentally and speak your truth. You can ensure others feel heard and that your perspective will also be heard and valued. Finally, you know how to deeply care for your personal well-being throughout both the difficult and easeful times, and in ways that naturally support those around you too. You no longer routinely second-guess your actions or feel guilty for prioritizing yourself when you do.

Now, imagine all of this coming from the same, heartfelt place—a natural source of care that gives you the courage, strength, outlook, and patience you need across many different situations. You can respect others' unique points of view while finding common ground. You move back and forth between self-care and other-care, staying in touch with others' needs as you look after your own and not losing sight of your own needs as you tend to others. You are an example of someone with a balanced approach that avoids unnecessary conflict, clarifies confusing social situations, takes good care of themselves, and advocates for positive changes and connections with mutual benefit.

This is the power of we-care in action.

So, is we-care an effortless walk in the park? Occasionally, yes—and in fact literally for me, as someone who regularly engages in we-care by taking a walk around a park near my apartment. But even when we-care does involve some extra effort, we can trust that it is on the side of creating more ease, peace, and joy in our lives. This is because we-care is about improving the overall effectiveness of our care, both for ourselves and others. It also opens us up to the possibility of receiving additional care from others—sometimes in surprising ways. However, we-care is not a quick fix or magic wand. It can be wonderfully complex and enigmatic at times. It can even get messy: No matter how humble, enlightened, thoughtful, or awake to our blind spots we become, people may still misunderstand us. We may misunderstand others. Our old, entrenched patterns may show up unexpectedly and hinder us again. Healthier patterns may take longer to establish than we hoped. All these challenges and more may occur. Some days, choosing we-care may feel like choosing the harder path.

Fortunately, like any practice, we-care becomes more natural over time. At its best, we-care powerfully transforms unwanted social dynamics, even in contexts where divided approaches appear dominant. With that in mind, let's consider one possible we-care response to what seems to be an especially divided situation. A few weeks ago, Eliza enthusiastically RSVP'd to attend her close friend's big birthday bash, and now the day of the party has arrived. Having just received the shocking news that her aunt passed away overnight, however, Eliza faces a dilemma not unlike that in the study introduced earlier. On the one hand, she wants to prioritize her friend's well-being, show up to celebrate their life, and ensure they feel her love and care. On the other hand, she feels devastated—so much so that she's struggling to make a cup of coffee without bursting into tears. She doubts if it's even possible for her to squash down her grief enough to be present and happy for a party, but she's also not quite sure what she needs to care for herself either.

Now, let's also imagine Eliza has some background and training in we-care. As she contemplates the two options laid out before her—suppress her feelings enough to attend the party or stay in and find a way to care for herself all night—she notices that neither one feels entirely right. After all, both options involve dividing her care, which goes against her commitment to we-care. Although she's too distraught to be present and cheerful for a big party, she also recognizes that thinking about supporting her friend's happiness is helping her feel more balanced and regulated. As Eliza reflects further, she realizes there is actually a third option. A hidden choice.

Enlivened by her insight, Eliza starts compiling an album of some of her favorite photos and videos of her close friend. A few quick texts to other friends about her plans result in being sent many more fond memories. And even though she has to take breaks now and then as she works with her grief, it's not long before she's arranged all the memories into a digital tribute, accompanied by her friend's favorite songs. She's even enlisted another friend to help with a surprise reveal and presentation of the tribute during the party. Relieved, tender-hearted, and justifiably peering through tear-filled eyes, Eliza takes one last action—sending a text to her friend to share why she's clearly not feeling up for the party, but that she's nevertheless created a little surprise to join in the celebrations.

Certainly, it is easier to discern a hidden choice like this from a distance, with ample time to contemplate and think beyond the binary. And yet, this example of a hidden third choice—one aligned with the principles of we-care—is worth reflecting on. It demonstrates the power of we-care to transform a divided situation, and it illustrates the kinds of profound changes that can occur when we commit to going beyond the either/or division of self-care or care for others, even in situations that seem to force us in one direction or another. After all, this we-care response would promote improved care for Eliza and her friend and possibly uplift the whole party for the better.

Why We-Care

We-care takes on many different forms, changing across different people, moments, and situations. For instance, if Eliza's grief were too overwhelming to even arrange a digital tribute, we-care might instead look like sending a heartfelt message to explain her situation and express regret that she cannot attend the party. An equally plausible case can be made that we-care could result in attending after all. This highlights how we-care can sometimes look a lot like divided forms of care from the outside—what is most essential is not the external appearance but how we-care changes our internal process and experience. More often than not, however, we-care transforms both our internal process and experience *and* our external behaviors. The true transformative power of we-care, then, lies in how it can catalyze profound inner changes alongside concrete and measurable improvements.

The choices set before us in everyday life are rarely as divided as those found in Batson's electric shock study or Eliza's birthday party dilemma. Yet the transformative power of we-care can be experienced in much simpler ways: an honest yet comforting conversation, a cup of tea, or a simple walk around the neighborhood. Therefore, as we near the end of this introduction, let's consider the broader relevance of we-care in the real world, with the goal of giving you a clearer idea of what to expect in the pages ahead. Overall, we-care can bring about three key benefits in daily life— what I think of as the *whys of we-care*:

1. *We-care enhances personal and social well-being.*
   The ultimate purpose of care is to foster well-being, so it follows that improving the strength and effectiveness of our care should translate into more well-being. Since we-care works to improve our self-care and other-care together as parts of a unified approach to care, it has the potential to promote more well-being not only for us personally but also for others with whom we interact. This dual focus can generate powerful feedback loops of mutually beneficial care and catalyze upward spirals of personal and social well-being.

2. *We-care promotes healthy boundaries.* Most people agree that having healthy boundaries is essential for well-being, but there is often little clarity about what healthy boundaries are or how to cultivate them. Robust we-care contains all the elements essential for giving rise to naturally healthy boundaries—skillful communication, discernment, authenticity, and more. In turn, these natural boundaries help to protect us from bad actors and the harmful behavior of others, as well as to advocate for our needs, goals, and values across all of our social interactions. We-care has the added advantage of enabling us to cultivate what I call *care-based boundaries*—that is, boundaries rooted in a foundation of care and connection, even in the face of conflict.

3. *We-care offers a path of healing and transformation.* As we grow more familiar with we-care, we begin to see that a lot of misunderstanding and harm in the world arises from overly divided views of caring for oneself, others, and the world. This applies to external actions and relationships as well as to our internal views and relationships with parts of ourselves. Reflecting this truth, many different paths of healing, growth, and transformation—from scientific to philosophical to spiritual—seem to converge on the value of overcoming divided views that hinder more interconnected ways of caring. By providing a framework, a set of tools, and numerous practices stemming from an undivided view, we-care serves as a practical path of healing and transformation.

These three whys of we-care are neither small nor short-lived. As you come to experience them in your own life, you will understand that we-care is more than just a concept; it is a call to action, a means to disrupt habitual patterns, and a comprehensive tool kit to positively reshape your outlook and actions. Throughout our social lives, we-care nurtures compassion, enhances interpersonal understanding, and strengthens community bonds. It helps us to better navigate both challenging and fulfilling social dynamics with other people, as well as in the systems and institutions to which we belong. Perhaps most essentially, we-care reconnects us to an undivided heart that is inherent in our shared human nature.

We-Care Practice 1
REVERSE SELF-CARE

Throughout this book, you'll find a novel we-care practice at the end of each chapter, aligned with the main lesson or themes of that chapter. As you work with these practices, they will invite you to experience we-care in many different forms and expressions, including activities with an emphasis on self-care, care for others, or both equally. For this first practice, we'll focus on self-care—but with a we-care spin. Typically, self-care is guided primarily, if not exclusively, by intentions to support one's personal well-being. Reverse Self-Care is designed to flip the script, inviting you to explore a more interconnected view of your self-care.

PRACTICE INSTRUCTIONS

1. *Choose a self-care activity.* Identify a self-care activity that you truly want to do and that you know will clearly foster your well-being.

2. *Who else might this self-care support?* Aside from yourself, bring to mind another, specific person

who might reasonably benefit from your self-care, either directly or indirectly. Maybe it's your romantic partner, child, family member, friend, or close work colleague—someone who will stand to benefit when you're more fully resourced.

3. *Do it for them.* Begin the self-care activity as you typically would, but instead of focusing on its benefits to you, see if you can source from your intention to benefit the other person you identified. If it's helpful, you can silently state or repeat an intention such as, *May this self-care of mine contribute positively to your life* or *May this act of self-care eventually bring about benefits for you.*

4. *Do it for you too.* As you engage in the activity, feel free to return your focus to primarily promoting your personal well-being. However, at least once more, bring the other person to mind, allowing yourself to feel care both for yourself and for them. In recognition that this self-care may support two people at once—you and them—see if you now can offer yourself even deeper and fuller self-care.

Reverse Self-Care is a highly flexible and customizable we-care practice. You can rely on it whenever you're already planning some self-care time or to spark your motivation to engage in self-care. Ideally, this practice will offer you glimpses of the potential for interconnected care and allow you to feel it in a few different ways. However, as always, insights and practices are intended as prompts or pointers. There's no one "right experience" to have when trying this practice. If a given practice ever seems like it's not supporting the quality and depth of your care, feel free to modify what's not working or skip it altogether.

To close, here's an example of what Reverse Self-Care could look like in action: It's a Friday night after a long workweek, and Kai has no plans. Having recently moved into his own studio apartment, he decides self-care could be found in listening to his favorite playlist and dancing around the living room, cardboard boxes and all. Kai may not be the best dancer around, but he knows that dancing at home has previously brought him many moments of joy, inspiration, and energy, so he can foresee how its mood-boosting effects could eventually benefit others too, especially his best friend, Morgan. So, as Kai cues up his favorite song, he thinks, *May all my silly dancing around this apartment somehow lead to more laughs for you.* He hits play and starts dancing, enjoying the space and time to himself. Now and again, he brings Morgan to mind, noticing that he can feel care both for himself and for her at the same time—a felt sense of interconnected care. What's more, every time he feels this extra care, Kai gets an extra burst of inspiration to keep on tearing up the dance floor of his new living room.

PART 1

WIRED FOR WE-CARE

We with our lives are like islands in the sea, or like trees in the forest. The maple and the pine may whisper to each other with their leaves. . . . But the trees also commingle their roots in the darkness underground, and the islands also hang together through the ocean's bottom.

—William James, "The Confidences of a 'Psychical Researcher'"

CHAPTER 1

The Superhero and the Hurt

Embracing Our Social Nature

> We have forgotten our belonging to one
> another and we've forgotten the realness
> of our connectedness.
> —TARA BRACH, "Revisiting Radical
>   Acceptance," *Tricycle Talks*

Seated in the grand assembly hall of the United Nations headquarters in Bangkok, Thailand, memories of the city in crisis flashed through my mind. I recalled suddenly receiving news of impending danger while I was having lunch at a restaurant, quickly paying in baht before rushing inside an acquaintance's nearby apartment to seek cover, closing the curtains for fear of rumored snipers, and filling the bathtub in case the water supply got shut off. Vivid details lingered—the acrid smell of rubber bonfires, the sound of sirens and shattered glass, and gunshots piercing through the enforced quiet of a citywide, shoot-on-sight curfew. It was May of 2010, and I had found myself unexpectedly at the geographical epicenter of Thailand's surging political turmoil.

At the time, I was a master's student and had been invited to Thailand to deliver a presentation on the science of meditation at an international conference, organized as part of the United Nations Day of Vesak celebrations. The conference aimed to explore topics such as how mindfulness, community harmony, and inner peace could meaningfully contribute to "global recovery." But upon my arrival, the need for recovery felt intensely local. The political chaos of Thailand escalated dramatically as the Thai government stormed an encampment of protestors, a tactic they hoped would put an end to months of demonstrations. Yet this move was like dousing a grease fire with water—protestors fled the encampment and took their fight to other areas of the city. They torched numerous buildings, including the CentralWorld mall, banks, and shopping centers. By the time the protests were over, 35 buildings lay in ruin, 86 people had tragically lost their lives, and 1,378 more had been injured.

It did not take long to realize the irony of my situation. I'd arrived to present an academic paper on the science of meditation for a conference on global peace, only to find myself in the midst of a real-life, deadly conflict. More salient to me than the irony were the two intense reactions that had emerged in me as the crisis unfolded—what I've come to call my *Superhero* and *Hurt*. My desire to analyze and understand these reactions has informed my career, research, and thinking ever since.

On the one hand, I felt emboldened by a sense of gutsy determination, with a heightened feeling of purpose for being in Thailand. Recognizing that I was at the epicenter of turmoil, the pull of a deeper call swept over me like a riptide tugging me out to sea. Maybe I could have a bigger positive impact, both at the conference and beyond. This inner response, however naïve, made me feel as if there was something I could personally do about Bangkok's social upheaval, even if I did not yet know what it was. On the other hand, I felt terrified by the immediate dangers I might face, alongside deep concern, even dread, for the people of Thailand. This part of me felt flooded by the magnitude of suffering.

I yearned to prioritize my safety and comfort by fleeing home to the United States and booking multiple sessions with my therapist. The clamorous juxtaposition of these two responses—each demanding my attention and presenting compelling arguments—led to an inner conflict in which my heart was being pulled in two completely different directions.

Much can and needs to be gleaned about care and compassion from those more directly impacted by traumatic events such as the one in Thailand I just described, as well as from the complex mix of factors that shape their occurrences and aftermaths. For the purpose of this book, I want to highlight how the Superhero and Hurt became a useful frame for describing my own divergent inner responses to this social crisis and for integrating key scientific findings, experiential truths, and applied insights about the nature of care.

Underestimating Our Social Nature

My first journey to Thailand resolved safely, and I was able to present at the United Nations conference as planned. Upon returning home, I embarked on an extensive quest to understand the two equally intense yet distinct responses I had experienced during that day of violent social turmoil. Reading countless books and journal articles, I generated and refined research questions that would come to shape and inform my scientific focus and thinking. Foremost, I learned that, despite everything I had already studied from social psychology and neuroscience, I was *still* underestimating what it means to be part of a social species. Research has since revealed how many people in modern times—especially those in more individualistic societies such as the United States—similarly underestimate this reality, and in ways that can profoundly work against mental health and social harmony.[1] As we will explore, the implications of underestimating our social nature are especially striking in relation to how we tend to think about and experience self-care, caring for others, and receiving care from others.

This brings us to the first layer of the Superhero and Hurt as distinct *care profiles* because they stand on opposite extremes of grappling with our innate sociality. Like two people locked in conflict, neither fully listening to the other, the Superhero and Hurt divide our social nature into cause and effect. For instance, I can now see times during the events in Bangkok when my Superhero took over. Despite the real dangers, I remember moments of dismissing my fears and internal process. I stayed in Thailand and gave my talk with even greater enthusiasm, focusing on the ways I could make a difference. And in the years following, my inner Superhero sometimes pushed me into imbalance while working on my dissertation and beyond, as I began my tenure as faculty. There was a definite drive in me to have an impact, even at the expense of my well-being. This is not to say I regret my decision to pursue an academic career nor the very interesting path it has carved out for me. Yet, looking back, I recognize ways I did not always listen to my inner Hurt's call for self-care, which led to various kinds of distress, health challenges, and blind spots regarding the care I offered myself and others. As we'll review in more detail later in this chapter, this relates to how the Superhero only ever wants to *cause* social effects, not be on the receiving end of them. By contrast, the Hurt feels trapped on the receiving end, inescapably porous to the social environment and incapable of effecting change.

It doesn't require a catastrophe to start acknowledging our fundamentally social qualities as human beings. We can deepen appreciation of our social nature in simple ways. Maybe you've noticed feeling more anxious after interacting with a worried friend. Or how distressing it can be to observe a heated argument, even when you're not invested in the outcome. It can be eye-opening to witness how such fleeting social interactions exert noticeable and, sometimes, lasting influences. Something that happens in a moment—say, you receive a passive-aggressive email—can haunt you long after. Or maybe it's not even personal. It could be a distressing news report that remains heavy in your mind, affecting your mood long after you scroll past it. The enduring influence of social situations may even be stronger when someone else you care about has been wronged. Perhaps you hear through the grapevine that a friend's being bullied, and you find yourself more outraged on their behalf than they even are.[2] Then again, fortunately, our susceptibility to being influenced by social contexts isn't all bad. On the positive side, we can feel tremendously inspired to grow into better people or engage in profoundly positive actions after simply witnessing the virtuous actions of others, even those of complete strangers.[3]

As these examples highlight, our brains are wired for a complex and varied social landscape, including many kinds of *social influence*—the flow and exchange of ideas, emotions, and behaviors from one person to another. While social influence can occur consciously through routes such as persuasion, in this context, I want to illuminate some of the less noticeable types of influence. Extremely subtle or subconscious social influences are by definition more frequently overlooked, but their impact on our capacity to care for ourselves and others can be surprisingly powerful. In my fields of psychology and neuroscience, we investigate these influences using terms like *emotional contagion, empathic distress, interbrain synchrony, mirror neurons,* and *vicarious trauma.* For example, research on emotional contagion has found that people tend to "catch" the emotions of others, even strangers, due to relatively subconscious actions of mimicking facial expression and body language.[4] These and many related phenomena point to the same truth: as a social species, much of what we consider to be

our private inner life is in fact shaped by the experiences and expressions of those around us.

One of my favorite studies uses a clever method to examine *fear
transmission*, demonstrating how our fears can be formed merely
through interacting with or observing others. The study reveals
how simply observing another person receiving shocks when
shown a neutral object—in this case, a blue square on a computer
screen—can cause observers to personally experience fear when
they are subsequently shown the blue square, reflected in the brain
as heightened amygdala activation.[5] A related study highlights the
downstream impacts of this kind of susceptibility to social transmission, finding that having a romantic partner with post-traumatic
stress disorder (PTSD) can increase one's own vulnerability to similar stress, almost as if one had experienced the trauma firsthand.[6]
Or consider a more positive example: When others help us manage our negative emotions by reframing the way we think about
stressful events (i.e., *social reappraisal*), it can have a bigger impact
than when we reframe those events on our own. Moreover, this
positive impact of social reappraisal sticks with us, protecting us
when we face similar events alone in the future.[7]

These influences go both ways, of course. Just as others influence us in conscious and subconscious ways, we too influence others through the same routes and social mechanisms. This means
that many of us go around underestimating our influence on others.
In fact, according to some remarkable research on social contagion, not only do we impact others we interact with directly, but
our actions and emotions can also ripple well beyond our immediate circle, up to three degrees of influence.[8] In other words, just
by living our lives, we are unintentionally influencing people we
have not met before and will likely never meet. Reflecting on my
potential influence in these ways can sometimes make me justifiably feel more cautious and concerned about my impact. At the
same time though, I feel more inspired and driven to cultivate

healthy behaviors and take better care of myself, knowing that any personal benefits I derive are likely to also benefit others, known and unknown to me.

Beyond these simpler forms of social influence, there's an abundance of evidence to confirm how much people *depend* on each other in conscious and subconscious ways. This may be obvious when we consider things like parenting, health care, or where the coffee in our mug comes from. But these are just the tip of the iceberg. For instance, research on loneliness consistently demonstrates the negative toll that simply feeling socially isolated can exert on our mental and physical health—findings that caught the attention of the US surgeon general, Dr. Vivek Murthy, in 2023, when he released an advisory on its destructive impacts. Relatedly, social rejection has been shown to generate neural activations akin to physical pain, such that taking something like acetaminophen can alter the pain of rejection.[9] Some of the most exciting advancements are emerging from *hyperscanning* and related neuroscientific methods that involve recording brain activity from multiple people simultaneously. This research has found that *interpersonal brain synchronization* can happen whenever people are interacting, and it is stronger when people are being honest with each other or cooperating.[10] Remarkably, this sort of interbrain synchrony even occurs when people are texting with each other, albeit to a lesser degree than during face-to-face interactions.[11]

These and many other findings suggest that our brains hold not only the capacity for shared processing with the brains of others but also the expectation of it. They describe a reality of being human that may be far from the individual emphasis through which many of us typically think about ourselves and instead reinforce the profound interconnectedness of people—stressing our identities as social beings in clear and quantifiable ways.

Even if we are intellectually aware of our inherently social nature, it is easy to lose sight of it in our day-to-day experience. Much of the human journey from the womb to adulthood involves gradual and meaningful growth toward increased independence, a developmental trajectory that can naturally cause people to downplay or filter out signs of one's innate sociality. This emphasis on independence from others becomes further ingrained in societies that emphasize self-reliance, celebrate individualism, and favor the view that our deepest nature is predominantly self-interested. Consequently, when social influences override the defenses that preserve our sense of independence, they may cause inner turmoil if we have not fully accepted our social nature. This dynamic amplifies the Superhero's urge to effect change, and intensifies the Hurt's pervasive feeling of powerlessness—a critical divergence in our care that we'll explore in more depth next.

Care, Divided

My quest to understand the divergent responses that first arose within me in Bangkok has led me to conclude that there are three critical trade-offs that can divide our care in detrimental ways:

1. Trade-offs between self-care and care for others

2. Trade-offs between feelings and actions

3. Trade-offs between vulnerability and strength

These trade-offs tend to go together in predictable ways along a shared dividing line—others, action, and strength versus self, feeling, and vulnerability—as they did for me in Bangkok. Yet they can also be experienced and expressed independently, and so, in upcoming chapters, we will explore these possible trade-offs in our care one by one, including the key scientific studies and findings that have informed my perspective. Through them, we'll learn about numerous interesting ideas related to divided care, such as *pathological altruism, secondary traumatic stress, unmitigated agency, compassion collapse*, and *care bypassing*. My conclusion is that these potential trade-offs pit different core elements of our overall care tool kit against each other, a shared feature of diverse social dilemmas.

Before we dive deeper into the details and the science though, it will be helpful to first get familiar with these trade-offs by more fully introducing what I mean by the Superhero and Hurt. In this context, the Superhero and Hurt are intended to represent two distinct care profiles for delineating when our care tool kit is split along a shared dividing line, such that the Superhero and Hurt each characterize a divided mode of care we might experience in daily life. As we will explore, these two care profiles can serve as mirrors, revealing imbalanced patterns of care-based thoughts, feelings, and behaviors when faced with suffering. Ultimately, what we see in them can guide us away from the inner conflict brought about by dividing our care and toward the more balanced approach of we-care.

Let's begin with the Superhero, a larger-than-life care profile that is intently other-focused, action-oriented, and strong when confronted with suffering. This was the part of me that, in the midst of Thailand's social turmoil, felt suddenly more driven to make a difference. At first glance, and especially as portrayed in pop culture, the Superhero may seem like the ideal care profile—and on rare occasions, when a situation demands swift action and self-sacrifice, its care profile and tool kit align with what's needed.

Consider the case of Nick Bostic, who, while driving, saw a stranger's house on fire, stopped and ran inside to check if anyone was trapped, and single-handedly saved the lives of five children.[12] There's no denying the extraordinary benefit of that kind of heroic action. However, when navigating the ordinary challenges of daily life, most situations aren't best supported when we try to push beyond our human limits—to be the Superhero. The inspiration we draw from Superhero narratives may inspire positive actions, but the stark, unfiltered Superhero care profile is rarely the right response to meet the nuanced situations we face.

Now for the Hurt, a care profile that brings self-care to the forefront alongside one's feelings and vulnerability. This part of us seeks solace and emotional support when faced with distress, especially when the intensity of suffering escalates. There are occasions, such as the sudden loss of a loved one, where the Hurt's wisdom of summoning us inward can be the right call. In the context of the Bangkok protests, the Hurt manifested in me as an overwhelming wave of feeling and emotion, pushing me toward a wish for comfort and a desire for dedicated time to focus on caring for myself. I could not help but imagine myself tucked safe and sound under the covers of my own bed, escaping reality through a Netflix binge.

The Hurt contrasts sharply with the Superhero, making it difficult to reconcile the two. Whereas the Superhero is urgently focused on others and self-sacrificing, the Hurt compels us to slow down and turn our focus inward. Whereas the Superhero springs into action without pausing and feeling, the Hurt is often immobilized by intense feeling. And whereas the Superhero boldly confronts challenges head-on, no matter the risks to themselves, the Hurt may struggle to even get out of bed.

The Superhero and the Hurt each draw on essential tools in our care tool kit, and, at times, their underlying abilities and propensities are the right fit for what we are facing. However, as distinct care profiles, the Superhero and Hurt oversimplify our potential responses in ways that cause adverse consequences for both us and others. Sooner or later, their divided approaches to care backfire, undermining our care in two directions at once. And interestingly, despite their contrasting styles, both the Superhero and the Hurt lead to similar adverse outcomes, such as empathic distress fatigue, ineffective helping, boundary issues, and burnout. This hints at how these care profiles may have more in common than initially meets the eye—after all, they are both expressions of divided care.

The Brain of a Superhero

For decades, research in social neuroscience and related fields has revealed significant variation in how people perceive and respond to suffering. These differences are rooted in an underlying *care circuitry* of the brain, shaped by both genetic predispositions and environmental influences. In subsequent chapters, we will explore the plasticity of the key regions and networks that make up this circuitry, including practices to catalyze *self-guided neuroplasticity* within your own personal care circuitry. Apart from such intentional practices, this research has confirmed that some people are simply less responsive to the suffering of others, and others more. Sometimes, *much* more. For instance, one research study found that extraordinary altruists—in this case, people who had donated their own kidneys to strangers—have a larger right amygdala that is also more activated by the fearful facial expressions of others.[13]

It may be tempting to question the level-headedness of those willing to donate an organ to a nonfamily member, but this kind of extraordinary altruism is not really what I mean by the Superhero care profile. This is because there's natural variation in people's capacity to empathize with suffering, including that of strangers. As a result, we should expect that a small percentage of individuals will exhibit other-oriented care that, while natural for them, may seem extreme to most. To peer into the brain of the Superhero, we have to instead look at when other-oriented care is driven by mostly subconscious motives rather than by deliberate intentions and actions. This means closely observing the brain during what researchers call *empathic distress*.[14] As summarized by the altruism expert Daniel Batson, empathic distress "does not involve feeling distressed *for* the other. . . . It involves feeling distressed *by* the state of another."[15] In other words, although Superheroes believe themselves to be acting in a self-sacrificing and other-oriented manner, they could be in fact driven by deeper motives to alleviate their own guilt, anxiety, and discomfort.[16]

When scanning brains of people that fit this description, researchers find evidence for the collapse of perceived boundaries between self and other. This includes lower brain volume in areas linked to distinguishing self from other, heightened connectivity between regions responsible for processing one's own versus others' distress, and neural markers of difficulty in regulating negative emotions.[17] All of this internal confusion can result in misguided and ineffective attempts to help, stemming at least partly from a desire to lessen one's personal discomfort in the process. This includes acts of *pathological altruism*, a scientific term that encompasses instances when altruistic actions cause unintended harm to the helper or those they're trying to help. Thus, studying the neural correlates of empathic distress offers an insightful window into the mind of the Superhero, revealing that beneath the surface, they may not be as other-oriented and self-sacrificing as they seem.

Looking at such neuroscientific research on altruism and empathic distress, another striking truth emerges: The Superhero brain overlaps considerably with that of the Hurt. Faced with suffering, a similar type of empathic distress that drives the Superhero to spring into action can instead block the Hurt from taking any action at all. As research has shown, the distress resulting from witnessing others' suffering activates neural networks similar to those activated by experiencing that pain and suffering personally. The associated negative emotions and difficulty regulating them can therefore lead to a self-focused state, less willingness to help, and social withdrawal.[18] Thus, although the Superhero and the Hurt appear quite different from the outside, their differences are not driven by fundamentally distinct patterns of brain activity and orientations toward suffering. Rather, what separates them has more to do with one's habitual, usually subconscious strategy to avoid the internal discomfort elicited by distressing situations. Despite their contrasting avoidance strategies and accompanying behaviors, both the Superhero and the Hurt can be traced back to similar underlying dysregulated brain states when faced with suffering. This is your brain on divided care.

The Many Faces of Superhero and Hurt

Before I share examples of how we-care differs from both the Superhero and the Hurt, I want to briefly review a couple other real-life examples of each care profile. These are drawn from the experiences of others I know, with identifying details changed, and are intended to enrich our understanding. By exploring the wider array of responses that fall within this frame, we can better comprehend how the Superhero and Hurt might uniquely manifest in different people across diverse situations. This will also help us to understand how we-care might address the set of adverse outcomes, such as ineffective care and burnout, shared by these two care profiles.

JOY'S SUPERHERO AND HURT

My colleague Joy and I recently met for a coffee chat. Given my research interests, she confided in me about a predicament she had encountered with one of her best friends. Joy had been trying to relax at home, waiting for her bath to fill after she received some concerning health news earlier in the day. But just as she was about to step into the water, her phone buzzed with a text message from her friend: "Need support. Can you talk?" Instantly, Joy felt torn. One part of her (what I would call her inner Superhero) wanted to call her friend back without delay and be there for her no matter how exhausted she felt. Her inner Hurt, on the other hand, wished to mute her phone, submerge in the bath, and pretend she had not seen the text until the following day.

DEAN'S SUPERHERO AND HURT

A relative of mine, let's call him Dean, is employed at a large technology firm. He recently called to share about a troubling situation in which a distressed colleague entered his office, sat down, and immediately started venting. The colleague expressed being on the brink of burnout due to escalating work and family stress. He had just finished meeting with their boss, who had agreed about the need to lessen his workload. Consequently, he informed Dean he would no longer be available to help with a significant project they had been collaborating on. Moreover, Dean's colleague made no acknowledgment of the potential implications for Dean and seemed not to have run that issue by their boss. Dean's inner Superhero was moved by the plight of his colleague's need for a break and wanted to simply reassure him by saying, "Got it and don't sweat it; I'll take it all from here." Yet his inner Hurt felt a wave of overwhelm and anger at the prospect of completing the entire project alone—especially given that Dean too was grappling with potential burnout, a concern that only grew more salient as he absorbed his colleague's distress.

Now let's review how Joy and Dean approached these social challenges by applying the principles of we-care, skillfully avoiding the extremes of the Superhero and Hurt.

JOY'S WE-CARE

Upon receiving her friend's text requesting a call for support, Joy paused to check in with herself. She technically had time for a call, but could she offer her friend the support she needed without first caring for her own needs? Having just learned about her health challenges, which she preferred to process in private, Joy decided she would offer her friend much better support after time to herself. However, if the need was urgent to the level of an emergency, she would prioritize that first.

Joy responded briefly stating she was available in an hour or so but could be sooner if it was an emergency. Within seconds, her friend replied, "No emergency! An hour or so from now sounds great!" Relieved and with clarity of intention, Joy muted her phone, stepped into the bath, and tended to her own emotions. After her bath, she called her friend, feeling ready to offer meaningful support. What's more, when her friend asked Joy how she was doing, Joy was prepared to share about her health news—opening the door to receive support in return.

DEAN'S WE-CARE

As Dean's colleague announced he could no longer assist with their collaborative project and started toward the door, Dean paused to reflect. He noticed feeling confused by his colleague's unusual behavior and unclear about what to do. More importantly, he could see that neither of his initial responses succeeded in balancing care for his colleague and himself. Although he was not yet aware of a better way forward, Dean was committed to finding a solution that would honor both the genuine care he felt for his colleague and for himself. So Dean said, "Hey—before you go. Thanks for updating me and sorry to hear about all the extra stress. That said, I think it's going to take a little time to digest everything before I decide what feels right on my end. I'll follow up with an email soon. Does that sound good?"

Dean's response seemed to snap his colleague out of a trance-like state. "Uh, yeah, sorry," his colleague replied. "I'll keep an eye out for your email. Thanks."

By the next morning, Dean had formulated a new plan that managed to maintain his workload while saving some deferrable tasks for his colleague. Furthermore, when Dean presented this new plan to his boss, it captured her attention and prompted her to assign a talented new employee to help Dean, ultimately reducing his workload beyond where it started.

If you imagined responding in a different way than Joy and Dean, that is completely understandable. What I appreciate about their responses is how they each help to demonstrate what is distinctive about we-care when compared to acting from the Superhero or the Hurt alone. After all, both Joy and Dean discerned a hidden choice—an alternate path forward that honored *both* their care for others *and* for themselves. Critically, taking this alternate path was also more effective in supporting everyone involved. In both cases, we-care promoted favorable outcomes and resulted in an unexpected additional benefit in the form of further support for themselves. This highlights the sort of positive, synergistic feedback loops that can occur when we choose to walk the path of we-care.

Our individual life experiences, social locations, worldviews, and use of language significantly shape how we perceive and express the Superhero and the Hurt as they relate to our personal lives. Therefore, to aid you in identifying and relating to your own unique expression(s) of the Superhero and Hurt, I have included some reflection questions below. I invite you to take some time contemplating and journaling about them if you find it helpful. And feel free to modify or reinterpret them to help you better understand your personal Superhero and Hurt.

EXPLORING THE SUPERHERO

- Do you ever feel the urge to take away other people's pain and discomfort, no matter the potential personal costs?

- Do you tend to sacrifice your own basic needs in order to support the well-being of others?

- Have you ever caught yourself trying to "rescue" others from their pain or struggles?

- When confronted with the suffering of others, do you sometimes spring into action before first pausing to feel?

- Do you tend to rush into "fixing" or problem-solving mode when others share about their difficulties, or when you personally face difficulty?

- As you reflect in this moment, do you sense a part of you that feels like you should be *doing* something more important to solve, fix, or otherwise assist others?

EXPLORING THE HURT

- Do you ever feel overwhelmed by the pain and suffering of the world or by specific challenging situations?

- Have you ever felt helpless in the midst of difficult situations?

- Does your heightened empathy, sensitivity, or vulnerability ever hinder your ability to fully support others?

- When you experience painful or negative emotions, do you find it challenging to offer care to yourself?

- Do you ever emotionally "check out" to avoid feeling, caring about, or absorbing too much suffering from others?

- Reflecting on your state in this moment, is there a part of you that seems to be currently feeling or shouldering the pain and struggles of others?

Embracing My Social Nature

More than a decade after the events in Bangkok, tragedy struck frighteningly close to home. On a cloudy spring afternoon in 2021, just minutes down the road from my apartment in Boulder, Colorado, a horrific mass shooting took place at a local supermarket. Upon receiving a text from a friend about the incident, I turned on the news to confirm what they had shared—a man with a gun, multiple casualties, and terrified shoppers being escorted to safety in lines from the store. What remains most piercing in my memory is the profound heartbreak I felt, and the surreal experience of watching alternating ground and helicopter camera footage of our town's familiar supermarket on national news. The incident left ten people dead, including a local police officer who was among the first to respond to the scene.

That day of the shooting, I experienced a number of difficult things that had nothing to do with the challenges I directly faced and that reminded me of the two different internal responses I had first felt in Bangkok. On one hand, I felt panic for those still trapped inside the market with the gunman, restlessness for the friends and families who had loved ones shopping at the time, and anger at the shooter for his ignorant and violent behavior. These challenging feelings clouded my mind, dampened my courage, and made me want to crawl under a rock and tend to myself alone—much like my desire to flee Bangkok during the violent protests.

But right there beside my panic, restlessness, and anger, another part of me felt the urge to take action and do something that might help. This desire was sparked in part by witnessing the bravery of those at the scene of the grocery store but also by something more deeply personal. I felt it as a drive to do something, anything, that could unburden those harmed. And this part of me wanted to act boldly, decisively, *right now*—even if I did not yet know what to do. It was the second familiar response to what arose in me back in Thailand, when I'd felt a greater sense of purpose and calling for being there in the midst of a crisis, as if I could do something to make a real difference.

This time, as I experienced these two different responses arising within me, rather than spiraling into inner conflict, I accepted and even embraced them as natural yet partial facets of me, inevitable manifestations of my social nature responding to the suffering of others. This perspective offered me an inner balance that allowed me to respond more effectively to both sets of needs without compromising my care one way or another. To respect my Hurt's need for feeling, self-care, and receiving care, I intentionally took time away from media and news, I rested and explored some of the more challenging thoughts and feelings that surfaced, and I reached out to loved ones for support. To respect my inner Superhero's urgent push toward action and other-care, I generated a list of possible actions that might make a difference and checked in with local friends. The next morning, I briefly did one of my we-care meditations and then took out my journal to reflect: How can I honor both of my heart's wishes—to help care for my local community while also caring for myself?

While sipping my coffee and journaling about my question, clarity dawned: What if I could find an accessible way to share about the tools and practices I'm resourcing from in the aftermath of this tragedy—things that are helping me to feel more centered and balanced in my self-care and care for others? By late morning, I had drafted an op-ed for our local Boulder newspaper, the *Daily Camera*, titled "Compassion in Times of Tragedy." It discussed research on two distinct responses that can arise in us when faced with suffering—what I would later call the Superhero and the Hurt—and the benefits of finding a balance of care between them. The article ended with a brief meditation practice I'd found supportive for cultivating balanced care in my personal process.

At that time, I did not realize writing the op-ed was also the start of writing this book. But I remember going on a walk days later, touching back into the pain of the shooting, and admitting to myself that I still wanted to do more to help heal divisions of our modern world. I was also aware that the most ideal scenario would involve finding something that complemented my work as a scientist and teacher, rather than getting pulled in an entirely new direction. Looking back, I see these reflections as my inner Superhero and Hurt in dialogue, trying to help me find the next step on my personal journey with we-care. As I reached our local park and saw some children happily running and playing on the jungle gym, my inner Superhero and Hurt—my care for others and for myself—found a meeting point: Given the gravity of the shooting and the broader issues it had raised for me, it no longer felt sufficient to write scientific articles or the occasional op-ed. I decided then and there to write this book and share the framework and practices of we-care with a wider audience.

We-Care Practice 2
FULL CIRCLE GRATITUDE

Most gratitude practices emphasize our individual experience, often through making a list or keeping a journal of what we are grateful for. This practice instead emphasizes gratitude as a *social emotion*, meaning we recognize and affirm its inherently social functions. This perspective on gratitude is bolstered by research on the power of gratitude in social contexts. For example, social gratitude incites altruistic actions and has been associated with higher oxytocin, a hormone linked to social bonding.[19] Additionally, simply receiving or listening to stories about social gratitude can boost one's mood and lead to more activation in the prefrontal cortex, an area of the brain critical for emotional and social functioning.[20] These and many other findings underscore that gratitude is much more powerful when we embrace its social side.

For the purpose of understanding and cultivating we-care, the following practice helps us to embrace our social nature. It also offers a counterbalance to some of the unhealthy aspects of both the Superhero and the Hurt. Specifically, experiencing gratitude as a social emotion tempers the Superhero's invincibility complex, which often guards against the vulnerability of receiving care from others or offering it to themselves. Conversely, this practice can counteract the Hurt's tendency to underestimate their potential for making a real positive impact, thereby motivating other-oriented action. Finally, as you will discover, the practice aims to generate an experience of shared benefits. Taken together, the practice of social gratitude invites us into a less divided way of seeing, allowing us to directly experience the mutual benefits of we-care. This enables us to see how our inner Superhero and Hurt are not in opposition but are simply two halves of one whole heart.

PRACTICE INSTRUCTIONS

1. *Reflect.* Identify a person in your life who has positively impacted you. It can be helpful to slow down and really consider a number of people before finding the one person you would like to focus on for this practice session. Note that it need not be the person who has had the biggest positive impact on you. Moreover, if you are having difficulty identifying such a person in a global way, see if you can think of someone who helped you with something specific, such as a work project.

2. *Journal.* Take some time to journal about your appreciation and gratitude for this individual. Aim to be specific, describing actual moments you are grateful for. Ideally, you could remember a story that helps to highlight why you are grateful and appreciative.

3. *Feel.* Notice how you are experiencing this gratitude and appreciation in your mind and body, breathing deeply to circulate any feelings that may arise. That said, although this practice is designed to foster positive feelings of connection, there are plenty of valid reasons why it may not. It is also common to feel a mixture of feelings, in which case, notice if gratitude and appreciation can coexist with any other feelings you may have.

4. *Express.* If it is both feasible and reasonable for you to do so, consider how to express your appreciation to this person in a thoughtful way, one that accounts for their personal preferences and needs. Maybe this looks like a simple handwritten note or letter, phone call, text message or email, or sharing with them over a coffee in person. Alternatively, it could show up in a less direct way, such as sending a small gift or simply doing them a favor the next time you have the chance. Whatever you choose, try to avoid the potential extremes of overwhelming them with positive words and deeds (like the Superhero might try), or conversely, holding back from expressing something meaningful (as with the Hurt). Additionally, if it does not make sense to express your gratitude in these ways, for any reason, you can modify this part of the practice into a visualization.

5. *Come full circle.* Be open to hearing how your expression of gratitude has had an impact. Remember that sometimes people find it hard to receive gratitude or appreciation, so it is important not to be on the lookout for something in return. That said, if you

do receive a positive response, take a moment to appreciate the benefits your practice has generated for another and yourself.

CHAPTER 2

Half-Hearted

The Real Problem with Self-Care

> This is what our brains were wired for:
> reaching out to and interacting with others. . . .
> Yet these social adaptations also keep us a
> mystery to ourselves. We have a massive
> blind spot for our own social wiring.
> —MATTHEW D. LIEBERMAN, *Social:*
> *Why Our Brains Are Wired to Connect*

Imagine you're out at your favorite café for some much-needed self-care. You're savoring a warm cup of tea and a sweet pastry, all while deeply engrossed in a book. Out of nowhere, a figure in flowing gray robes rushes past you and disappears out the door. You look back toward your book only to notice an envelope now sits beside your teacup. Did the mysterious figure really rush past just now to hand deliver you this envelope? Sealed with gray wax and stamped with alternating 1s and 0s, it has your full name elegantly written in calligraphy on the front.

Upon opening it, you discover an invitation to a "tournament of character and wit," promising a $5,000 prize. Little more detail is provided but for an address, date, and time. No special preparation or attire is specified. But as the date of the tournament approaches, you hear whispers that others around town have also received surprise invitations—each delivered in the midst of their own self-care activity. The mystery gets the best of you. You summon your courage and travel to the tournament's location, in the basement of the city's old downtown library. There, by a side door, the mysterious figure in the gray robes stands waiting. He greets you warmly by name, ushers you through the library door, and guides you to an antiquated 1980s computer. On the screen, the tournament rules glow in vivid green letters:

Your Objective: Engage in a series of computer-based interactions with another player, your opponent. Try to maximize your own points in each interaction. Before the tournament's end, you will play many different opponents. Your points will accumulate across these matches, and the player with the highest total score will win $5,000.

Rules: You'll play multiple rounds against each opponent. However, the exact number of rounds will be unknown in advance. For each round, you and your opponent will independently decide between two choices: We or Me.

Although you cannot communicate with your opponent during the game, you will be informed about your opponent's choice after each round.

Scoring: In each round, your score is based on the following outcomes:

- **5 Points:** If you select Me, and your opponent chooses We, you receive 5 points and they receive 0 points.
- **3 Points:** If you both choose We, each of you receives 3 points.
- **1 Point:** If you both choose Me, each of you receives 1 point.
- **0 Points:** If you choose We, but your opponent selects Me, you receive 0 points and they receive 5 points.

Ready to play? Your first opponent is ready and waiting in another room. Press Enter to begin.

You sit back and let out a sigh, reflecting on the strangeness of all that's led you here, and then turn your attention back to the rules of the tournament. The rules reward choosing We, but only if both you and your opponent choose it. Otherwise, choosing Me is clearly the better option. Without knowing your opponent, will you choose Me or We in the first round? If your opponent chooses Me, how will that shape your responses in subsequent rounds? Is there some sort of strategy you can adopt that will work across the different opponents?

Your finger hovers over the Enter key. Suddenly, it hits you. A flash of recognition. You have read about this game before, albeit with slightly different rules and terminology. It's the classic game scenario known as the prisoner's dilemma. And crucially, you might just know how to win.

Confronting the Prisoner's Dilemma

In the 1980s, the political scientist Robert Axelrod hosted a real-life prisoner's dilemma tournament at the University of Michigan.[1] Sharing many features with our imagined tournament, this competition attracted scholars, mathematicians, and other enthusiasts of *game theory*—the overarching category for games, such as the prisoner's dilemma, that can be useful for investigating how people make decisions in social contexts. Prior to the tournament, each participant was tasked with designing a computer program that would compete in multiple rounds of the prisoner's dilemma, facing off against others' computer programs.

As with our imagined tournament in the library, the real-life tournament included the aim of maximizing one's score across matches. However, instead of We versus Me, the choices in Axelrod's tournament were named *Cooperate* or *Defect*. In the end, the tournament was a clear triumph for the social sciences, shedding new light on the dynamics of cooperation versus competition, revealing not only the winning strategy of a game but also lessons that can apply to how we approach caring for ourselves and others in daily life.

What new insights emerged from Axelrod's tournament? Foremost, the overall pattern of findings helped to problematize what's been called the *selfishness axiom*—the assumption that people will always seek to make the most of their own gain and thereby expect others to be equally selfish. In the imagined tournament, this could mean choosing Me more frequently, in an attempt to steal the largest share of points in a round.

It turns out that people are driven by a more varied and complex set of factors than the selfishness axiom would predict. Beyond strictly rational concerns about maximizing personal gain, people navigate their social worlds with what sometimes seem to be irrational social preferences for fairness and cooperation. These preferences can be strong enough to outweigh self-interest, even to the point of considerable cost to oneself as an individual. Thus, the selfishness axiom is an oversimplification of people's motives that fails to accurately predict people's actions in the prisoner's dilemma, or in daily life.

Secondly, the tournament highlighted the relevance of short-term and long-term thinking to social decisions. Whereas a single round of the prisoner's dilemma could go either way, repeated rounds increase how much people choose to cooperate—the choice of We in our fictitious tournament. This is because choosing Defect, or Me, can decrease how often other players choose We in future rounds. So while the choice of Me can create the temptation of immediate payoff (5 points), it trades off against a possible longer-term payoff of repeated cooperation. This emphasis on long-term thinking can be made even stronger if players can get to know each other across opponents, through a kind of reputation system—something that more strongly mimics our social lives in the real world.

Third and finally, the winning strategy in Axelrod's tournament highlighted the value of erring on the side of trust, cooperation, and forgiveness—while nonetheless looking out for oneself. This is because the winner prioritized We, while still relying on Me as needed. So then, what was this winning strategy? It was actually quite simple: it was a strategy called tit for tat. The strategy began each match by choosing to cooperate (We) but followed by mirroring the decision of the opponent on all subsequent rounds. So, if one's opponent chose to defect (Me), the tit-for-tat computer program would choose to defect (Me) in the next round. However, if the opponent switched back to cooperating (We), the program would shift back to cooperating again (We).

Considered together, these three chief lessons from Axelrod's tournament point to a more fundamental truth about human social life: Always choosing and prioritizing yourself is a bad strategy for getting what you want. Yet so is never putting yourself first.

Life is not a winner-takes-all tournament, but effective strategies for navigating it depend on wisely selecting between decisions that reflect both Me and We—rather than always choosing one or the other.[2] As demonstrated by the winning strategy of tit for tat, intelligent or wise cooperation appears to be the most successful approach over the long run, partly because it is more aligned with our social nature and our preferences for getting along. This has obvious implications for how we approach our social lives and especially our self-care. Without mindful consideration, however, the immediate takeaways of Axelrod's tournament can overshadow deeper insights about the *real* problem with self-care.

Is Self-Care Selfish?

In April of 2023, an article on Bustle titled "Is Therapy-Speak Making Us Selfish?" circulated widely online. Scholars praised its insightfulness. Influencers doubled down, amplifying its message to thousands. And writers lauded its astute author, Rebecca

Fishbein, all the while wishing they had penned the article themselves. Writer Ej Dickson summed up her feelings in a social media post: "I firmly believe that therapy is tremendously helpful for like 90% of people and turns the other 10% into soulless monsters."[3]

Clearly, the article struck a chord.

To me, however, the feverish attention wasn't at all surprising. Throughout my years studying care in its various forms, I've consistently witnessed this sort of response—from students to colleagues to viral memes—toward messages aimed at the selfishness of concepts like therapy-speak, boundaries, or self-care. On one hand, I take this to be a meaningful signal that people have been personally burned, or at least underserved, by the widespread adoption of these ideas and related behaviors. And more specific to the idea of self-care, I think we have all encountered ways the concept gets misused and co-opted by selfish motives. If we're honest, maybe even by us personally.

On the flip side, I believe we've all also experienced moments when genuine self-care, however we personally define it, truly helped us—whether through keeping us going when we needed it most, bringing us back to center when we felt overwhelmed, or giving us the right words to communicate and prioritize much-needed personal time and space. Without a doubt, the concept of self-care has even contributed to saving many lives, if only by helping to reverse slippery slopes of addiction and other destructive behaviors. Reflecting on self-care in these ways, it seems far from selfish. It rather looks like a common-sense choice that protects our health, safety, and sanity. Even if we put all the personal benefits aside, through self-care, we grow more resourceful and ready to meet the challenge of showing up more fully for others.

How can we reconcile these two very different perspectives on self-care? To answer this question in any satisfying way, we first need to travel back in time to understand the origins, evolution, and seemingly nonstop rise in the popularity of self-care.

Self-Care: The Good, the Bad, and the Ugly

Self-care as most know it today carries a number of meanings. But back when it was first popularized in the 1950s, it had a fairly singular meaning as a medical term. Back then, self-care was essentially a supplement to professional health care, especially for patients who had chronic health problems or needed long-term care. For example, self-care for diabetic patients meant monitoring their own blood sugar levels and regulating insulin dosage based on daily blood sugar readings. Over time, the scope of self-care outgrew its narrow medical use, expanding alongside the recognition that certain helping professionals—such as social workers, therapists, and nurses—tended to put others first to an extreme degree, which came at their own expense and, over time, compromised the quality of care they provided. This wider scope for self-care also subtly shifted its meaning. Now self-care was not only a helpful supplement but also a balancing force—something that could protect against common discrepancies in care patterns among specific types of professionals.

The next consequential expansion of self-care's meaning occurred during and in the wake of the Civil Rights Movement of the 1950s and 1960s. Leaders and activists such as Audre Lorde and Angela Davis declared self-care to be something revolutionary, a political act of profound importance—especially against the backdrop of rampant and escalating inequalities in health care based on gender, race, sexual orientation, and class. Thus, its meaning transformed again, from a counterbalance for certain helping professions into a force needed to address imbalances embedded in society's care for its citizens. Critically, this made self-care a personal necessity as well as something that could serve as an instrument for political resistance and a driver of social change.[4]

Through subsequent decades, seemingly endless wellness promotion has steadily broadened the relevance of self-care far beyond any of its previous meanings. Today, even as policymakers, researchers, and activists continue to emphasize more specific uses of the term, self-care is being widely trumpeted as essential for literally *everyone*—and especially anyone seeking greater ease, beauty, energy, inner peace, or well-being. And beyond its use as a mainstream term and science-backed wellness strategy, self-care has become big business, with public companies such as Calm and Headspace valued at billions. Viewed in this way, self-care is about more than addressing internal or external imbalances. It is an assumed feature of a modern life well-lived.

But if that still weren't broad enough, there's one last trend that's expanded self-care's meaning all over again. It's the idea that self-care is a comprehensive approach encompassing the many aspects of one's well-being—the tendency to use self-care to describe not only specific actions or activities, such as a relaxing bath, but equally the broader feeling of looking after and choosing one's personal self. This can include things like setting boundaries, deciding to start therapy, validating one's emotions, or even just saying no to an event. In this broadest sense, self-care is any attitude or decision that prioritizes one's personal well-being.

This broadest sense is where self-care's shadow side can most easily take over, for if self-care is whatever you want it to be, it can end up being indistinguishable from unchecked personal habits and cultural fads. Yet it's this broadest meaning of self-care, in its true sense, that best fits with how I am using it throughout this book. I believe the tasks of caring deeply for oneself are simply too critical for well-being in modern life to limit its use. Furthermore, self-care does not occur in a social vacuum, making it impossible to separate any narrower meaning of self-care from the daily decisions we make about our social lives and the care we provide to others.

Despite its proven benefits for many, self-care is not a panacea for protecting and promoting well-being. There are countless examples of how self-care can become misinterpreted and misused. Some instances of misuse appear harmless, yet others may risk undermining the deeper meaning of self-care that social justice leaders such as Audre Lorde advocated for—that self-care can be about preservation, not mere indulgence. Watering down the meaning of self-care through emphasizing its more superficial expressions is part of what I consider to be the "bad" of self-care. When self-indulgent forms of self-care abound, people can grow mistrustful of self-care, maybe even dismissing it altogether. Consequently, they might criticize the self-care of others, neglect their own well-being, and increase the risk of poor health for themselves and those around them.

Examples for the bad side of self-care may seem easy to spot for some, but naming them in any consensus way can be tricky, partly because we never can know what intentions are behind people's actions. Fortunately, comedy and satire can help. In the hit show *Parks and Recreation*, the characters Donna and Tom preach, "Treat yo' self." Check out this exchange between the two characters as they introduce viewers to their philosophy:

> TOM: Once a year, Donna and I spend a day treating ourselves. What do we treat ourselves to?
> DONNA: Clothes.
> TOM: Treat yo' self.
> DONNA: Fragrances.
> TOM: Treat yo' self.
> DONNA: Massages.
> TOM: Treat yo' self.
> DONNA: Mimosas.
> TOM: Treat yo' self.
> DONNA: Fine leather goods.
> TOM: Treat yo' self!
> DONNA: It's the best day of the year.[5]

Before you start writing me a letter, I'm not saying it's always bad to treat yourself. *Phew!* I am, however, pushing against the very real risk of eclipsing the deeper meaning and real-life value of self-care through an overemphasis on self-indulgence and materialism of various kinds.

Let's move beyond the bad manifestations of self-care toward the downright ugly ones, when self-care really is selfish, exacerbating all sorts of confusion and harm. Selfish self-care usually occurs when a person is avoiding something or someone. They're not merely trying to balance their allocation of care but rather operating with the goal of shirking personal responsibility or taking advantage of others. When we're confronted with this ugly kind of self-care, we might not always be able to differentiate it from healthy self-care. In its wake, however, we may find ourselves feeling confused and upset, maybe suspicious, without fully knowing why. After all, they said it was about their self-care, right? Shouldn't we support and advocate for the self-care of others?

Let's consider an example to reflect on selfish self-care—though fair warning, such expressions of self-care are rarely as straightforward as they initially seem.

Betsy and Tara are siblings. Their mother, in her late eighties, had been experiencing deteriorating health and memory problems, demanding more time, attention, and care. As the older sibling who also lived closer, Betsy initially felt like it was natural to take on the uptick in responsibilities of caring for her mother. But as days turned into months, the caregiving demands only grew more intense. Eventually, many of Betsy's relationships began to suffer, and her boss issued her a warning about her seeming lack of engagement at work.

Following this warning from her boss, Betsy decided it was finally time to connect with Tara about helping to care for their mother too. On the phone, Betsy carefully explained her dilemma and openness to many different ways Tara could aid in caring for their mother. But right away, Tara got defensive. She said she was not able to help care for their mother due to her need for more "self-care" to recharge, manage her stress, and attend her exercise classes, which she "barely has the energy for" as it is.

Given what I've shared so far, I expect many would agree that Tara's use of self-care appears selfish. However, when it comes to judging the self-care of others, the specific external words and actions someone uses can be less important than their inner experience and motives. Therefore, it's critical we try to clarify what lies beneath people's actions before passing final judgment. In this case, although Tara offered Betsy some of the rationale behind her view, there's still a possibility that Tara was *trying* to do the right thing. As research indicates, people can act selfishly without being aware that they are doing so, partly due to inaccurate perceptions of the situation.[6] Moreover, they can distort or rationalize selfish actions, coming to genuinely believe they are not acting selfishly. All of which brings us right up to edge of what may be the worst of self-care in modern life. What I call its *real* problem.

Half-Hearted

In the esteemed corridors of University College London, an eminent chemist-turned-biologist named George Price once had an office—all thanks to an equation. In 1970, Price published a truly groundbreaking equation with profound implications for understanding altruism. In elegant mathematical terms, it proposed that selfless, prosocial actions could occur even outside the context of genetic similarity, a view that went against prevailing understanding at that time. Before his equation, the dominant view was instead that altruism was merely an outgrowth of looking after one's relatives. Beyond these scientific impacts, the equation's effects on Price personally were wide-reaching, and getting an honorary appointment at University College London was just the start.

Shortly after writing his equation and receiving his professorship, Price's life took another unexpected turn. He experienced a profound religious awakening and became a devout Christian. This spiritual conversion, coupled with insights from his equation, led him to begin engaging in acts of altruism some may consider extreme, such as welcoming houseless individuals from London into his own home—choices rooted in his care for others that would ultimately leave Price without a home himself. What's more, beneath his unyielding altruism lay mounting mental struggles and underlying health issues. Tragically, the weight of his internal battles was too much to bear, and Price died by suicide in 1975.

Looking back on the full context of Price's death, it would be an oversimplification to attribute it solely to his extreme selflessness. Nevertheless, his haunting legacy is a powerful illustration of the potential dangers of what researchers call *pathological altruism*.[7] Pathological altruism is just one of many terms needed for the different ways people can be *too* other-oriented—that is, they can push themselves to help, or keep helping, far beyond what is healthy for them. Research has shown that it can also lead to less effective helping or even cause harm to those one is trying to support. While this is plenty interesting in its own right, what I find most fascinating about pathological altruism is what it shares in common with its seeming opposite—selfish self-care.

That's right. In a parallel to what we see with the Superhero and Hurt, at the extremes of both self-care and other-care lies the same fundamental problem. Both extremes are, in fact, symptoms of an underlying either/or mindset about care—that is, a way of thinking about self-care and other-care in an either/or, this-or-that fashion. This either/or mindset is out of sync with our innate sociality, leaving us half-hearted in our care each time we view it as *either* self-care *or* care for others. The result is misperceiving our social lives as riddled with *false dichotomies*—the erroneous view that there's only two, binary options to any social problem or dilemma. Consequently, someone may care in ways that do not seem to make sense from the outside, such as undermining their care for a loved one by neglecting their own self-care or bashing the selfishness of another's self-care, while never once reflecting on the selfishness of their own self-caring decisions.

The real problem of self-care, therefore, is the way in which its rapid rise and popularity activates and reinforces the either/or mindset in the context of our care, exacerbating unhealthy expressions of *both* self-care and care for others. Like water to fish, the either/or mindset hides in plain sight. Reflecting back on the prisoner's dilemma tournament from the outset of this chapter, understanding the either/or mindset can help us see how self-care's appeal and popularity as a concept, in research and beyond, lies partly in how it oversimplifies the complexity of social life into a series of binary choices. It plugs into the either/or mindset, with insights about whether to choose Cooperate (We) or Defect (Me), making one feel like they now understand how best to approach their entire life. In the end, thinking simplistically about whether to choose self-care or care for others is not all that different from preferring stories that have clear good-versus-evil narratives. However entrancing, once we head back to reality, we quickly rediscover that our social lives are much more complex and nuanced than the either/or mindset could ever handle.

When the either/or mindset takes hold, we all pay the price for its oversimplification of the reality of caring. The detrimental downstream influences of this mindset are many, but they can be summed up as heightened conflict—both inwardly in terms of dueling perspectives, values, and emotions, and outwardly in the form of relational stress and struggle. Consequently, the extremes are not just bad for us in a single direction, such as selfish self-care undermining other-care or pathological altruism undermining self-care. Ultimately, care rooted in an either/or mindset restricts care flowing in both directions, with damaging impacts on personal and social well-being. We are left in a half-hearted state that compromises the full potential of our natural caring capacities.

Divided Mind, Competing Brain

Each time we divide our care, we are simultaneously dividing an underlying natural care circuitry that functions better the more it's communicating and connected. The unique vantage point offered by neuroscience can help us understand how the either/or mindset drives literal inner conflict—a duel between brain regions and circuits weighing individual self-interest and concern for others. The most critical brain structures, regions, and networks depend on the particular situation you're facing and where you choose to direct your focus. Therefore, no one study can give us a complete picture of the workings of the either/or mindset. Nonetheless, we can return to the simplified context of games like the prisoner's dilemma for a meaningful glimpse into how the either/or mindset manifests in the brain.

During games like the prisoner's dilemma, scans reveal evidence for the brain being in a state of internal conflict known as *neural competition.* Areas of the brain linked with reward, like the striatum, and those involved in long-term strategy or social thinking, such as the dorsolateral prefrontal cortex (dlPFC), become activated alongside the anterior cingulate cortex (ACC), all signals of a brain trying to resolve conflict between two or more potentially rewarding choices, such as whether to choose Cooperate (We) or Defect (Me) in the prisoner's dilemma.[8] Moreover, when people have to choose either self-interest or other-interest in such game theory scenarios, doing so demands mental effort to suppress inclinations toward the nonchosen option, as demonstrated by top-down control of amygdala activation.[9] Yet unlike choosing between self or other, one of the more consistent findings in social decision-making neuroscience is that mutually beneficial cooperation (e.g., both players choosing We) is intrinsically rewarding, activating specific reward-related brain regions even when external rewards are absent.[10] This deeply ingrained mechanism of positive reinforcement underscores how our brains are naturally inclined toward actions that benefit both ourselves and others, whenever such options are available.

It's important to note that neural competition is not inherently bad and can instead be understood as a more general principle of how our brains work, supporting not only effective and caring decisions but also basic functions and adaptability in daily life. However, when brain areas and networks are in intense rivalry, it can be metabolically costly and subjectively exhausting. This is especially striking in light of the inherently rewarding nature of brain activity focused on mutual benefit. Ultimately, what's vital to understand about the link between the either/or mindset and neural competition is the biological reality of inner conflict. It's when we needlessly divide ourselves that we incur costs that accumulate, lose out on the rewards of mutual cooperation, and reinforce neural patterns that keep us conflicted. Appreciating this fully requires viewing the brain as always situated in a nuanced social context: It's one thing to endure the inner conflict and divide one's care when there are truly only two binary options. It's entirely different when there are several more straightforward paths that can benefit everyone involved. In situations where the outcomes genuinely matter to you, learning to identify and embrace those paths can save you from an exhausting neural tug-of-war.

Beliefs behind the Mindset

The either/or mindset is essentially embedded in the term *self-care*. While adding *self-* to *care* provides a useful distinction or emphasis compared to just saying *care*, the way it triggers the either/or mindset can cause problems. It's especially problematic when it is used to shield, mask, or justify selfish or otherwise unhelpful decisions and actions. So, although I think it's overall good news that self-care has outgrown its original, narrower meanings, we have to relate carefully to the implications of its new semantic breadth and ubiquitous use in our culture. We desperately need to update and recalibrate our views of how self-care fits within the broader picture of balancing care for ourselves and others.

If people were already inclined to think in more nuanced ways about their care, it wouldn't matter whether or not we used the term *self-care* so pervasively. Unfortunately, the opposite is true. Research has consistently found that people hold either/or mindsets across diverse social situations,[11] and common negative features of modern life—fear, scarcity, time pressure—readily exacerbate this tendency, serving as either/or mindset *triggers*. Thus, whether it's our default or context driven, the either/or mindset collapses the world of possibilities into self versus other, us versus them, winner versus loser. And it does so even when mutually beneficial outcomes are clearly possible. Like two players continually choosing Me, and thereby both ending up with fewer points, the either/or mindset limits the strength, scope, and effectiveness of our care, for others *and* ourselves.

Let's explore one more layer of the either/or mindset to see what specific beliefs may lie beneath it. Viewed in this way, we can think about a mindset as partly reflecting an underlying mental model or set of concepts about care. Mind you, many of the concepts that guide and shape our care may lie hidden beneath the surface of conscious awareness. Nevertheless, the divided model is based in certain assumptions that, when made clear, can be examined and held up to the light of our conscious awareness. In this spirit, I've listed below five possible statements that reflect this divided view, along with a rating scale so you can weigh and explore your own level of agreement with each:

Across our lives, care is frequently an either/or choice—either you care for yourself or for others.

Strongly Disagree   Strongly Agree

| 1 | 2 | 3 | 4 | 5 |

Care is a scarce resource, such that extending care to one person can readily diminish the care available for others.

Strongly Disagree   Strongly Agree

1   2   3   4   5

Approaching care in an either/or fashion is a good strategy for handling the complexity of our social lives.

Strongly Disagree   Strongly Agree

1   2   3   4   5

If you are naturally inclined toward caring deeply for others, you should aim to correct this imbalance by lessening your care for others.

Strongly Disagree   Strongly Agree

1   2   3   4   5

Your own and others' well-being frequently trade off against each other, so the best you can usually hope for is either a compromise or only one person getting what they want.

Strongly Disagree   Strongly Agree

1   2   3   4   5

As you can infer from this list, there could be many possible beliefs that intersect with an either/or mindset about care, only some of which are presented here. Moreover, since the intention here was about personal reflection, there's no benchmark score I can provide you for direct comparison. Despite this, I believe it can be helpful to get specific like this about aspects of the either/or mindset. On its own, each statement sheds light on our personal beliefs in relation to those that may underlie a divided mental model of care. Considered together, they highlight the varied ways an either/or mindset may find its way into our beliefs about care. Thus, in examining the extent to which our own views align with these statements, we begin to push against oversimplified storylines in which self-care is always selfish and other-care spells saintly.

Tara's Either/Or Mindset

To briefly review all we've covered so far, let's revisit the scenario involving the sisters, Tara and Betsy, in which Tara had relied on the language of self-care to deny support to both Betsy and their mother. Remember how I said Tara may have been *trying* to do the right thing? Now that we've reviewed the real problem of self-care, it should be easier to understand what I meant by that statement. Indeed, Tara's selfish thoughts and actions could have been motivated by a healthy, if misguided, desire to choose self-care. Imagine, for instance, that Tara had recently talked to her close friend Emma about her struggles with depression and anxiety. Emma asserted that Tara is struggling emotionally because she needs to get better at setting boundaries. According to Emma, Tara is always putting others before herself and therefore needs more self-care. If Tara did not start putting herself first, Emma claimed, her mental health and emotional well-being would continue to suffer.

Following this conversation, filled with well-intended advice, Tara came to believe she needed to resist her tendencies toward empathy, kindness, and compassion in order to put herself first—no matter how guilty it made her feel. Thus, when Betsy asked Tara for help, Tara did her best to suppress her natural care for her sister and mother, to focus solely on her own needs, and to set boundaries for the sake of her own self-care. In other words, the concept of self-care became fuel for Tara's either/or mindset, providing her with both a motive and rationalization for acting selfishly.

Glimpsing Your Care Blind Spots

When driving a car on the highway, you can usually rely on your view out the windshield, in the rearview mirror, and via side mirrors to provide you with multiple perspectives on your surroundings. Checking through these different points of view is useful because it integrates the unique information from each source into a more complete picture. And yet, all these views together are still limited. Without taking the time to look over your shoulder—or on newer cars, relying on technological assistance that provides that function—visual blind spots persist in which a nearby vehicle could be traveling out of sight. Knowing this, we have to compensate as we drive, putting in some extra effort and due diligence to check our blind spots. Or else.

Similar to the role of blind spots while driving, our minds can overlook important details about ourselves and the social worlds we inhabit. And just as visual blind spots matter more on the road than in the comfort of our homes, these sorts of personal and social blind spots matter much more when we are making decisions about how we approach caring for ourselves and others. In the context of our care, we can speak in terms of *care blind spots*— gaps in awareness that end up negatively impacting our self-care or care for others. As in driving, failing to acknowledge and check our care blind spots can be disastrous, resulting in harms such as neglect, abuse, abandonment, aggression, and more—toward others and ourselves.

Below are two sets of examples of how these critical care blind spots can manifest in everyday life. As you read through them, notice how, despite their differences, both could cause similarly detrimental, even disastrous, consequences.

SELF-CARE BLIND SPOT EXAMPLES (I.E., WHEN PEOPLE OVERLOOK THE NEED FOR SELF-CARE)

- Working to the brink of exhaustion, all the while forgetting to nourish oneself with food, water, or breaks.

- Insisting that others decide on the details of upcoming plans for the weekend, even when asked sincerely to voice one's own preferences.

- Giving all of one's savings to an estranged friend who calls out of the blue, desperate for financial assistance.

- Always saying yes to requests from friends asking for favors, such as babysitting or helping them move, even when it is highly inconvenient.

OTHER-CARE BLIND SPOT EXAMPLES (I.E., WHEN PEOPLE OVERLOOK THE NEED TO CARE FOR OTHERS)

- Treating a server at a restaurant like one's personal servant, then leaving no tip due to something outside of their control.

- Thinking about how to approach a hard conversation solely in terms of what is most easeful or convenient for oneself personally.

- Venting about one's problems to a friend without checking in if it's okay to do so or offering them much of a chance to speak about themselves.

- Always saying no to requests from friends who ask for favors, even when they have repeatedly supported you with favors.

Exploring the Causes of Care Blind Spots

In the complex, messy reality of caring in everyday life, care blind spots are frequently specific to certain people and situations. For instance, someone could have a self-care blind spot in their romantic relationship but not in their friendships. Or they might fail to express care for their coworkers while being quite other-oriented and prosocial outside the office. In my own ongoing exploration of my care blind spots, I recently uncovered one I hadn't sensed before: I have trouble fully listening to someone when I disagree with part of what they're saying—even if it's only a small part. I get fixated on where I disagree and tune out the rest. In reflecting on the source of this blind spot, I noticed how long I'd been identified with being a "good listener," having received this feedback from others throughout my life. This made me believe I was almost always a good listener, when in fact my listening skills vary quite a bit from one person or situation to the next. Looking more closely for the "why" of this blind spot, I recalled a core memory from childhood in which I decided not to listen fully to others sometimes, since naming the subtleties of what others were saying could get me in trouble. This explanation feels satisfying, but I know it is far from complete. I suspect that, like many others, I sometimes struggle to listen fully simply due to general issues of inattentiveness, selective listening, mental rehearsal of what to say next, or perhaps even an underlying fear of being changed by what another is sharing.

When exploring the origins of one's care blind spots, it's vital not to oversimplify or rush to conclusions. For any one blind spot, there's bound to be a staggering number of factors to weigh—from personal history to learned patterns to genetics to quirks common to nearly all human minds—all of which may hold explanatory value without being the whole story. Finding one root, we may come to believe we fully understand the entire root system. Yet, if we keep exploring, we uncover an intricate network of intertwined roots, each representing another contributing factor and causal pathway.

Common care blind spots, such as the general tendency to overlook either self-care or other-care, may result not only from the either/or mindset broadly but also from a mixture of highly specific "features" and "bugs" of the human mind and brain. This is because a lot of different neural and mental processes have to work in concert for our care system and circuitry to function optimally. For example, as I mentioned earlier in relation to Tara's example, the science of selfishness supports the view that someone can act selfishly yet be unaware they are doing so.[12] This is because what we call selfish is highly subjective, context-dependent, and frequently inferred with degrees of uncertainty. Accurately recognizing selfishness, both in ourselves and in others, is therefore an advanced skill that depends on the coordinated functioning of various mental processes, brain regions, and interconnected brain networks. It's no wonder, then, that people sometimes fail to recognize their own selfish behavior.

Similarly, regarding self-care blind spots, research has consistently shown that people can be partly unaware of their tendency to compromise their own well-being while pursuing the goal of supporting others.[13] Beyond certain cultural factors and the either/or mindset, the ubiquity of such self-care blind spots points to more universal explanations. For instance, empathy-based guilt is an evolved response not only in humans but also in other mammals, with plenty of research to demonstrate that it can serve as a precursor to pathological altruism that harms the altruist and sometimes those they're trying to help.[14]

Fortunately, we need not know all the reasons why our care blind spots exist to avoid many of their negative consequences. What's more essential is acknowledging they exist, then doing our best to remain aware of them—much like remembering to look over your shoulder while driving and switching lanes. In recognizing that, by virtue of being human, we're bound to have care blind spots, we can take an important step toward reducing the harms they may cause us and others. Beyond this basic awareness, it can be helpful to underscore that a care blind spot in one direction frequently diminishes care in both directions. Understanding this provides an extra incentive to address both sorts of common blind spots, no matter which direction we may lean.

How Do You Spot the Unseen?

Starting to become aware of and work with our care blind spots sounds nice, but when we get right down to it, how does one actually start to notice something that one has been habitually unaware of? This is an essential question for understanding the challenge of counteracting our care blind spots. Catching a first glimpse of a care blind spot may well be half the battle. The other half, occurring after this initial awareness, connects back to the metaphor of blind spots during driving. When switching lanes, we rely on our memory—a secondary awareness or prospective memory that something could be hiding in our blind spot. This motivates us to take extra precautions such as checking over our shoulder. In a similar fashion, we can learn to anticipate and check our care blind spots before it's too late.

By now, you may also be pondering the care blind spots of others. Rest assured that, in future chapters, we will relate more fully to this topic. However, as the great philosopher Seneca noted, "We hold the flaws of others before our eyes but turn our backs toward our own."[15] Therefore, in this section, I want to provide three categories of methods or tools that can help you to grow more conscious of your personal care blind spots. Some of the methods listed may help you to spot the unseen—that is, to grow your primary awareness of a care blind spot. Others may work more on your secondary awareness of your blind spots, helping you to anticipate their inevitability, proactively lessen their influences, and moderate some of their unwanted consequences when they do arise:

1. *Self-inquiry.* Although one cannot rely solely on one's own perspective to sense blind spots, the right combination of self-inquiry can still make a difference. At their best, these kinds of methods offer new angles and more truthful perspectives for observing ourselves and others. Personally, I recommend a combination of training in mindfulness and compassion, alongside some sort of embodiment practice such as dance or yoga. Additionally, I've found tremendous value in journaling, making art, writing, spending time in nature, traveling, and exercising. If it can support you seeing yourself in new ways, it may help you catch a glimpse of your care blind spots.

2. *Social feedback.* There are few moments in life more challenging to work with than the surprise of unexpected negative feedback about a care blind spot, especially if you have inadvertently caused harm. To avoid this, you can proactively seek out feedback about yourself, be it from loved ones, close friends, mentors, or trusted colleagues. The feedback we get from others is always filtered through their own subjective lenses, so it's critical to balance what you hear with what you know is true for you. Moreover, because of the complexity of care in our lives, others' feedback can sometimes be completely off target, even when it is delivered with care. As a general rule, if you're feeling at all defensive about social feedback, it could be a clue that there's something there worth taking a closer look at. One

final idea in this category involves trying to spot others' blind spots and then turning the mirror back on yourself: Is the care blind spot you're seeing in another potentially a blind spot for you too?

3. *Experts, professionals, and trusted guides.* Healing modalities and systems of many kinds—from evidence-based and scientific approaches to alternative and spiritual ones—converge in their interest in strategies that can reveal areas of conflict or division within ourselves. This could be seen as partly a shared view about the importance of uprooting the either/or mindset. Accordingly, I believe there's distinctive value in exploring diverse approaches and systems from many kinds of experts and guides, since different modalities can reveal unique insights. This could take the form of reading books, attending workshops, or engaging in longer-term trainings. In my view, however, there's no substitute for one-on-one work with a professional or trusted guide, and perhaps especially with a skillful, qualified therapist or counselor. Whichever direction you explore, be wary of anyone who claims they have no blind spots or refuses to take responsibility for them—similar to how we should remain skeptical if we ever start to think we're free of them.

The Most Common Care Blind Spot

Many people report having care blind spots that predominantly cause deficits in either self-care or other-care, leading them to frequently neglect caring for themselves or others in an unintended manner. However, the most important care blind spot appears more ubiquitous than either of these alone. It's a care blind spot that causes us to miss the broad and varied territory *between* self-care or other-care, the territory of we-care.

Throughout the chapters ahead, our exploration of we-care will broaden far beyond care blind spots. But at this juncture, it makes sense to name we-care as a blind spot all its own—one that's evident whenever people fail to perceive the possibility of combining self-care and other-care to promote mutual benefits. In overlooking we-care, people are left to believe there is no choice but to act from the either/or mindset, opting for divided forms of self-care or care for others. Too much emphasis on the value of self-care not only reinforces the either/or mindset and its divided expressions, it eclipses we-care. Said another way, the we-care blind spot and either/or mindset are two angles on the same underlying problem—the real problem of self-care.

If Not You, Who?

One week before beginning to write this chapter, I signed my contract with the publisher. Enthralled by the opportunity to publish my debut book, an old care blind spot of mine got the best of me. I wouldn't fault you for laughing. Ironically, in writing too intensely about self-care, I forgot to practice it myself. Pushing well beyond my limits too many days in a row, it caught up with me in the form of insomnia fueled by racing thoughts of looping, meaningless sentences—a kind of writer's hangover. For days after, my sleepy state diminished my well-being and the care I was able to offer to myself and those I interacted with, especially my wife. I vowed not to miss this self-care blind spot again.

Only one week later, I again found myself approaching the same frazzled state of mind. Fortunately, it set in right as I was editing a sentence about self-care blind spots. A simple truth dawned: no one was going to tell me to take a break from writing but myself. I immediately stopped and, knowing I'd better distance myself from my laptop, invited my wife to join me for a night hike. Less than an hour later, as we reached the top of the trail, we were delighted by a rising, honey-colored supermoon.

Tracing the history of self-care from its roots in the medical world to its modern ubiquity, we see a general trend of expanding the scope of what counts as self-care and for whom self-care is needed. Reencountering my self-care blind spot in these ways reminded me of another reason why, despite its downsides, I nonetheless embrace and value the expansion of self-care in modern life: Self-care belongs to everyone. After all, there are certain caring actions no else can perform for us but us. And yet, as we've explored, the downsides of self-care matter. They include not only its superficial or self-indulgent manifestations but also the potential for encouraging selfish and harmful actions as well as masking them. Most of all, the term *self-care* can reinforce the either/or mindset and perpetuate harmful care blind spots. So, where do we draw the line between the good of self-care and its bad or downright ugly expressions? What ultimately distinguishes healthy, unselfish forms of self-care from unhealthy, selfish ones?

Healthy Selfishness

A couple of years ago, I was scanning the references of a scientific paper when my eyes did a double take on the title of another paper I'd not yet read: "Healthy Selfishness and Pathological Altruism: Measuring Two Paradoxical Forms of Selfishness."[16] I dropped what I was doing, looked up the paper, and got to reading. The study introduced two new measurement tools, one for what the authors called *healthy selfishness* and the other for pathological altruism. Their findings showed how healthy selfishness was linked not only to personal well-being but also to being more other-oriented and prosocial. By contrast, pathological altruism was linked to lower personal well-being and behaviors aimed at helping that might actually be harmful to others.

So far, so good—the results tracked with what I would expect, based on my understanding of the either/or mindset. But, I wondered, how exactly did the researchers distinguish healthy forms of selfishness? For this, I needed to look at the statements they relied on to measure it. Here are a few examples from the paper:

- "I have a lot of self-care."
- "Even though I give a lot to others, I know when to recharge."
- "I balance my own needs with the needs of others."
- "I have healthy boundaries."
- "I have a healthy form of selfishness (e.g., meditation, eating healthy, exercising, etc.) that doesn't hurt others but brings me greater happiness."

Can you spot any patterns or themes related to what we've reviewed so far in this chapter? As I read through them, I realized that what these researchers were calling *healthy selfishness* was not far off the mark from what I'd come to call *healthy self-care*.

The Key to Healthy Self-Care

Part of the challenge in wrapping our minds around self-care in modern times is the sheer diversity of phenomena it can now encompass. The thoughts, feelings, and actions people may identify as their unique versions of self-care vary as much as the people who wield them. Such a diverse range of self-care makes it difficult to say anything universal about what it means to have healthy self-care. Yet somehow, despite this tremendous diversity, the term retains a measure of meaning and potency.

Fortunately, the real problem of self-care puts the right target in focus. Flipping this real problem of self-care around, we find that healthy expressions of self-care accomplish all the good stuff we typically ascribe to self-care but without reinforcing the either/or mindset. In other words, the key to healthy self-care is fundamentally about a shift in mindset: self-care is not divorced from our care for others; the two are naturally interconnected. From this interconnected view of care, we can readily see the potential for our self-care to support ourselves *and* others.

This could be as simple as knowing that our chosen self-care holds the potential to benefit someone we love, even if the connection isn't immediately obvious. Frequently, however, this interconnected view of self-care entails raising our gaze and looking past the short-term consequences of our self-caring choices or actions. Consider how the short-term impact of a new mother choosing to leave home for a massage might look to a crying baby and a stressed-out father. Internally though, the mother knows that prioritizing her own well-being is going to benefit her whole family. Therefore, even if she feels guilty as she drives away, she's likely to return home buoyed by her sense that her self-care is certain to have longer-term mutual benefits.

This perspective offers us a line in the sand for assessing the health of your own self-care: healthy self-care honors your care for others while still prioritizing your personal well-being. This means recognizing the ways in which caring for yourself can positively influence your care for others without requiring sacrifice or compromising your own needs. In this way, you maintain a healthy balance, ensuring that you do not feel stuck in an others-versus-myself dilemma. And because you're awake to the interconnectedness of self-care and other-care, you are likewise motivated to avoid unhealthy forms of self-care that don't align with your care for others. By contrast, unhealthy self-care is fundamentally disconnected from our care for others, and may even run counter to it. This disconnect starts at the level of awareness, and it ultimately weakens our overall care system—allowing more divided thoughts, feelings, words, and actions to incite and maintain all kinds of conflict and harm.

Bearing this in mind, here are a few simple reflection questions for you to begin evaluating healthy self-care for yourself:

- Does this act of self-care honor my care for others while still prioritizing my personal well-being?

- Can I feel the interconnectedness between this self-care and my care for others?

- Could this self-care create any strong blocks or interference in my care for others?

I'm not suggesting you need to analyze and uncover an other-oriented motive for all your self-care, nor is it about catering to specific people who may misunderstand your needs and values. Healthy self-care is beneficial for reasons beyond its ability to support others or its alignment with our inherent sociality. Rather, it is healthy primarily because it is *more effective self-care*. Healthy self-care should therefore do all the things you would typically expect self-care to do, but better. This includes prioritizing your long-term well-being over the demands of others, generating moments and memories that are deeply enjoyable or pleasurable, protecting yourself from harm and needless suffering, and lessening the likelihood of exhaustion and burnout. After all, self-care is naturally bound up with our care for others, so an interconnected view of self-care equips you with a more accurate compass for navigating the reality of care in your daily life. Then there's the fact that an interconnected approach to self-care is more likely to succeed in fostering the well-being of others—catalyzing powerful positive feedback loops of care that strengthen the social fabric and reciprocally benefit you. Lastly, all of these benefits together free you from the grip of the either/or mindset. Consequently, you find yet more benefits such as improved relationships, naturally healthy boundaries, and an expanded tool kit for effecting personal and societal change. You come to realize that the key to healthy self-care has unlocked an inner door to something much greater. In embracing healthy self-care, you have stepped clearly onto the path of we-care.

We-Care Practice 3
BOTH/AND SELF-CARE

Healthy self-care is rooted in interconnectedness—the felt sense that one's own self-care can benefit others too. This can be as simple as being aware that your self-care will resource you in ways that will improve the quality of your relationships and work. However, it's also possible to take this a step further through a more deliberate approach to your self-care. At its best, this kind of both/and self-care creates a special kind of synergy, where caring for yourself and others enhances both together. In this spirit, the following guidelines will help you choose a both/and self-care activity that can create the right conditions for you to directly experience this special care synergy.

PRACTICE INSTRUCTIONS

1. *Choose a Both/And Self-Care activity.* A Both/And Self-Care activity is one in which you consciously aim to care for yourself and another person. However, the benefits from the activity do not have to be exactly the same, equal, or occur at the same time. There are many different varieties and approaches to Both/And Self-Care, including the practice of

Reverse Self-Care outlined in the introduction. To help you brainstorm, here's a few more types and examples:

a. ABUNDANT SELF-CARE. Instead of purchasing or making something only for yourself, consider someone else who may also appreciate it and make or buy it for them too. For instance, you can bake cookies or prepare a nice meal that you would personally delight in that you can also share with a family member, romantic partner, friend, or roommate. Alternatively, you could double the self-care by benefiting a stranger, paying for both your coffee and that of a person in line behind you, or offering a meal similar to yours to a person experiencing houselessness.

b. FORWARD SELF-CARE. Whereas Reverse Self-Care can focus on anyone in your life, here the attention is on the very next person you care about who you'll be interacting with. Looking *forward* to this encounter, see if you can identify a self-care activity that will deeply support and nourish you in the here and now, so that you will feel more resourced and present when you see them.

c. PARALLEL SELF-CARE. During free time on weekends, my wife or I will sometimes confess our need for self-care and alone time. Rather than seeing this as an insult, we've come to welcome it as a natural invitation for the other to do the same. Occasionally, we'll drop in and visit each other during the time. But almost always, after a few hours, we find ourselves naturally reconvening with fresh energy, excited to share about what reflections, insights, or simple joys we experienced while off by ourselves. More broadly, Parallel Self-Care involves linking others' self-care time to our own, supported by check-ins before and after time and space to oneself. This can provide a supportive structure and container for enhancing both self-care and connection.

d. TANDEM SELF-CARE. Many self-care activities can be done in the presence or company of others who are also seeking some dedicated time for self-care. For example, if you're eager to curl up and read your favorite book with a cup of tea, why not ask a friend if they want to come over with their favorite book and join you for a couple hours? Or maybe you and a friend each want to listen to your favorite music with headphones in, bopping around while doing something crafty? Many tandem self-care activities can also be adapted for a phone or video call.

e. MATCHING SELF-CARE. Sometimes, the same self-care activity you want to do can be done with another person who also sees it as self-care for them. Simply invite a friend or loved one to join you for a self-care activity, communicating your intention to experience some needed self-care time together. This could include joint activities like going to a yin yoga class, getting a pedicure, or meeting for ice cream. In this way, you still get to enjoy each other's company while simultaneously experiencing self-care.

2. *Do the activity with a both/and mindset.* Decide on a timeline and way that make sense for you and carry out the Both/And Self-Care activity you identified. Throughout the activity, try to remember that you are doing this activity not only as a form of self-care but also as a both/and act of caring that can support others too.

3. *Notice impacts, short and long.* Shortly after completing the activity and into the future, keep an eye out for its effects. Not every Both/And Self-Care activity will succeed in producing benefits for us and others. It's therefore helpful to be in a mindset of experimenting rather than expecting, letting go of attachment to any specific outcome. Ideally, however, your chosen activity will generate benefits for yourself and at least one other person, as well as create a kind of synergy or positive feedback loop, amplifying benefits all around. Did the act of caring for someone else enhance your own experience of self-care? Might it lead to additional positive outcomes that you hadn't anticipated?

CHAPTER 3

An Undivided Heart

Discovering We-Care

> If our small minds, for some convenience,
> divide . . . this universe, into parts . . . remember
> that nature does not know it! So let us put it
> all back together.
> —RICHARD FEYNMAN, "The Relation
>   of Physics to Other Sciences"

During the tumultuous 1960s, as the Vietnam War escalated, the revered Vietnamese Zen master Thich Nhat Hanh was in pursuit of the perfect word. Amid the chaos and suffering of the war, Thich Nhat Hanh—affectionately known as Thay, meaning "teacher"—sought an English word to express a profound concept. This teacher and scholar—who, only years later, would be nominated for a Nobel Peace Prize by Dr. Martin Luther King Jr.—wanted to find a way to express that all things in the universe are deeply, radically interconnected. In Thay's words, "Everything relies on everything else in the cosmos in order to manifest—whether a star, a cloud, a flower, a tree, or you and me."[1]

The word he sought would need to be consistent with Zen teachings on *emptiness*. Emptiness is an easily misunderstood

Buddhist concept, as it points not to the lack of anything meaningful or good in our lives but rather to the absence of truly isolated or independent things. While I'm not an expert in Buddhist philosophy, I've personally always found emptiness to be a helpful term within the context of Buddhist practice, but its meaning can get lost in translation outside it. So, in a way, Thay might have been aiming for a more accessible synonym for emptiness. However, in knowing the word he landed on, as well as the teachings it inspired, it's clear there was more to Thay's search than translating emptiness. He aimed to capture not only the absence of absolute independence but also the radical, omnipresence of *inter*dependence.

Now, if Thich Nhat Hanh had not been limited to searching within English for the perfect word, he might have had more choices. Many cultures and belief systems around the world include words or phrases that express similar ideas about the deeply interconnected nature of the world and our lives. The word *ubuntu*, for example, originates from the Nguni Bantu languages in Southern Africa and is often translated as "I am because we are," emphasizing communal interdependence and shared humanity. Similarly, the Sanskrit term *vasudhaiva kutumbakam* from ancient Indian scriptures epitomizes the perception of the world as one family, stressing the importance of communal harmony and the holistic well-being of the individual and the collective. Or consider that *mitakuye oyasin*, a phrase from the Lakota Sioux, may be translated as "all my relatives," expressing the interconnectedness among humans as well as with all beings and elements of existence. Then there's *aloha* from Hawaiian culture, the Filipino concept of *bayanihan*, and numerous other examples in use today, with yet more lost to time.

Whatever your native language(s), you've likely experienced ways in which words are limited, unable to perfectly describe the varied world we inhabit and explore from within. There are gaps between what we mean and what we say, such as between the diversity of colors and one's limited color vocabulary. Searching in this experiential terrain, Thay at first landed on the word *togetherness*. But still feeling that the gap between togetherness and what he wanted to convey was too large, he decided to get more creative, looking beyond the bounds of existing words.

He boldly invented a new English word—*interbeing*—that would go on to become a central aspect of his teaching, scholarship, activism, and peacemaking. As Thay would later write when reflecting on what led him to invent this new word, "The verb 'to be,' can be misleading because we cannot be by ourselves, alone. 'To be' is always to 'inter-be.'"[2]

For me, Thay's invention of *interbeing* is all the more powerful and inspiring when considered against the backdrop of the divisive war in which he conjured it—a simple yet profound teaching on finding the courage to look past the limits of existing words when something more is needed to express deeper truths.

Thay's being Buddhist was undoubtedly a crucial aspect of his process in coining *interbeing*, yet that was only part of his complex identity. Other aspects of his background likely also informed his quest for the right word. Born in 1926 in central Vietnam, he developed a worldview deeply influenced by the culture and environment of his upbringing. As is true of many East Asian cultures, the culture of Vietnam is high in collectivism, meaning that the goals and preferences of groups and community are typically prioritized over those of the individual. While the exact relationship between collectivism and Buddhism is complex and not merely cause and effect in East Asian societies, there are many shared ideals that emphasize seeing oneself and others as more interconnected than is the case in individualistic societies, such as that of the United States.

Now for what I consider to be a vital question: Can Thay's perspective of reality as deeply interconnected be reduced to an outgrowth of his Buddhist study and collectivist cultural upbringing?

In other words, do the values and lifestyles found in more individualistic societies mean that the interconnected view he aimed to share cannot take root in them? Or were Thay's views about deep interconnectedness born from insights about the world that span across religions and cultures—things that are true and verifiable, no matter one's country or creed?

One way to approach this question is through the lens of science. What if Thay had been a scientist back in the 1960s? Back then, it would have been much harder to make a compelling scientific case for the view that everyone and everything is deeply interconnected. Science in the 1960s focused more so on isolated phenomena and linear relationships. Today, however, it is much easier to find scientific perspectives and evidence aligned with the essence of Thay's message. Breakthroughs in fields ranging from systems ecology to quantum physics to social neuroscience have contributed to a paradigm shift in understanding toward a more interconnected view of the world and humanity.

As one well-known example, although it is frequently oversimplified, the *butterfly effect* has helped popularize important insights about the nature of deeply interconnected systems. As a metaphor, it refers to how even a very small or subtle change, such as a butterfly flapping its wings, could have effects that ripple into significant impacts elsewhere, such as a tornado in Texas.[3] To scientists, however, this effect concerns more nuanced, tractable ideas situated within the broader field of *systems theory*—a transdisciplinary area of research that emphasizes emergence, interdependence, and complexity rather than reductionism. This holistic, sum-over-parts approach has proven enduringly generative for diverse scientific fields, from meteorology to computational biology to theoretical physics, to this day. For example, in my own fields, systems theory has been instrumental in elucidating the complex interactions among brain regions (e.g., network neuroscience) and between people (e.g., social contagion effects), underscoring the fundamental role of interconnectedness at multiple levels of analysis. Yet despite its eventual widespread adoption within science, systems theory was still proving its relevance in the 1960s, around the same time Thay was searching for his perfect word.

Given the resonance between Thay's ideas and those found within modern science, I've never taken his quest for the right word to be fundamentally about making religious or cultural scripts more palatable to the Western mind. Instead, I see it as his effort to share a perspective born from his own careful observations about what the world is and how it all works. While there are many important differences between Zen Buddhism and contemporary science, they strongly converge in their pursuit of understanding and describing how deeply interconnected the world really is.

Carving Care

Notwithstanding the increased acceptance of and orientation to interconnectedness in recent decades, much of science still operates with the principle of "carving nature at its joints"—an idea introduced by Plato to convey the ideal of dividing one's concepts about the world according to their natural structures or "joints." Based on this principle, scientific thinking frequently entails conceptually "carving" phenomena of interest along lines that make it easier to study them scientifically. However natural and pragmatic these conceptual lines, carving a deeply interconnected world can lead to misperceptions, as well as contradictions that exist in the description of the phenomenon being studied but not in the phenomenon itself.

It's exactly this kind of contradiction that stopped my mind one day, a few months after commencing my role as research director of Naropa University's Compassion Initiative. For more than a decade, I had been fascinated by the topic of healthy boundaries. I found it personally relevant and practical for addressing many of my problems, and I had observed in various settings—from classroom disruptions to counseling sessions to meditation retreats—that boundaries often played a key role in the social dilemmas people reported. However, in looking to the science, a place where I'd often found clarity about other topics, I was surprised to find only scattered pieces of a puzzle, with a lot of uncertainty as to how they might fit together.

Most puzzle pieces I encountered over the years came from familiar sources—scientific papers on social emotion regulation, experiential practices like Buddhism's *tonglen* ("sending and taking") meditation, or clinical insights on the need for permeable boundaries.[4] However, the missing piece, the transformative one, was not in any of these usual places. It was instead hidden closer to the center of the science on care and compassion. It was there I uncovered a contradiction, rooted in the scientific tendency to "carve nature at its joints," with far-reaching implications.

Scientists are not immune to the biases we uncover. Like anyone else, when given new information to consider, there can be a *binary bias*[5]—a tendency toward thinking in ways that divide, which I previously called the either/or mindset. This biased mindset can lead to the perception of *false dichotomies*. Consequently, over decades of studying care and compassion, scientists and others had carved these topics at what seemed a natural joint—self-care or other-oriented care. As the field progressed, with study after study relying on this same binary view, a body of scientific tools and findings amassed that appeared to reinforce the value of carving care (and compassion) at this self/other joint. Literature has blossomed around this conceptual distinction, countless conferences have been convened, and numerous academic and professional careers have been shaped by it. However, amidst all this development, an important problem persisted: the initial distinction between self-care and care for others wasn't natural in the first place.

One could employ many different strategies to substantiate this claim. However, to fully understand the rationale behind my conviction, it is critical to shift from searching for supportive evidence to weighing what evidence would have been needed to initially justify carving care in such a binary, self/other way. One may, for example, investigate the brain activity and structures associated with individual self-awareness and the perception of others, showing discrete areas of the brain that are activated when individuals think about themselves versus when they think about others. However, the bulk of data within neuroscience shows how interconnected these processes are, with overlapping neural regions and networks (e.g., the dorsal and ventral medial prefrontal cortex) underlying the perception of both self and other. This is not to say our brains fail to distinguish between self and other but instead that its default orientation to representing them occurs via shared, not discrete, neural structures. As the social neuroscientists Jamil Zaki and Kevin Ochsner concluded from their careful review of the evidence, "Separating brain activations by the target of processing [self versus other] alone might resemble trying to slice a cake into the flour and sugar that went into it: although one can contemplate the separation conceptually, in actual practice, the two are hopelessly intertwined."[6]

Upon realizing that the self/other joint in care had never been scientifically verified despite its use in so much of the literature, all the other thoughts I had about care and compassion began to rotate into new configurations, revealing a new and very different way to complete the puzzle. Instead of starting with an assumption of division between self-care and care for others, I tried building from an undivided foundation, one that assumed self-care and care for others were parts of one unified care system. Fitting the pieces together over the coming months and years, I discovered new convergences between the pieces I'd already gathered. These convergences opened my eyes to perspectives and findings I hadn't previously considered to be relevant.

Whereas the assumption of division had led to more complexity, this undivided approach was equally simpler and more comprehensive. Completing the puzzle, initially undertaken as a journey to understand healthy boundaries, was revealing itself to be about something bigger.

Now I just needed a word for it.

What Exactly Is We-Care?

As first stated in the introduction, we-care entails caring for a *we*. Since that initial discussion, we have explored several broader ideas about we-care, including how it can reveal hidden choices between self-care and care for others, how it differs from extremes of care represented by the Superhero and the Hurt, and how it may relate to healthier forms of self-care. At this point, I think it will be helpful to home in on a simple definition of *we-care* to center our focus and give us an anchor to circle back to, as needed:

> *We-care:* A broad form of care in which self-care
> and care for others are experienced as essential
> and interconnected.

Let's slow down to reflect on each of its key elements in turn:

> *A broad form of care . . .* We-care is a wide-ranging category of care. As with self-care, we-care manifests in a large variety of ways. This includes specific activities that look just like self-care from the outside, consistent with how *healthy self-care* was described in chapter 2. But we-care may also look like *healthy other-care* or some combination

of the two. More broadly, like self-care, we-care can encompass any and all caring thoughts, feelings, decisions, and actions that fit with the rest of its definition. There's also a range of depths to we-care, from basic caring at the level of awareness to courageous acts of compassion. All of these different expressions make up its broad and varied scope.

In which self-care and care for others are experienced as essential . . . The type of care described involves, first and foremost, the presence of care for oneself and at least one other person. But more than mutual presence, the definition highlights that self-care and other-care are both *essential.* In other words, both are experienced as indispensable to we-care. This dual focus protects against both extremes of an either/or mindset, including some of the most critical care blind spots (e.g., selfish self-care, self-sacrificing care for others). Here, "essential" also means that both self-care and other-care matter enough to inform and inspire our caring thoughts, feelings, and actions to some degree. Lastly, it's worth noting that the definition does not specify an ideal proportion or balance point. Self-care and other-care are both present and essential in we-care, but they need not shape one's care equally in a strict fifty-fifty split that somehow holds across various situations.

And interconnected. This final element of our definition highlights how, in we-care, care for oneself and care for others are not experienced in opposition or tension but instead as parts of one underlying care system. In fact, we-care spans a wide range of felt interconnectedness. At deeper levels, we-care may manifest in unified experiences in which distinctions between self-care and other-care seem to fall away. This may sound profound, and indeed it is often experienced that way, but it need not be mysterious. An experience of deep interconnectedness or unified we-care can be as familiar as what we mean when we use the word *we*.

The *We* in We-Care

The word *we* is so commonplace that we typically avoid reflecting more deeply on its layered meaning. After all, at its most basic, *we* is just a word used to refer to oneself and another person or set of people. This is the meaning as in, "I live with my roommate, Jackson. *We* live in the building on the corner of 9th and Spruce." On the other hand, *we* can sometimes point to a more profound kind of relationship, such as, "The incident happened only last week, but I can already tell, *we* will never be the same."

In the first use of *we*, there is clearly oneself and one other person included, but there's no explicit sense of deeper relationship between the roommates. In the second example *we* points to a deeper kind of connection in which oneself, another, and the relationship are all affected in lasting ways. There's no denying these two uses of *we* are very different. However, in both, *we* communicates an *essential* and *interconnected* nature to oneself and another—consistent with all of the key elements of our definition for *we-care*.

The dual utility of *we* is evident globally—*noi* in Italian, *hum* in Hindi, *watashitachi* in Japanese—each representing an underlying concept that is remarkably consistent in meaning and exhibits similar flexibility to the word *we*. For me, this underscores how we-care is not some new concept we have to strive to understand but is rather something built into the fabric of our languages and the inner experiences of felt interconnectedness they represent. With appreciation for our differences, *we* are nonetheless all human beings.

Let's complete this discussion with a brief reflection activity that can help to ground these ideas about *we* in your own feelings and body, alongside your thinking mind. To begin with, I invite you to reflect on *we* as you experience it in your life. Consider the different relationships or groups you already refer to as *we*, repeating the word as you reflect on each of them. What do you notice as you apply *we* to different people, groups, and maybe even the whole of humanity or all sentient beings? Does *we* feel the exact same to you across these different social contexts?

You may have noticed that some elements seem to stay the same across relationships and groups of people, while other elements change. Perhaps you can feel into a varied and nuanced range of *we*, reflecting degrees and varieties of interconnectedness. For some, the *we* may feel more faint, reflecting only the presence of both self and others. With close others, however, you may experience a much richer and more complex felt sense of *we*.

Undivided Care, Undivided Brains

While I frequently write and speak about we-care in terms of how it feels in our hearts, from a scientific perspective, we-care is still primarily determined by what's happening in our brains. And although neuroscience has traditionally focused on studying brains in relative isolation from other people, prevailing views and methods in the field are increasingly adept at examining the social brain. In other words, there's ever more acceptance within both psychology and neuroscience that, to understand human minds and brains, you must study them in social contexts. Accordingly, as these disciplines have steered their focus in a more social direction, I've witnessed an increasing number of paradigm-shifting discoveries that are aligned with core principles of we-care—discoveries that capture and showcase our innate sociality and preference for mutually beneficial relationships.

One of my favorite examples comes from the innovative work of James Coan, a social neuroscientist at the University of Virginia. In 2006, Coan and colleagues published an important study with counterintuitive results.[7] They discovered that, when alone, women who were anticipating the onset of a threatening, painful stimulus had greater activation in their prefrontal cortex, particularly in regions of the brain linked with down-regulating the negative emotions that occur when we're faced with some kind of threat or painful event (e.g., in the moments leading up to a flu shot). By contrast, when holding the hand of their romantic partner while facing the same threat, there was overall less activation in these common regulatory areas of the prefrontal cortex, especially when they reported being in a higher-quality romantic relationship. Thus, instead of *enhancing* one's ability to dampen feelings of threat, the presence of a trusted other appeared to actually *diminish* it.

Why might holding a loved one's hand lead to *less* prefrontal activation to down-regulate one's negative emotions when faced with a threat? The explanation revealed something truly fascinating: when quality social support was present, there was less down-regulation because there was less of a threat to begin with. In other words, the presence of social support actually lowered one's underlying perception of threat, decreasing the need for the brain's effortful management of fear and anxiety.

Further research since this initial study has helped fill in the gaps, eventually building to an intriguing new theory about our innate sociality, known as Social Baseline Theory. It posits that, since human beings evolved in close proximity to other humans, our brains now function in ways that are optimized for social proximity.[8] Consistent with Coan's initial findings, the presence of trusted others naturally down-regulates threat through the expectation of social support, helping us to face and navigate whatever challenges may come—not just in the laboratory but throughout our lives. This explains the broader context for why, when holding the hand of a loved one in the face of threat, there is less need to rely on costly, effortful regulation mediated by the prefrontal cortex. After all, when we're surrounded by others we know and love, our brains get to function in the sort of context they evolved to thrive in.

We-Care Strengths, Unlocked

There are three vital features, or *we-care strengths*, that may be thought of as primary routes through which we-care's basic elements positively transform one's care. Rather than thinking of these features as add-ons or learned skills, I understand them to be natural capacities of our overall care system that can easily get blocked, weakened, or distorted by divided approaches to care. In other words, because we-care better aligns with the inherent qualities of our underlying care circuitry, it unblocks access to natural capacities that can augment the effectiveness of our care. Accordingly, each we-care strength may be seen as part of our evolutionary legacy as social beings—something deeply ingrained in us through millennia of people developing and interacting in social settings.

The first strength derives from how, in a moment of we-care, self-care and care for others are both present and interconnected. This allows for *flexible emphasis* on self-care or care for others, without abandoning the orientation that's not currently emphasized. Secondly, because we-care takes us beyond the binary of caring for either one's individual self or others, it unlocks a full *continuum of interconnected care*. This includes healthy expressions of self-care and other-care, as well as many possible synergies between them. Finally, the third strength unlocked by we-care involves *an adaptable we* that improves our capacity to promote and prioritize healthy relationships. Rather than feeling stuck in one-sided dynamics, we-care helps us foster more mutually beneficial relationships as well as build and value new connections in which there's greater mutual care and interconnectedness.

The combined powers of these natural care capacities are especially striking when we compare them with self-care or other-care alone. Wielding the undivided approach of we-care, we can accomplish all the good that divided approaches to care do—protection, advocacy, resilience, cooperation, reciprocity, and more—but with fewer harms and more effectiveness. Furthermore, because we-care exists at the meeting point of self and others, the rewards from this type of transformation of our overall caring capacities can ripple beyond us, strengthening our connections, promoting mutual benefits, and perhaps even reinforcing the broader social fabric with kindness, compassion, and unity.

Because the influences of these three we-care strengths are so important for understanding we-care, the next three sections will delve deeper into each in turn.

Emphasis without Division

We-care helps us to transcend but integrate either/or care, meaning we experience the possibility of emphasizing self-care or care for others, while nonetheless lessening division and conflict. This we-care strength of *flexible emphasis* makes it so we can foreground one direction or flow of our care—toward self or others—while still respecting the other primary direction. This is important because, in practice, we-care is rarely as simple as an equal fifty-fifty split between our self-care and care for others.

Moreover, at times, care for oneself or others will need to be strongly emphasized. For instance, if someone is aiming to cause you harm, we-care could take the form of protective acts of self-care—setting strong boundaries, ending a relationship, or blocking a phone number.

However, even when our we-care does lean strongly in the direction of self-care, we need not close our hearts to everyone and everything. At minimum, we can stay awake to how our self-caring actions will support those we care about. And in most if not all cases, we can also set clear boundaries without burning bridges, end a relationship without the personal insults, or block a number without seeking revenge. Similarly, when extending our care to others, we can still look out for ourselves. This flexible emphasis of we-care enhances our capacity to support others and navigate complex social dynamics, all the while shielding us against the tendency to neglect our needs, goals, and values in the process.

Beyond emphasizing one orientation at a time, the flexible emphasis strength of we-care affords fluid and dynamic movement between emphases, such as the back-and-forth of care during a social interaction. Maybe you've had the experience of "losing yourself" in a conversation, only to realize afterward that you got overly other-oriented, caught up in another's perspective or emotions. With we-care, you can more readily alternate between care for yourself and others, which lowers the risk of getting hooked and confused and improves the overall balance between connection and protection, relationship and autonomy, empathy and compassion, or love and freedom. Then, as your confidence grows in your capacity to flexibly open and come back to yourself, you'll find it's easier to listen to others more deeply. Equally, you will feel more comfortable taking up space in conversation and speaking openly about what's true for you, bolstered by the knowledge that the best kinds of conversations make room for care to flow in all directions.

The We-Care Continuum

One seeming advantage of the either/or mindset is the way it appears to simplify decision-making. By turning the world into a set of binary options, ignoring its complexities and shades of gray, the either/or mindset can sometimes make it all feel a little less daunting. Still, it's not hard to see that constantly oversimplifying the reality of caring in a complex world, and thereby making simplistic binary decisions about one's care, would catch up with anyone eventually. What this all comes down to is the willingness to pause and reflect on the wider set of possible options. In fact, insufficient deliberation is one of the key factors research has shown to cause or exacerbate the either/or mindset.[9] Might there be a way to streamline decision-making about our care without oversimplifying it? This is the essence of the second we-care strength, which offers us access to a more nuanced and varied *continuum of care*. One way of depicting this continuum is through the we-care continuum shown below.

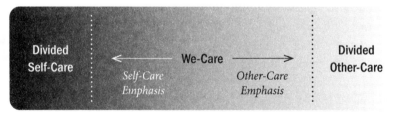

The essential idea is to reimagine divided self-care and divided other-care not as binary options but as opposing ends of a continuum, with ample space for we-care between them. This highlights just how wide-ranging and diverse we-care is when compared to the overly simplified either/or of divided self-care (e.g., selfish self-care) and divided other-care (e.g., pathological altruism).

The we-care continuum can be easily understood in relation to the defining elements of we-care. Like bookends framing each side of we-care, the dotted lines on the left and right mark its starting points—the territory in which both self-care and other-care are experienced as *essential* to one's care. Outside these lines, on either extreme end, exist the divided expressions of our care, territories of the either/or mindset. Within these lines, however, the essential nature of both self-care and other-care keeps us from moving into unhealthy extremes, even when, at times, we strongly emphasize one orientation or another. The we-care continuum is also meant to illustrate the potential range of *interconnectedness* that's possible in we-care. As illustrated, this spans from relative emphasis on self-care or other-care toward an emphasis on both nearer the center. Keep in mind there's tremendous diversity that falls within the centermost section of the we-care continuum, including the potential for both/and solutions and synergistic relationships between self-care and other-care.

At the midpoint of the continuum, it's tempting to imagine a fifty-fifty split in our care. However, that's an echo of the either/or mindset. Even though we-care can take the form of a fifty-fifty compromise sometimes, the most ideal midpoint in we-care represents a unified and harmonious combination of self-care and other-care, where both are strongly felt and fulfilled simultaneously. Consider the example of two people in the early stages of falling in love. Each person not only finds personal fulfillment in prioritizing the blossoming relationship (self-care) but also willingly adjusts their schedule and life to accommodate the needs of their partner (other-care). This adjustment isn't a sacrifice or compromise—it's a reciprocal act that enhances their own well-being while likewise nurturing the relationship.

Now that you've got the basics down, let's take a look at a few more examples of how we-care can manifest at different points along the continuum. See if you can spot how, in all the examples below, self-care and other-care are clearly present and are experienced as essential and interconnected. And note that while I'm still using the terms *self-care* and *other-care* to describe differences that fall within the boundaries of we-care, there's a subtle shift in their meaning. Within the bounds of we-care, these terms now reflect an emphasis of one's care rather than a division within it. Then again, we-care introduces the possibility of not needing to use the terms self-care and other-care, even when emphasizing one or another. As represented in the we-care continuum and evident in the examples that follow, differing emphases can simply be called we-care.

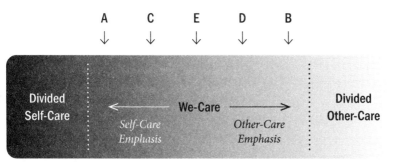

A. We-care: healthy self-care.

After two weeks in a row of particularly stressful work, Travis decides to make the upcoming weekend all about his self-care. He plans out a schedule with some of his favorite activities, maximizing time and space for himself. But as tempting as it is to completely clear his schedule, he decides against canceling the lunch plans he'd already confirmed with his good friend, since he knows the friend has been going through some major life changes and could likely use Travis's support. Reflecting on the chance for his own self-care weekend to also support his friend and to revitalize his own engagement with work the following week, Travis feels even more inspired to design an ideal self-care weekend.

B. We-care: healthy other-care.

Leading up to an election, Sasha decides to volunteer a few weekends of her time to help campaign for a local candidate she believes will bring about benefits for her entire community. She's always enjoyed similar volunteer opportunities in the past, although it's hard work. Sasha makes sure to request two different weekend dates that are farther apart on the schedule because she knows two weekends in a row would feel like too little rest alongside her full-time job.

C. We-care: emphasis on self-care.

It's Wednesday night and Marta isn't feeling very good, and she fears she could be getting sick. Rather than doing some planned household chores, she decides to scroll through her streaming services for a good movie. She can't seem to find anything genuinely interesting, which only makes her feel even worse. That's when she remembers that her mother has been urging her to watch a particular movie she really enjoyed. As she imagines the excitement her mother will have if she shares that she watched the movie, Marta begins feeling genuinely excited by the idea of watching the movie herself. She presses play, finding herself with a warm heart and beginning to rest.

D. We-care: emphasis on other-care.

While at work, a colleague emails Michael for some help with a task that is clearly outside the responsibilities of his job description. While he's tempted to simply decline the request, Michael can tell by the tone of the email that his colleague is desperate. Reflecting further from this place of empathy, he remembers that a meeting scheduled for later in the week had been canceled, providing a window to get the task done without too much additional stress. Before confirming his support, however, Michael takes a moment to feel into his own needs and goals. He realizes the task could also provide him with an interesting opportunity to accrue relevant experience for an upcoming promotion opportunity, making it all the easier to say yes.

E. We-care: unified self-care and other-care.

Rani returns home late from work, ready to roll up her sleeves to cook dinner for the family, only to discover her teenager has made a terrible mess of the kitchen with their latest cooking experiment. Before running upstairs to her teen's room in a burst of anger, she pauses and takes a few mindful breaths. She remembers how much her teen has been struggling recently, all the while staying connected to what she personally needs to remedy the situation. A lightbulb goes off: Her teen seems to love cooking and has been struggling partly because they have to work extra hours at a part-time job they hate. Interestingly, Rani, as a single mother, has also been feeling challenged to cook for the family, especially when work keeps her late. What if she offered her teen an allowance to cook for their family—and clean the kitchen afterward—a few times per week?

The we-care continuum can be thought of as a tool for helping you to scaffold your thinking in ways that simplify decisions about care but without oversimplifying them anywhere close to the extent of the binary world of the either/or mindset. Because of this, thinking of your care along a continuum can be powerfully consequential, transforming it from an either/or proposition into a spectrum of possibilities. You can therefore better embody and benefit from all of the natural strengths unblocked by we-care. This allows you to balance the straightforward decision-making favored by the either/or mindset with your longer-term commitment to reducing inner conflict and avoiding the harms that inevitably come when you sacrifice your self-care or care for others along the way.

An Adaptable We

Lately, Brianna's longtime friend Nola seems checked out—or something. Weeks pass before she replies to texts, and all but one of Brianna's recent phone calls have gone unreturned. Despite these warning signs, Nola has consistently reassured Brianna that everything's good in her life and in their friendship. Brianna doesn't want to let go of her friendship with Nola, given all the good times they've shared, but as weeks turn into months, she's finding it harder to keep investing energy into a connection that's not supporting her in return. Touching into what feels best for her personally, Brianna decides to dial back how often she reaches out to Nola, while nonetheless staying open to rekindling their friendship. With the extra time and energy, she leans into a new friendship she's excited about and that has been more consistently providing her an experience of mutual benefit and good times.

As Brianna's example highlights, the *we* in we-care is adaptable because it can encompass ourselves and others of our choosing, rather than being fixed to one person or group of people. This isn't to say we have total control over who gets priority in every aspect of our lives. For instance, unless you work for yourself or own a company, the *we* of your coworkers may be mostly out of your control. And the parents of a newborn baby often find that the *we* of family can feel all-consuming for a time. But the strength of *an adaptable we* in we-care makes it easier to promote and prioritize connections that are serving both us and others. Part of this natural power of we-care comes from greater recognition of opportunities to combine, blend, and unify care for ourselves and others. But it's also found in the inherent flexibility of the word *we* itself, underscoring the fluid nature of where our care can be expressed on any given day. Over time, the adaptable *we* in we-care supports us in fostering relationships rooted in beneficial intentions, positive impacts, and the organic rewards of mutual empowerment and care.

When we realize and enact we-care within ourselves, we may find that we are more naturally drawn away from one-sided dynamics toward those connections and relationships that are clearly reciprocal and mutually supportive. Yet equally so, the adaptable *we* can help us to steer existing relationships in a healthier, more mutually beneficial direction. This is made possible not only through meaningful changes in our overall approach to self-care and caring for others but also in how we-care supports an expanded tool kit of effective strategies to improve our social discernment, communication skills, boundaries, and more—all of which we'll explore more fully in future chapters. As daunting as transforming a relationship for the better may sound, it can be as simple as updating our expectations about what we want or need from a certain connection.

It's important, however, not to sugarcoat the real challenges of certain relationships. Even with the view and tools of we-care, there are no guarantees. After all, we cannot force others to change, grow, or show up more fully for us, no matter how clear and easy it all seems through our perspective. But this again is where the adaptable *we* can support us. The *we* in we-care is not specific to one other person, or even to a group of people. Therefore, if a given relationship is interfering both with our self-care and care for others more broadly, we-care can help us to let go and move forward. This does not mean we have to entirely give up on the possibility of an improved relationship in the future. However, there are times when we have done all that we can do to foster a truly healthy relationship—that is, a relationship that does not require abandoning our heart's wish to feel care flowing in two directions. When this occurs, we may decide it's best to dial down our investment of time and energy until we see evidence of constructive changes, or even to end a relationship altogether. Doing so may allow us to prioritize a different *we* that's better for us and for everyone else we care for too.

One important caveat before we move on: sometimes it feels necessary or preferable to remain in very challenging relationships, and although we-care can help us even in those cases, I strongly encourage anyone who is faced with a particularly difficult social situation to seek out professional support and guidance before deciding what's best. More often than not, there are multiple paths forward that will be better for everyone, and there are people out there who can help you to identify and carefully navigate those paths.

What's *Not* We-Care

I suspect that at this point in the book you've been able to identify instances of we-care in your own life—maybe even many of them. In my research, I've found that, even in the absence of any kind of formal training in we-care, many people are able to identify moments of it in their daily lives, with some reporting it as a common occurrence. This reinforces that we-care is something quite natural to us as human beings—a feature of how we're wired to care. And yet, despite this naturalness of we-care, it's important not to confuse minimal experiences of combining self-care and care for others with the full expression of we-care in our lives. As illustrated by the we-care continuum, there's tremendous breadth and depth to we-care. Therefore, approaching we-care more consciously can help you to identify where it's already present and supporting you and also where you could increase its frequency and potency. After all, the we-care journey will only ever be as meaningful as you make it personal.

Equally as important as noticing when we-care is already present for you is ensuring you don't conflate it with other, similar experiences—especially when you're first learning about we-care. In other words, it's possible to mistake certain experiences for we-care that are *not* we-care. To avoid this, let's review a few examples, beyond the usual suspects like selfish self-care and pathological altruism, of what's not we-care.

We-care is *not* . . .

- *Being everything to everyone—including yourself.* Along the path of we-care, you may begin to feel your capacity for care expanding. This includes enhancements in your self-care, as well as an increased capacity to care for your loved ones and possibly even new acquaintances or strangers. It's a positive sign that you're growing more genuinely resourceful. Yet, no matter how fully realized your care capacities, no one can do it all. As with many good things in life, the idea of perfect we-care is the enemy of good we-care. This includes recognition that our own self-care will sometimes fall short, and habitual patterns will reemerge. Knowing this, we can stay mindful and not let the perfectionist or people-pleaser in us co-opt we-care for its purposes and at your expense. After all, genuine we-care includes *care-based boundaries*, a topic we'll focus on more in chapter 8. Additionally, we-care includes promoting and prioritizing mutually beneficial relationships, meaning receiving care in return may become more of the norm than the exception. So, while we can't be everything to everyone with we-care, we still get to be more of ourselves and show up more fully for others.

- *A collection of "shoulds."* If we are not attentive to our thoughts, it is possible for our study and practice of we-care to turn into a bundle of *shoulds* (e.g., "I *should* be

ensuring that all my self-care benefits my romantic partner"). Related to this concern, research indicates that
people who struggle with a "loud" self-critic may have
a harder time offering and receiving care.[10] Rather than
letting self-critical thoughts hinder your care, you can
learn to see their arising as a byproduct of deepening
your journey of we-care, like smoke plumes rising from
a fire. Viewed in this way, you can stay awake and caring
when your self-critic shows up, not believing its false,
uncaring storylines.

- *A system for keeping score.* As mentioned earlier, we-care
  is rarely an even split. Why is this? Even if someone held
  the view that a relationship should be fifty-fifty, it would
  not mean every instance of care would be so. There's a
  natural back-and-forth to caring for oneself and others,
  however subtle it may be experienced. Similarly, we-
  care rarely looks like a compromise, which implies we
  must give up something to achieve balance. Thinking
  in terms of percentages, or otherwise keeping score, is
  not the spirit of we-care. Not only is care too subjective,
  nuanced, and mysterious for that, but also, over time,
  we-care reveals there's frequently more than enough
  care to go around.

- *The same for everyone.* What constitutes an ideal approach to caring for ourselves and others depends on
  countless factors. Because of this, I have little doubt
  there are exceptions to nearly every statement or principle named in this book. Fortunately, the view and
  methods of we-care need not fit perfectly to be useful—
  so long as we are willing to study, apply, and adapt them

to our own personal needs, goals, and values. This is also why I will repeatedly emphasize and offer practices for cultivating we-care from within. By focusing on the most essential, inner aspects of we-care, rather than on its outer expressions, there's room for every person to discover we-care for themselves. This understanding can also help us avoid the temptations of judging others' care or comparing our we-care to that of others.

- *Whatever we want it to be.* Finally, although we-care looks different for different people and different situations, there are core features of we-care that must be present. It's critical to reflect on whether our we-care is producing the benefits we are aiming for, which includes staying open to feedback about our impact, and more ideally, proactively seeking feedback from those we trust. Openness to feedback about our we-care honors the truth that we-care is an inherently social act. Moreover, as care blind spots reveal, our own subjective appraisals of our care can be biased or limited.

Your Undivided Heart

We-care is a new word. Yet, similar to *interbeing*, the essential truths it highlights have long been understood by countless human beings across many different times and cultures, including Thich Nhat Hanh. As he once said about the connection between interbeing and care, "We are all interconnected. By taking care of another person, you take care of yourself. By taking care of yourself, you take care of the other person."[11] Hopefully, it's now clearer to you why statements like this one, enacted through we-care, can reflect something not only as profound and complex as interbeing but also as everyday as looking after ourselves and our loved ones. This is because all forms of we-care share key elements, as we've reviewed in this chapter.

The next steps of this we-care journey will focus more specifically on exploring we-care from within, as you uniquely experience it. Through growing more familiar with and increasingly sourcing from your undivided heart, you'll have a chance to uncover your personal touch with we-care. No one can do this for you, and all the words and sentences in this book can only point to it. In that spirit, as we begin the transition from the *what* to the *how* of we-care, let's close with a few questions:

- Are there any self-care activities you enjoy that could also be considered or easily evolve into forms of we-care for you?

- Have you ever experienced we-care before in a social situation or relationship, even if you didn't yet have a name for it? If so, what did we-care look and feel like for you?

- In what area(s) of your life do you see the potential for we-care to support you uniquely? How about others you deeply care about? Others more broadly?

- How might getting clearer about we-care's definition and key elements inform and deepen your day-to-day experiences and expressions of self-care and care for others?

- Are there any potential drawbacks or downsides to we-care that you'd like to steer clear of as you continue to explore its relevance to your life?

- Is there a trusted person or two you can identify who can offer you valuable input and feedback on your unique journey with we-care?

- If others in your life adopted we-care, can you imagine ways it might possibly lead to benefits for you too?
  If yes, can you imagine the same happening in reverse, with your we-care leading to benefits for you and for others you care about?

We-Care Practice 4
UNDIVIDED HEART BREATHING

We-care and the either/or mindset invite reflection on the interplay between how we conceptualize our care and how we embody and express it. As research into our profoundly social nature has revealed, we are wired for we-care more clearly than we are wired for self-care or other-care alone. In other words, our natural care system and care circuitry already reflect the inherently social nature of care. Consequently, although concepts and the either/or mindset may divide our care into self-care *or* other-care, our natural care is undivided and readily equipped to experience self-care *and* other-care together in interconnected forms. With this in mind, the next we-care practice aims to get you out of your head and into your heart, seeing if you can experience your heart as a natural gateway into an experience of undivided care.

PRACTICE INSTRUCTIONS

1. *Get comfortable.* For this practice, feel free to sit or lie down, aiming for a balance between relaxation and wakefulness.

2. *Breathe mindfully.* Breathe naturally while inviting your attention to the rise and fall of your chest and abdomen. It can take time for our attention to settle,

so stay with this stage of the practice for as long as needed to feel more present with your breathing. As is standard with mindfulness practice, it's only natural for the mind to wander away, and sometimes quite a bit. Each time you notice your attention has drifted elsewhere, simply bring it back to noticing the sensations of breathing in your chest and abdomen. In this context of mindful breathing, we can ideally experience a more relaxed and open quality of attention.

3. *Feel your caring heart.* Mindfully guide your attention and awareness from noticing sensations of breathing in your abdomen and chest to the level of feeling in and around your heart center. More specifically, see if you can feel the natural presence of care, often arising as subtle qualities of warmth and affection. If you can, tune in to these feelings and allow your breath to help you feel them more deeply. However, if you're having trouble noticing these qualities in and around your heart center, don't worry. You may simply need to spend some more time cultivating mindfulness of feeling or perhaps even learning how to self-generate feelings of warmth and affection. Therefore, if this seems to describe your experience, feel free to pause the practice here, return to mindfulness of breathing, or simply explore whether and how you might connect to caring feelings. In the next chapter, we'll review some relatable methods for self-generating caring feelings.

4. *Breathe in self-care, breathe out other-care.* Sensing into your natural care, use each inbreath to direct this care toward yourself, taking however much time

you need to experience self-care as you breathe in.
Next, turn your attention toward the outbreath and
imagine your care radiating out from you toward
others. You can imagine this in a general sense or
picture a specific other you care about. Finally, try
synchronizing your feelings of care with each inbreath and outbreath, feeling care for yourself,
then for others, respectively.

5. *Feel undivided care.* In this last step, see if you can
   drop any sense of direction or orientation in your
   care—that is, no more self-care on the inbreath and
   other-care on the outbreath. Instead, simply rest in
   a felt sense of undivided care in and around your
   heart. You may experience this as a unified feeling of
   warmth and affection or visualize it as a field of light
   or energy that includes and connects you and others.
   Ideally, when compared to alternating between self-
   care and other-care, this final step will feel less effortful. You may even feel a sense of relief. In relaxing
   the divided mind, you are connecting to the more
   essential nature of your undivided heart.

PART II

WE-CARE
FROM WITHIN

To put everything in balance is good, to put everything in harmony is better.

—Victor Hugo, *Ninety-Three*

CHAPTER 4

The Empathy-Compassion Gap

Bridging Feeling and Action

> Suffering is the fuel of compassion,
> not its result.
> —B. ALAN WALLACE, *The Art of
> Transforming the Mind: A Meditator's
> Guide to the Tibetan Practice of Lojong*

My years of studying the mind and brain have been replete with twists and turns. The vast scope and ceaseless rate of discovery within psychology and neuroscience means that I'm frequently confronted with findings that challenge my understanding of what it means to be human and with ideas that stick with me long after first encountering them. One of my favorite "sticky" lessons revolves around an activity I enjoy sharing in classrooms and workshops. Designed to provide firsthand insight into one of the more counterintuitive ways our minds operate, it has roots dating all the way back to 1863, in the writings of Dostoevsky. The activity is simple, with just a few steps, and I invite you to try it out yourself now:

1. Set a timer for thirty seconds.
2. Close your eyes.

3. Try your best to *not* think of a white bear until the timer goes off.

Maybe you're not too surprised by how difficult it can be. As Dostoevsky himself put it, "Try to pose for yourself this task: not to think of a polar bear, and you will see that the cursed thing will come to mind every minute."[1] Having now done this activity in a variety of settings, I have observed that some people do succeed at first, often through some kind of strong-minded distraction technique. However, most struggle to keep the image of the white bear out of their minds for long. What's more, the activity is not quite over when the timer stops. Now that you have finally stopped trying to keep the bear at bay, might it be flashing in your mind as you read this sentence?

This phenomenon, known in psychology as the *white bear problem*,[2] highlights the sometimes paradoxical effects of attempting to avoid or suppress an internal experience. Specifically, when we try to avoid thoughts and feelings, we can end up experiencing them even more, whether in the moment or later on. Even if suppression works for a short while, research on the white bear problem indicates there is often a *rebound effect* in which the suppressed material eventually asserts itself even more strongly. Perhaps you have experienced the white bear problem in other areas of your life, such as trying to resist tempting foods while dieting, attempting to stop thinking about a work problem while on vacation, or pushing away anxieties about an upcoming public speaking event. As you might expect, the white bear also holds significance for mental health: those suffering from depression tend to rely on more avoidant approaches toward their emotions, whereas reversing this tendency through greater acceptance of one's emotions can decrease depressive symptoms.[3]

In the context of we-care, the white bear problem has a number of interesting implications. To begin with, it underscores that attempts to suppress our heart's care from flowing as it wants to—

for ourselves *and* for others—can lead to exhaustion, heightened inner conflict, and rebound effects. Due to the underlying architecture and functioning of our minds and brains, the either/or mindset and its typically divided approaches to care ultimately work against us, no matter how successful we may be initially in suppressing our natural self-care or care for others. In this chapter, however, we're going to focus on another aspect that targets the foundational, bottom-up feelings associated with we-care, namely how the white bear problem relates to the distinction between *empathy* and *compassion*. Although empathy and compassion are often used interchangeably, their differences are centrally important to the science of compassion and to its training in programs like our Mindful Compassion Training at Naropa University. Most critically, as we move from the *what* to the *how* of we-care, you will see how bridging the empathy-compassion gap can make a world of difference for the cultivation and follow-through of we-care in daily life.

What's an Emotion?

Think back to a recent situation that triggered a strong emotional response in you. What came first—thoughts or feelings? This question has been central to the science of emotion, known as *affective science*, since its inception. And while it can be fascinating to tour through all the competing scientific theories, like we do in my university course on emotions, I'll jump straight to the punchline: In contemporary affective science, researchers view emotions as most often being initiated not by thoughts *or* feelings but from something more entwined from the start—the dynamic, even blended, interplay of thoughts *and* feelings. Disentangling these aspects of an emotion is not unlike trying to separate nature (biology) from nurture (environment) in explaining why and how someone communicates in the ways they do. Beyond the many exacting studies that have led to this understanding, the view has been further bolstered by neuroscientific evidence that emotions are not localized to one specialized region of the brain but instead recruit diverse and widely distributed brain regions that also participate in nonemotional mental states.[4]

Adopting this perspective, we find a very different view of what an "emotion" is. Rather than fitting neatly with common ideas—that our emotions are a truly distinct type of experience—each instance of emotion can be better understood as a holistic state emerging from an underlying mixture of psychological "ingredients."[5] These ingredients include thoughts and feelings, as well as a wider variety of general cognitive and embodied functions like memories, attention, interoception (our internal sense of the body's physiological state and signals), autonomic arousal, and action tendencies. Even the words we use guide and shape emotions, influencing the very thing they're aiming to describe. Thus, emotions are not simple, isolated things within us but dynamic states, richly woven from a variety of more universal mental processes and bodily experiences.

Although we-care is not an emotion, this more nuanced view of emotions provides a model to understand it. By recognizing the dynamic interplay of thoughts, feelings, and actions in something as familiar as an emotion, we can learn to appreciate why a comprehensive approach to cultivating we-care may similarly require attention to an interplay of elements. Just like an emotion, the thoughts we rely on to understand our care can guide and transform our care-based feelings, yet these feelings can likewise stir and reshape the thoughts and words we find true to our actual experience. Moreover, both can go on to inspire our caring actions—which then in turn reciprocally inform our caring thoughts and feelings. This dynamic interplay may seem obvious, but it can be overlooked when it comes time to actually cultivate we-care from within. Some people clearly favor the cool distance and rational arguments that come with thinking, while others prefer the depth and warmth of affiliative feelings and bodily sensations. Still others may stress the concreteness and clear impact of specific we-care actions and their measurable consequences. If we are not mindful of the critical interplay between all of these different elements right from the start, each can become a hiding place that keeps us from experiencing the fullness of we-care's healing and transformative power.

Defining Empathy and Compassion

In my experience of studying and teaching on the topic of care, I've seen a tendency—not universal, but noticeable—to think of care mostly in terms of visible actions rather than as the feelings and intentions that underlie them. Fortunately, psychology and neuroscience have developed many robust methods to make the unseen more visible, whether through on-the-spot smartphone surveys, tracking subtle differences in response times to index cognitive performance, or using advanced neuroimaging to precisely map activated brain areas. These and many other tools have contributed to a science of the mind that's adept at observing how transforming your inner experience can profoundly inform and guide your behavior and interactions with the world.

In the science of care, researchers have identified two interconnected inner states—empathy and compassion—that can steer our caring actions in very different directions. Therefore, learning to distinguish between them can be tremendously supportive for cultivating we-care from within. The reason for this is twofold: First, empathy and compassion each play a distinct role in we-care. Second, one of these two states is the clear frontrunner when actively practicing and engaging in we-care. Let's briefly review how scientists typically define and differentiate empathy and compassion before learning to distinguish them within our lived experience.

Empathy is a complex term that encompasses a variety of related experiences, such as feeling what others are feeling or putting ourselves in someone else's shoes. However, at its core, empathy pertains to the capacity of our nervous system to pick up cues about others' inner states and to subsequently experience a similar state ourselves—a tendency referred to by researchers as *experience sharing*.[6] This aspect of empathy can happen without conscious awareness or effort, such that empathy (as experience sharing) is a process that occurs largely outside of our control. You can even give people complex math problems to solve while they view images of others' emotional expressions, and they still end up experience sharing.[7]

Compassion, by contrast, is a more conscious emotional state that builds from empathy. It begins with empathy for someone experiencing suffering but soon moves beyond feeling *with* what they're feeling to actively feeling *for* them. What do I mean by feeling *for* someone who is suffering? Typically, it's experienced as an other-oriented state of concern alongside a felt sense of warmth and affection, much like you might feel naturally toward a puppy yelping or a loved one's infant who starts crying. But compassion is not only a feeling; as with any emotion, it is a more complex mental state of varied psychological ingredients. The specific mixture of compassion includes three main components, which we'll circle back to later in this chapter: (1) mental and felt awareness that someone is suffering, (2) feeling *for* the one who is suffering; and (3) motivation to take caring actions that might alleviate suffering.[8]

The Empathy-Compassion Gap

Imagine yourself stepping into the clean, clinical environment of a neuroscience research lab, heartbeat quickening as you reflect on just how little you know about what will happen next. You are instructed to lie down on a stretcher near a hefty machine, before being thrust headfirst into the enclosed, dim, noisy world of a functional magnetic resonance imaging (fMRI) scanner. As the hum of the machine fades into the background, footage from documentaries and news reports begins to play on a screen, each portraying challenging clips of adults and children in clear distress—scenes that are real, raw, and jarringly intimate. Naturally, your heart aches as you witness the pain and suffering of others. Then you remember the researcher's instructions—to try empathizing even more with those in the video—so you consciously try to feel *with* the distress you see.

So went the first of two fMRI sessions for participants in a pioneering scientific study led by Tania Singer and colleagues, in which participants were first trained in empathy for suffering and later in compassion.[9] After their compassion training, participants again underwent this fMRI procedure but with new video clips and different instructions—this time, to instead try generating compassion for those they witnessed suffering. The study's findings revealed a striking difference in the patterns of neural activation between the empathy and compassion conditions. Specifically, empathy led to activations in areas of the brain linked to pain and negative emotion, namely the anterior insula and anterior midcingulate cortex, whereas compassion led to activations in the ventral striatum, pregenual anterior cingulate cortex, and medial orbitofrontal cortex—areas linked to reward, affiliation, and positive emotion. In other words, the study showed that empathy and compassion rely on distinct brain networks, each with a very different trajectory for how we feel, think, and respond when confronted with human suffering.

This study, alongside others that have since compared empathy and compassion, highlights what I have come to refer to as the *empathy-compassion gap.* To summarize this research and elucidate this gap, consider the following figure:

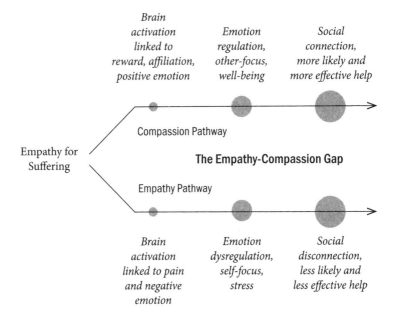

When faced with human suffering, both empathy and compassion begin with empathic resonance—feeling with those who are suffering. Yet this shared beginning is already the peak point of similarity between these two care-related states. If empathy or suffering is not transformed into compassion, its continuation can easily spiral into empathic distress and a more individually self-oriented, dysregulated, personally detrimental, and socially disconnected state.[10] On the other hand, compassion can readily change empathy into a more other-oriented, regulated, personally beneficial, and socially connected state. As illustrated, the gap between empathy and compassion widens with time, as each sends us on a divergent pathway of corresponding brain activations and downstream effects on our thoughts, emotions, and actions. Ultimately, this widening gap reveals how, when compared to empathy, compassion is more strongly aligned with care for both oneself and others—with we-care.

Balancing Feeling and Action

When Jess went through her challenging breakup, she found herself having two very different experiences when sharing with her friends. With Eduardo, her empathetic confidante, the air became heavy with shared sorrow. Eduardo mirrored Jess's grief with tear-brimmed eyes, deep sighs, and frequent hugs. Yet, Eduardo also seemed to hold back his words, offering silent solidarity instead of advice or insight. In contrast was Anne, who treated the news with a cool, analytical approach. As soon as Jess finished her story, Anne seemed spring-loaded into problem-solving mode, offering a barrage of "what next" strategies while missing the raw wound of Jess's emotions in her hurry to strategize and get Jess back to her usual, happy self. Jess found herself torn between these two extremes. She realized that she craved both the empathy of Eduardo and the effective advice of Anne, but that neither approach alone provided the balanced support she really needed.

Unfortunately, many people report having experiences similar to Jess. They find themselves navigating a sea of imperfect emotional support, where well-intended friends and loved ones either immerse too deeply into shared feelings or remain aloof, striving to solve problems without truly attuning to them first. Rare is the listener who interweaves feeling and action to offer us care that not only meets us on an emotional level but also provides valuable insight for our journey forward. When it does occur, however, it becomes clear that the care we're most seeking is not of one type or another alone. We prefer instead a dynamic balance of heartfelt understanding and constructive reflection or actions, even if we may favor one or the other at times. Clarifying the need for this ideal balance can help us to further appreciate the distinction between empathy and compassion, revealing a path for becoming that rare, balanced confidante for others—which, in turn, can increase the quality of support we receive in kind.

When encountering the pain and struggles of others, it is only natural for our hearts to resonate with them, and for good reason. Empathic attunement heightens our awareness of others' difficulties and boosts our motivation to help. But if we stay with simply empathizing for too long, our caring responses can err on the side of feeling. Having taken in the suffering of others, we are also now suffering—at times, intensely so. Researchers refer to this state as *empathic distress*, highlighting that our empathy has led to a marked increase in our personal distress levels. In a state of empathic distress, we actually become more self-focused due to the need to regulate our own negative emotions. Consequently, we are less likely to help.[11] Alternatively, if we do try to offer support, our caring actions may be more driven by motives to alleviate our own distress, resulting in less effective help overall.

Compared to empathy alone, the downstream effects of compassion on our brains and behavior are aligned with taking action that can help to alleviate the struggle and difficulty we are empathizing with. Critically, taking action is not only supportive for those on the receiving end of caring action, but research indicates it can have a self-regulating influence for the actor. But of course, not all caring actions are equally beneficial. The benefits of acting from a place of care all depend on the effectiveness of the actions we take. If you have ever been on the receiving end of someone's misguided attempt to help, then you know how uncomfortable and challenging it can be. So, the compassionate impulse and intention to take caring actions is generally good—but rushing into action-oriented mode without first pausing to feel can cause us to overlook mission-critical information. Thus, without first allowing the embodied resonance of empathy, even the most well-intentioned actions can deviate from what's truly needed. They may even cause harm. Ultimately, effective we-care is best supported by a dynamic balance of feeling and action—a balance made more likely in states of authentic compassion.

Doesn't the World Need More Empathy—Not Less?

Based on what I have shared so far, I would not blame you for thinking this chapter is mounting a case against the benefits of empathy. However, aren't many of our problems in society primarily driven by a lack of empathy for the troubles of others? Wouldn't the world be much better off if people focused on increasing their empathy for suffering? An informative longitudinal study found a marked decline in empathy in college students from 1979 through 2009, just one data point of many that spotlight a concerning trend toward less empathy within modern society.[12] And, as mentioned, empathy is the starting point of compassion—so if our empathy is compromised, it is likely to weaken our compassion as well.

Although it's important to reflect on declines in empathy, formal compassion training includes cultivating empathy, especially where it appears to be lacking most—particularly in the context of resonating with the pain and struggles of others, including those we don't like or know. The reason this is central to compassion training is because genuine compassion includes a dynamic balance of resonating with the struggles of others and taking caring actions that may alleviate suffering in the world as a whole. Therefore, if we are serious about cultivating compassion and effective we-care, we cannot bypass the role of feeling *with* the pain of others. Critically, however, this feeling dimension in compassion is seen to be instrumental to our broader goal of alleviating suffering. For these reasons, compassion trainers and scientists tend to see compassion training as an important antidote to the social dilemmas of our times. Training in compassion allows us not only to enhance empathy but also to bolster other critical capacities that increase the effectiveness of our actions to alleviate suffering.

Consider how people often report concern about a lack of empathy among those in authority, consistent with studies on how the experience of power can blunt empathy.[13] Research on thousands of leaders, however, found that those with a tendency toward compassion outperformed leaders who favored empathy, and that proved true in ways that benefited both the followers and the leader.[14]

Even though empathy is not the ultimate aim when cultivating we-care, there is an important truth embedded in concerns about the need for more empathy—one that speaks to how you can start to close the empathy-compassion gap in daily life. Paradoxically, closing this gap involves learning to embrace your natural empathy *more*. To understand why, we need to revisit the activity from the outset of this chapter.

Let's Think about a White Bear

We can now return to our white bear and understand its connection to distinguishing empathy from compassion. To bridge these concepts, consider this: The struggles we encounter when attempting to suppress thinking about a white bear parallel our efforts to avoid the uncomfortable feelings of empathizing with the suffering of others. Just as we cannot avoid thinking about a white bear without significant efforts, most individuals cannot easily avoid empathy when witnessing suffering. Sure, there is variation in how naturally empathic people are as well as strategies that can mitigate certain aspects of empathy—but in the end, for most people, it is much more effortful to resist being empathic than it is to accept and allow empathy. Compassion acknowledges this simple truth. Accordingly, bridging the empathy-compassion gap starts with consciously embracing your identity as a social being, including the inevitability of your empathic resonance with suffering.

Remembering the role of empathy in compassion can also help us to see why empathy and compassion are so often conflated.

Even researchers, who we assume to be experts in the field, can fall prey to this misunderstanding. One notable example in the science of care is the term *compassion fatigue*, often used in the literature and throughout many applied settings to describe the exhaustion and weariness that result from repeated exposure to and care for suffering, especially suffering that urgently demands attention. Although well-intended, this term is misleading. For instance, someone who identifies with compassion fatigue may come to believe the solution lies in resisting their natural tendencies toward compassion even more, compromising their care for others and likely exhausting themselves even further.[15]

Fortunately, there is an alternative to this term that risks less confusion and is likely to promote not only more care overall but also more effective care. Instead of *compassion fatigue*, we could say *empathic distress fatigue*.[16] Indeed, the symptoms of so-called compassion fatigue are much more consistent with the downsides of empathic distress and trying to avoid empathizing with others' pain and difficulty. When people try to avoid their natural empathy for suffering, they exert significant efforts and rely on costly strategies that backfire—similar to the mental effort and rebound effect that happen when trying not to think about a white bear. Ultimately, the drive to control and suppress our natural processes of empathy could contribute more to fatigue than the empathy itself.

To experience this more directly, there's another activity you can try out with a partner:

1. Designate one person as the listener and the other as the speaker.

2. Have the speaker share a mildly distressing event from their recent life, such as something relatively small that is causing them excess anxiety or struggle.

3. The listener should attempt to listen *without* showing any supportive social cues—no nodding, making facial expressions, or offering verbal responses.

4. Swap roles and repeat the process.

5. Finally, swap roles again to repeat the activity. But this time, allow the listener to express natural social cues as they normally would.

6. Reflect on the differences between the two: Which kind of listening felt more effortful? Was it possible to completely suppress your supportive social cues? What did this teach you about empathy and the effort it might take to suppress it?

As you can see, beginning to close the empathy-compassion gap requires an approach that can initially seem counterintuitive, or maybe even paradoxical. The fundamental shift lies in changing our internal response to suffering—rather than avoiding and suppressing our automatic tendency to empathize, compassion involves learning to accept and embrace it. The good news is that once we stop wasting our efforts on avoiding empathy, we can shift our energy further downstream, relying on the power of compassion to relate more consciously and skillfully to suffering whenever and wherever we encounter it.

The Healing Fire of Compassion

Learning to embrace your empathy is a critical first step to bridging the empathy-compassion gap, putting you into alignment with your natural, caring response to suffering and thereby freeing precious mental resources from the wasted efforts of empathy avoidance. Building from this foundation, there are a few further steps you must take to transform empathy into a more conscious state of compassion. Even though compassion is natural to us as human beings, it is also a more complex state than empathy, involving the interplay of mental, emotional, and motivational factors. Fortunately, with the right view and methods, you can make compassion more of a default response.

Let's start by gaining the right view of compassion, using the analogy of a fire. What is fire, truly? In the constant glow of electrified modern life, it's possible we take this question for granted. But imagine observing fire with the awe of a beginner's mind, perhaps much like our ancestors encountering its mysterious brilliance for the first time—dancing light, transparent oranges and blues, radiant warmth, transformative power. Fire, as physicists tell us, results from a precise combination of three things: oxygen, heat, and fuel. For example, a campfire draws oxygen from the natural air, heat initiated from matches or a lighter, and fuel in the form of wood or kindling. Looking closely, in which of these things do we find the fire? As we know, none of them alone contains the fire. Instead, fire is an *emergent property* of its three separable components—oxygen, heat, fuel.

Like fire, compassion similarly emerges from the interplay of three separable components: (1) awareness of the presence of suffering, (2) feeling *for* the one who is suffering, and (3) motivation to take caring actions that can alleviate suffering. Extending our metaphor to think of building a fire of compassion, awareness of suffering can be likened to the oxygen. Just as a campfire cannot exist without oxygen, compassion cannot flourish without our conscious awareness of suffering. This awareness is not only a cognitive process but also includes the felt sense of empathizing and feeling with others. Although sometimes cognitive empathy is sufficient for compassion, more often both cognitive and affective attunement to suffering are needed for compassion to be genuine.[17] Thus, both mental and felt recognition of suffering should be thought of as the oxygen, vital to enlivening and nourishing the luminescent potential of our compassionate response.

Next, we have the component of feeling *for* whoever is suffering, which can be likened to the heat needed to spark and sustain the fire of compassion. Feeling for is about generating a felt sense of warmth, good will, and care that extends out and toward those who are suffering. In scientific terms, feeling for involves the interplay of both *emotion generation* and *emotion regulation*. Together, these aspects support a more conscious relationship with our emotions, rather than feeling constantly on the receiving end of their powerful yet unpredictable nature. With training, we can grow more confident in our capacity to generate and maintain caring emotions and feelings that warm and awaken our hearts to the needs of the moment, keeping us focused on our compassionate intention to alleviate suffering if possible.

Finally, the third component of prosocial motivation to alleviate suffering can be likened to the fuel. We are in touch with a sincere desire and intention to ease the struggles and difficulties we perceive. This can generate vital energy for taking compassionate action, sometimes experienced as a sudden burst of willpower and drive. With merely a glimpse of our potential to lessen someone's suffering, compassion makes us ready to act. This said, external action is not a strict requirement of compassion, and as mentioned earlier, we must learn to pause, feel, and take in situations before leaping into action. What's primary is our inner readiness and intentional stance toward less suffering. At times, instead of taking outward action, you may take inner actions such as silently wishing for others' well-being or setting an intention to act in the future if the opportunity arises. As fuel sustains a fire, our ongoing motivation to alleviate suffering is crucial for keeping the flame of compassion burning brightly.

Ultimately, the fiery experience of compassion illumines and serves as a beacon, helping to light our way through the shadowed landscapes of suffering. But unlike the hot sting and thick smoke of an ordinary fire, the fire of compassion warms and heals. It can even cool and clarify, if that's what is most needed. Its influence radiates within and beyond us, beaming in multiple directions at once. And in the illuminating glow of compassion, we find the capacity to transform pain into healing, setbacks into resilience, and challenge into growth. As the Roman emperor and Stoic philosopher Marcus Aurelius once remarked, "A blazing fire makes flame and brightness out of everything that is thrown into it."[18] Similarly, the fire of compassion is so powerful because it allows us to stay present with, and thereby more consciously relate to and transform, many different kinds of suffering.

Where does this view of compassion as an emergent property, akin to a healing and clarifying fire, leave us in terms of bridging the empathy-compassion gap? While comparing compassion to a fire in this way may not immediately provide an answer, the metaphor has a number of additional instructive implications and actionable insights. Most notably—as with fire—the healing and transformative flames of compassion can begin with a *spark*.

Your Compassion Spark

Through my years of studying and teaching on compassion, I have discovered that each of us possesses one or more inner sparks that can help to ignite the flames of compassion—our personal *compassion spark*. Once you discover your own compassion spark, you will find it is much easier to close the empathy-compassion gap, especially when this discovery is paired with ongoing practice. This is because your compassion spark will help you to self-generate the *feeling for* component of compassion, which tends to be the least familiar—and perhaps most critical—factor when learning to cultivate compassion. This will further allow you to consciously shift your default response to suffering, sending you upward along the pathway of compassion toward more positive emotions, improved emotion regulation, and greater social connection. Without a compassion spark, you are more likely to instead follow the empathy pathway, spiraling into empathic distress and social disconnection.

The first step toward finding your compassion spark is to experience an *empathy spark*, as this will aid in differentiating the two. To spark empathy, I invite you to simply recall a person or persons going through a difficult time—maybe it is a group you read about in the news, a friend going through a breakup, an evocative character from a film or novel, or even a stranger you've come across whose story moved you. As you hold this person in mind, take note of what this empathy feels like for you. Observe your facial expressions and bodily sensations, your emotions, and your thoughts. Does your body feel lighter or heavier? Are you more inclined toward feeling or action? Pay attention to the nuances of this empathic response and register them in your awareness.

While an empathy spark is effective in helping us to be aware of suffering and feel *with* another's struggles, it tends not to result in also feeling *for* who is suffering. Accordingly, your compassion spark will be something that helps you to invoke feeling for directly, which you can eventually use alongside your natural empathy for suffering to generate compassion. To find your spark, simply bring to mind someone or something that elicits an inner sense of warmth, affection, good will, and care. It could be a cherished pet, a small child, a loved one, or a specific memory, such as receiving kindness from a stranger. Interestingly, research has found that people may have an easier time naturally feeling warmth and affection toward an animal than a human being, so do not worry if this works better for you too.[19] Personally, I do not currently have any pets, but my brother's dog has long been a reliable spark for me, especially when I recall him as a small puppy, rolling around in the grass. And you need not limit yourself to one spark, as it can be helpful to try a range of potential sparks—a treasured childhood toy, a favorite place in nature, a meaningful song, the sound of a favorite instrument, a quote, or the comforting gesture of your hand on your heart. The key point is to find something that, whenever you call it to mind, it spontaneously invites inner warmth and natural affection.

Just as you did with the empathy spark, take time to really observe your physical sensations, emotions, and thoughts associated with this compassion spark. Again, does your body feel lighter or heavier? Are you more inclined toward feeling or action? Comparing between the empathy spark and this compassion spark, what similarities and differences do you notice? Ideally, your compassion spark should feel quite distinct from your empathy spark, allowing you to touch into what it is like to feel *for* alongside feeling *with*. Perhaps you feel it as though there is a source of light at your heart, radiating out from within. Additionally, your spark may also bring about a quality of inner resourcefulness, in the sense that you feel in touch with your own capacity to offer effective support.

If you are having difficulty finding a compassion spark that seems to evoke these qualities, do not be discouraged. It is not every day we are asked to reflect on what sparks inner warmth, and it may be something that takes time to uncover, maybe even with the help of a trusted friend or mentor. Over the next few days, simply keep an eye out for something that touches your heart and connects you to a natural sense of care.

Remember that your compassion spark is not meant to bring about all the components of compassion at once—it is focused primarily on the second component of feeling *for*, or what we explored earlier as the element of heat. At the end of this chapter, you will find a compassion practice that relies on your compassion spark to ignite the fire of compassion and thereby close the empathy-compassion gap within your own experience. That said, once you have identified your unique spark, you may well have what you need to begin bridging the empathy-compassion gap in daily life. The next time you notice feeling empathy for someone who is suffering, first simply allow it to be there, perhaps taking a couple deep breaths. Then, call to mind your compassion spark, helping you to self-generate feelings of warmth, good will, and affection. Let the feelings of your natural empathy mix with those generated by your compassion spark, connecting feeling *with* and feeling *for* the person(s) suffering. In contrast to empathy on its own, this combination should help you feel more resourced and balanced, as you both recognize the suffering and feel ready to offer something supportive in return—radiating out the healing warmth and clarifying light of compassionate care.

Self-Compassion with an Undivided Heart

Much of what we explored in the previous chapter about we-care likewise applies to understanding *self-compassion*, a term commonly used to describe the practice of directing care toward oneself as an individual. We must commit to growing our view of compassion beyond simple self/other distinctions. That caveat notwithstanding, I want to briefly highlight how self-compassion can be instrumental in the cultivation of a more holistic experience of compassion that supports we-care and that can help protect you from many confused kinds of care, such as enabling someone's bad habits under the guise of caring for them, or people-pleasing to make someone like you. So long as you are grounded in a more expansive view, both self-compassion and compassion for others can be expressions of the same compassion, arising from the same three components: awareness of suffering, feeling for the one who is suffering, and motivation to alleviate or ease the suffering. The key difference of self-compassion is then just a matter of emphasis, similar to how healthy self-care is an emphasis of we-care.

Your struggles and sufferings do not need to be more intense or worse than those of others to merit directing compassion toward yourself. Suffering is suffering, even when it's as subtle as noticing the presence of anxiety, confusion, or dissatisfaction within your experience. As the Buddhist teacher Jack Kornfield famously said, "If your compassion does not include yourself, it is incomplete."[20] Similarly, if your compassion excludes certain types of suffering, it is incomplete. Noticing both pronounced and subtle ways you personally struggle is one way self-compassion can simultaneously enrich your compassion for others. You can thereby better attune to and care for both kinds of difficulties experienced by others. More broadly, an emphasis on self-compassion can help you to realize and embody a dynamic balance of feeling and action when caring for yourself, similar to these benefits of other-oriented compassion. You can honor and tend to the inner dimension of your struggles even as you seek and traverse a path toward less suffering.

From Self-Compassion to We-Compassion

Growing familiar with compassion offers a way to cultivate we-care from the inside out. This stands in contrast to approaches for enhancing care that emphasize the externals—such as the case of doctors relying on conversation scripts generated by ChatGPT to express more empathy with patients.[21] Here, I have emphasized an internal shift away from empathy toward compassion, a more complex emotional state that transcends and includes empathy and completes a natural process that empathy for suffering is meant to serve. When we deeply train and ground ourselves in both compassion for others and self-compassion, we cannot help but begin enacting we-care. However, applying the lessons of we-care, it is also beneficial to home in on the essential interconnectedness of these two orientations of compassion. This can help us hold both our own pain and that of others within our hearts.

There's a view common to compassion researchers and practitioners alike: one should emphasize training in self-compassion if predisposed toward excess other-oriented care, and other-oriented compassion when there's a bias toward prioritizing one's individual self. However, from a we-care perspective, even as we train in one orientation, we are also working to support the other. The two are not really separate after all, which is especially clear when we are able to hold a view that keeps both self and others in mind. At the same time, given the interconnectedness of self-compassion and other-compassion, focusing exclusively on one type of training is inherently incomplete. Therefore, whether we start with self-compassion or compassion for others, we are aiming to cultivate and deepen both types of compassion as pillars that can support the development of *interconnected compassion*—or *we-compassion.* Through the practice of we-compassion, self-compassion and other-compassion are seen as essential and interconnected aspects of compassion more broadly. And as with we-care, we can learn to flexibly emphasize one orientation of compassion without losing sight of the other—or, alternatively, we can blend and integrate them in diverse combinations. There's a distinct feel and uniquely transformative quality to holding one's own and others' suffering in mind simultaneously. Our awareness of interconnection broadens and expands, providing us with a stable, energizing foundation for experiencing and expressing we-care.

We-Care Practice 5

COMPASSION COMPASS

The following practice is designed to teach you how to cultivate compassion, so that you can get familiar with bridging the empathy-compassion gap anytime you encounter suffering. As you will see, it is structured to evoke and combine the three core components of compassion reviewed in this chapter, and it can begin either with an emphasis on other-oriented compassion or self-compassion, before eventually spanning both. Per the compass metaphor, the purpose of this practice is to provide you with a foundation needed to establish and orient compassion in any direction—toward yourself, others, both at once, and more widely. The practice also follows a simple mnemonic of NSEW—like north, south, east, and west on a compass—but here corresponding to notice, spark, extend, and wish.

PRACTICE INSTRUCTIONS

1. *Notice suffering.* Find a comfortable posture that feels both supportive and wakeful. You may keep your eyes open with a soft gaze or closed. Decide whether you would like to begin this practice session by emphasizing other-oriented compassion or self-compassion. If starting with other-oriented compassion, bring to mind someone who is having difficulty that you have recently encountered or simply heard about. If you are trying this practice for the first time, it can be ideal to choose something that sparks empathy without feeling overwhelming. See if you can feel whatever you are feeling while also mindfully noticing what it's like to empathize with the struggles of another person or group of people.

    If you chose to instead start with an emphasis on self-compassion, bring awareness to your own recent or current suffering. It could be something obvious, like the discomfort of having recently had conflict with a loved one, or as subtle as wanting to feel something other than what you're feeling right now. Let yourself open to your own experience of struggle through a kind of self-empathy and attunement.

2. *Spark compassion.* Allow awareness of suffering to
fade into the background as you bring to mind a
compassion spark—a person, animal, memory, image,
idea, or gesture that warms your heart, helping you
to connect with a sense of inner warmth, affection,
and care. For instance, you might think of a pet,
child, other loved one, or special moment from your
past. Hold your chosen compassion spark in your
awareness and allow the natural warmth it evokes
to grow and deepen as you breathe.

3. *Extend compassion.* Grounding yourself in the
inner warmth and care elicited by your compassion
spark, bring your awareness back to the suffering
you initially focused on—whether that of another
or your own. See if you can now hold this suffering
within the container of the warmth and affection you
have cultivated—feeling *for* the one who is suffering.
Imagine this warmth and care flowing out with each
exhale, carrying the capacity to alleviate suffering to
wherever it flows. If you'd like, you can try visual-
izing light or other healing imagery, but remember
that staying attuned to the feelings of warmth and
compassion is most essential.

4. *Wish for alleviation.* Join the felt sense of warmth
with an inner wish that you can repeat silently as you
practice. For example, when practicing for others,
you could repeat, *May you be free from this suffering,*
or *May you experience some relief.* If practicing for
yourself, you can substitute an "I" into these phrases,
such as *May I be free from this suffering,* or create a
unique wish that's tailored to whatever suffering you

are focused on, like *May I awaken more self-acceptance
and patience.*

After some time practicing, if you initially focused
on compassion for another, begin to acknowledge and
welcome your own discomforts or struggles too. If
you initially practiced self-compassion, broaden your
focus to include the other orientation by bringing
to mind someone else who is struggling, perhaps
in a similar way as yourself. As you contemplate the
suffering of yourself and another together, generate
a new wish for you both as part of one "we." This version of the wish may sound something like, *May we
find relief from our struggles* or *May we all find greater
ease in the midst of the challenges we are facing.*

The primary purpose of this practice is to cultivate each
core component of compassion and to eventually experience
them together as one emergent feeling state—the healing and
clarifying inner fire of compassion itself. Take as much time
as you need for each step, and see if you can personally find
joy, comfort, and ease in the practice. If you lose touch with
your inner warmth, return to your compassion spark to help
you reconnect with genuine affection and care. Once you
have reestablished this sense of warmth, you can continue to
silently repeat your chosen wish or let it fade into the natural
glow of compassion.

CHAPTER 5

The End of Divided Care

The We-Care Mindset

> Every now and then a [person's] mind is
> stretched by a new idea or sensation, and
> never shrinks back to its former dimensions.
> —OLIVER WENDELL HOLMES, SR.,
> "The Autocrat of the Breakfast-Table"

In the small dining hall of a meditation retreat center, high in the mountains of Red Feather Lakes, Colorado, I recognized a face I'd not seen in over a decade. It was an old housemate of mine, Gabriel.[1] I stopped by the table where he sat and said hello, catching him by surprise. As greetings unfolded, it quickly became clear that Gabriel's decision to come to the retreat center wasn't about seeking a relaxing getaway. He confessed to being there for a personal retreat in the throes of an incredibly trying time—a multilayered storm that had been brewing for years. Facing numerous mental health and life challenges, including a condition affecting his speech, he shared his profound sense of isolation and loneliness. Even before I knew all these details, I immediately sensed his struggle. Faint was the carefree, joyous Gabriel I knew from the past. In his place was someone grappling with numerous real, heartbreaking problems, searching for meaning and a place in the world.

I, on the other hand, felt overwhelmed by how little alone time I would have available while on retreat. Rather than flying solo, I was there as the faculty lead for our undergraduate psychology program's annual meditation retreat—a longstanding and unique feature of our BA program, when students and faculty alike leave their usual lives behind, make the two-hour trek from Boulder to Drala Mountain Center, and engage in various activities and contemplative practices together. As faculty lead as well as department chair, it had been primarily my responsibility to plan that year's retreat. During most of the planning period, I hadn't realized that the first morning of the retreat's group practice would be set against the backdrop of an incredible celestial event. Just a couple of weeks before the retreat, another faculty member informed me that a solar eclipse would occur that first morning. This meant I needed to find a way to acknowledge the stellar occurrence and integrate it into our retreat schedule. Fortunately, my colleague agreed to brainstorm how to do so. But then, less than a day before the retreat, right before we were to meet and finalize the schedule, this colleague had a family emergency that meant they could no longer make it.

Self-doubt turned to overwhelm as it dawned on me that I was now largely on my own, not only to fill in fresh gaps in the schedule created by their absence but to decide on something fitting for the eclipse. My practice of we-care helped me relate to my overwhelm and prioritize what was most essential before leaving for the retreat center, but in the midst of other more critical changes to the schedule, I eventually arrived to the land without a plan for how to integrate the eclipse into the first morning's practice session.

This brings us back to that first night, when I recognized Gabriel. Early the next morning, I saw him again at breakfast and he asked to sit down with me. We got to talking about the eclipse— now just an hour away. I explained how I'd managed to coordinate with the staff of Drala Mountain Center to help us mark the event by holding a *lhasang*—a sacred smoke offering ritual consistent with the Tibetan Buddhist lineages primary to the retreat center's history—but nothing like the direct observation of moon over sun that might get our students particularly excited. Gabriel responded by sharing a story about a time when, as a boy, he looked directly into the sun during an eclipse, resulting in permanent damage to his vision. He wondered if he might help to support our ceremony by devising a way for students to safely view the eclipse, using a device made from materials in the kitchen. I happily agreed.

An hour later as we encircled the fire, Gabriel was nowhere in sight. I shrugged it off, reminded students not to stare at the sun, and proceeded with the ceremony. As I suspected, the students' participation in the ceremony didn't feel all that enthusiastic, and I wondered if they wished they could interact with the eclipse more directly. We then made our way to the meditation hall in silence to begin our morning sit. Partway through the first period of mindfulness meditation, my eyes softly open, something caught my eye outside the expansive floor-to-ceiling windows of the meditation hall. A man wearing a backpack was sprinting across the field behind the meditation hall, his swift motion creating a striking contrast as he traversed from left to right across all the windows. Aiming to model nondistraction for my students, I resisted raising my gaze for a better look.

I couldn't ignore the man for long though, as moments later, he entered the meditation hall through the doors behind us. It was Gabriel. "Sorry—to—interrupt," he said, catching his breath between words. "I drove to the local library where they had free eclipse sunglasses available, and got enough for—everyone. The eclipse is still happening—if you want to look."

The students looked at me eagerly, their eyes saying, "Can we please?"

I smiled and nodded. They stood and rushed out the meditation hall, slowing only to grab their pair of glasses from Gabriel, who eagerly handed them out by the handful. The next half hour was spent gathered outside, watching the cosmic spectacle with eyes (safely) wide with wonder, hearts sparked by the gift of a stranger's kindness. And for that brief time, Gabriel's personal retreat intertwined with our collective experience, creating an unexpected highpoint in everyone's time on the land.

Reflecting through the lens of we-care, Gabriel's actions—driving to the local library, fetching enough glasses for us all, and sprinting to the meditation hall—raise an important question for me: Were his efforts completely selfless, such that Gabriel had been driven by pure, other-focused care? Or might there have been self-caring intentions embedded in his actions too—a way for him to counter his isolation and loneliness, perhaps even to strike a note of retroactive self-care for the trauma to his vision he'd suffered when younger?

With a *we-care mindset*, a single caring action is rarely, if ever, solely for the benefit of others *or* oneself. In Gabriel's case, his caring actions that morning not only helped me and him, they uplifted the entire energy of our community retreat for the better. As the sun and moon aligned in the sky, casting a mesmerizing dance of light and shadow across the landscape, a powerful and transformative convergence of care unfolded right there among us.

Kindness Feels Good—That's Not a Problem

Imagine that, one month ago, we measured the mental well-being of three hundred people before randomly sorting them into three groups. The first group was given the task of completing three random acts of other-oriented kindness every week—things like doing a chore for a family member, helping an elderly person, or writing a thank-you note. The second group was tasked with carrying out acts of self-kindness, such as spending time on a beloved hobby or enjoying a massage. Finally, the third group simply had to keep track of whatever activities they were naturally drawn to.

Now, a month later, imagine we again measured the well-being of these three hundred people. Knowing what you do so far about the we-care mindset, take a moment to reflect: Do you think the well-being of any of these groups would increase significantly more over the month?

A similar study conducted previously found that there was, in fact, one clear winner among the three groups.[2] Specifically, the largest and most lasting change in psychological well-being was among those tasked with other-oriented kindness. What's more, there was no measurable improvement in well-being among those assigned to self-kindness. And these findings are not outliers. Many other studies have found similar results, whether through kind acts reducing symptoms of anxiety and depression[3] or through better outcomes among those who spent money to benefit others compared to spending it on themselves.[4]

How should we think about the implications of these findings in relation to we-care? From one perspective, they demonstrate alignment with some of the central ideas we've reviewed so far, such as the potential for mutual benefits and intrinsic rewards when caring for others. From another perspective, they reveal something paradoxical that we haven't discussed: When directly comparing the benefits that accrue to the caring individual, acts of other-care often outperform self-care. In other words, for some outcomes like one's overall sense of well-being, the best self-care may be found in caring for others. This is consistent with a popular quote by His Holiness the Dalai Lama, "If you want others to be happy, practice compassion. If you want to be happy, practice compassion."[5]

We-care equips us with a new looking glass for viewing and making sense of the aforementioned studies and the scientific literature on care at large. For instance, I imagine many people, including some researchers, would look at the above results and conclude that divided forms of other-care are superior to self-care for promoting well-being. An alternative explanation—and the way I read these study results—is that people's approach to caring for others frequently *includes* sufficient care for oneself quite naturally, especially when they have autonomy to choose what acts of other-kindness they carry out. Acts of self-kindness, on the other hand, do not as readily integrate care for others without explicit instructions or training to do so. They may even diminish other-oriented care through subtly encouraging divided forms of self-care. Therefore, participants tasked with other-kindness may have been more likely to spontaneously experience we-care than those assigned to self-kindness, despite the researchers' not framing it this way.

Using the we-care looking glass can help us understand why studies that rely solely on an either/or distinction of care can yield genuinely puzzling results. For instance, people sometimes hesitate to engage in acts of other-oriented kindness because they focus too much on the effectiveness of their actions and feel self-conscious about the personal gratification it brings them.[6] This leads them to underestimate how meaningful their kind acts could be for others. Consequently, aware that their acts of kindness can result in personal benefits but underestimating the social impact, they may talk themselves out of doing them. The we-care perspective shows us that such decisions, sadly, are shaped by the idea that true other-care excludes self-care. Without a we-care mindset, people may avoid acts that could achieve and integrate both kinds of care.

If you'd like to explore for yourself some of these less intuitive aspects of kind actions, there's a wonderful practice from Zen Buddhism called *inji-gyo*, which translates to "secret good deeds." The basic idea is to do something kind for another stealthily, without them knowing it was you. For instance, you could clear a neighbor's driveway of snow when they're away at work, cover the cost of the next person at a toll booth, pick up trash at the local park, or leave an uplifting note or gift card inside a book at the library. Although inji-gyo is valued as a practice within Zen for reasons organic to that tradition, I've long found it useful for reflecting on theories within the science of care. Embedded in the practice's design is the removal of the most obvious causal pathways—such as direct reciprocity, praise, or recognition—that link performing an act of kindness to experiencing personal benefits. Consequently, you're left with a pure experience of what it's like to act kindly without these elements. You can therefore use the practice of inji-gyo for an intriguing personal experiment. Does performing a secret act of kindness nonetheless yield personal benefits for you? If no, why not? And if yes, how so?

What Makes a Mindset?

Many lessons and insights related to we-care point to a basic truth: how we think about care impacts the quantity and quality of care we have to offer. And yet, on its own, the thinking mind can only ever take us so far. As we've seen, the nature of our care can be counterintuitive, even mysterious. No matter how hard we try, experiences of care will never fit perfectly with the concepts and mental models we rely on to understand them. Obviously, I find transforming our thinking about care interesting and important—I'm writing a whole book on it. But there are important layers of care that are less conceptual, such as those in the realm of caring feelings and compassionate actions. Consider how much trust you might place in a psychotherapist who has seen countless clients versus one whose training was limited to only reading training manuals and academic papers about it. Direct experience with clients not only enhances intellectual understanding but also deepens care-based feelings and improves the effectiveness of actions necessary for impactful care.

Accordingly, direct experiences and applications of we-care both counterbalance and support our conceptual understanding, such that the interplay of thoughts, feelings, and actions together lead to a more personal and embodied realization of we-care. To encompass this broader and more complete approach to we-care, it's helpful to think about cultivating a *we-care mindset* that blends thoughts, feelings, and actions aligned with we-care.

But what makes something a holistic mindset, rather than simply a collection of ideas, emotions, and action tendencies? In other words, how can we mix and blend the essential elements of we-care to give rise to a broader we-care mindset? For this, we can turn to two key brain-based insights that have emerged from cognitive and affective neuroscience. Specifically, *psychological constructionism*, an insight we first touched upon to understand emotion in chapter 4, reveals how the we-care mindset can incorporate many different psychological "ingredients" into a cohesive whole that is greater than the sum of its parts. In fact, the human brain is remarkably good at integrating diverse neural and psychological processes into more complex and holistic states of being. This functional integration is a vital feature of brain functioning, occurring across multiple levels of analysis. It increases in both its complexity and the number of emergent properties it exhibits, from the nuances of basic sensory awareness to the entirety of one's moment-to-moment, subjective experience. Similarly, the we-care mindset emerges from the interplay of essential elements and qualities at multiple levels, each contributing uniquely to the formation of a coherent and comprehensive whole.

The concept of *neuroplasticity* explains how these brain states can then turn into enduring traits—stable aspects of our character—over time. The brain does not change uniformly across all the varied experiences of our lives, nor is it always choiceful. Instead, the science of neuroplasticity has discovered that the brain naturally grows and transforms to varying degrees across different kinds of experiences, from one-off events to chronic life challenges to consciously pursued and cultivated qualities of mind. Whether framed in terms of neuroplasticity or not, any path of personal growth partly involves self-guiding our brains into states aligned with the kind of growth we're aiming for.

A few key principles about how neuroplasticity works can help us to understand this in ways we might use to our advantage. To begin with, neuroplasticity starts with our awareness and attention. The more conscious we are of our goal and intended process for change, the more our brains muster the neural resources needed to grow and transform. Although one-off events can sometimes change our brains in lasting ways—for example, the moment you realize you are falling in love or receiving an acceptance letter from your dream university—they're not a predictable or reliable way to self-guide neuroplasticity. Rather, we should focus on repeatedly cultivating desired mental qualities and states, deliberately carving new neural pathways that are reinforced by the naturally rewarding feedback loops of progressing toward our goals. Like the way a fresh footpath toward our favorite spot in a dense forest becomes easier to recognize and follow with each use, repeatedly experiencing specific brain states will make it easier for your brain to click back into them.

Considered together, psychological constructionism and neuroplasticity reveal insights about cultivating the we-care mindset that are remarkably practical. There's both a science and an art to crafting a holistic mindset. We can build and fine-tune the we-care mindset through study, practice, and application of any one element or quality, based on the understanding that strengthening any one aspect can contribute to an overall stronger mindset. Yet we are likely to transform even more if we also prioritize cultivating two or more aspects at a time. In fact, those properties of an interconnected system that are considered "emergent" can only ever arise through the dynamic interplay of its parts. There's thus distinct value in exploring and embracing higher-order expressions of we-care that arise through the interaction of its constituent elements.

Consider the journey of Elena, who began practicing we-care to manage stress from her demanding job in graphic design. Initially, her practice focused on emphasizing self-compassion, particularly on being kinder to herself during moments of high stress or failure. As Elena became more attuned to her needs and feelings, she started seeing her creative process as an expression of her we-care. She found that it was possible to embrace the creative aspects of her job as opportunities to deepen we-compassion, lessening her resistance to the stress they sometimes brought and leading her to design more inclusive and emotionally resonant projects. Her inner experiences felt increasingly like a springboard for innovation, especially as she learned to approach creative blocks with more curiosity and acceptance. Elena's holistic we-care mindset therefore fostered a unique synergy that both enhanced her well-being and transformed her professional output.

Expanding Your We-Care Mindset

Beginning in the following section and continuing through the rest of this chapter, I will delineate some of the most important emergent qualities of the we-care mindset—qualities that can bring focus to a new set of targets on the path of cultivating we-care from within. In spotlighting them, my hope is that you can better notice and embrace their roles as you cultivate and apply the we-care mindset throughout your life.

To track your progress along the way, it can be helpful to have a benchmark of where you stand that you can circle back to. I've therefore devised a short set of statements to represent beliefs aligned with the we-care mindset, in contrast to those presented for the either/or mindset in chapter 2. While these statements are not drawn from any formal scientific assessment tool, rating your agreement with them and recording your responses in a journal or similar space may help to scaffold reflection on your we-care mindset.

Across our lives, the decision between self-care and care for others is rarely a matter of either/or.

Strongly Disagree   Strongly Agree

1   2   3   4   5

Care is an abundant and continuously replenishing resource; it's possible to offer a lot of care to others and still have plenty for self-care.

Strongly Disagree   Strongly Agree

1   2   3   4   5

How best to approach we-care varies from one situation to the next, so it's important to be mindful of the context while also paying attention to your personal needs.

Strongly Disagree   Strongly Agree

1   2   3   4   5

One person's genuine expression of we-care may not look and feel like we-care to others.

Strongly Disagree   Strongly Agree

1   2   3   4   5

*Your own and others' well-being are interconnected, so
seeking mutual benefit is often practical and worthwhile.*

Strongly Disagree   Strongly Agree

    1   2   3   4   5

Both/And and Beyond

Anytime you have an experience in which your self-care and
other-care are essential and interconnected—an experience of
we-care—you are drawing on and leaning into the mind's capacity for *dialectical thinking*, which is the ability to entertain multiple perspectives at once, even when they appear contradictory
or opposing. But while the we-care mindset is most certainly
dialectical—embracing a both/and approach—it also extends far
beyond simple expressions of dialectical thinking. Even in the
basic, everyday expressions of we-care, there are clearly times
when both/and doesn't quite cut it. As we've explored, we-care
can involve strongly emphasizing self-care or other-care, meaning
there's a need to reintegrate either/or thinking alongside both/
and thinking. For instance, if someone's trying to take advantage
of you, it would be unwise not to strongly emphasize self-care in
ways that thwart their attempted manipulation.

This highlights the value of *paradoxical thinking*, a more advanced expression of both/and that involves more fully embracing
contradictions, finding distinctive value in them, and capitalizing on this unique understanding to yield innovative solutions.
With a mindset that embraces paradox, we may, for example, find
ourselves enjoying the process of rooting out even the subtlest
residual fragments of conflicted care. Take the case of Jamie, who
often found it challenging to listen over dinner to his partner's
stress-inducing stories from their high-powered job. Intrigued by
his resistance, Jamie began leaning into the conversations more,

eventually uncovering a paradoxical benefit: By actively engaging and exploring meaningful solutions for his partner's work dilemmas, he realized he'd not been sufficiently standing up for himself at his own job. Thus, the act of supporting his partner not only helped them and deepened their romantic relationship, it eventually inspired Jamie to apply for and receive a promotion.

But even as we deftly wield the eccentric tool of paradoxical thinking, the path of we-care beckons us further. After all, intrinsic to the notion of both/and, as well as paradox, is the assumption of two distinct things. By contrast, we-care frequently blurs the lines between what counts as caring for oneself and caring for others, manifesting in unified experiences in which self-care *is* other-care, or other-care *is* self-care. These experiences put us in touch with an even deeper sense of mystery surrounding our care, one where any and all concepts, even paradoxes, prove inadequate.

Care Yoga

Imagine that, right now as you read this sentence, the words on the page begin to move and rearrange themselves. At first, you rightly feel befuddled. But then, as you confirm the ever-shifting page isn't merely a trick of your eyes, you recall having heard about such experiences—that transforming text like this could, in fact, be a sign of something quite explainable. You look around you, confirming that you do not quite remember how you ended up here, of all places. You take out your phone—it's glitching. Another sign. Could it really be? You remember a simple test you once learned for this exact situation, pinching your nose and trying to breathe. Miraculously, despite your fully pinched nose, your breath passes easily through.

You are dreaming.

As strange as this experience may sound, at some point in their lives roughly 50 percent of the population will have a *lucid dream*—defined as a dream in which they recognize they are dreaming in the midst of the dream. This clear recognition allows one to perform feats that would be impossible in waking life, such as changing the color of the sky, flying, or walking through walls. Such experiences can seem endlessly fascinating, yet, more frequent lucid dreamers sometimes experience a sort of disillusionment after countless such dreams, when the novelty fades and they run out of ideas for what to do next: What's the point of continuing to do this? Are these exceptional dream experiences at all supporting who and what I care about in my waking life?

I've long had an interest in the science of dreaming, tracing back to the first lucid dream I experienced when I was a senior in high school. After facing a similar what's-the-point contemplation of my own, I discovered *dream yoga*, a practice originating from Tibetan Buddhism that helped me find a deeper why for lucid dreaming. Dream yoga taught me that it's possible to use the lucid dream state to engage in exercises to stretch and expand the mind, making it more flexible and open, similar to how physical forms of yoga work to transform the body. I could now see how walking through a wall in a lucid dream was not just fun and interesting, but it could help me enhance my *psychological flexibility* in waking life.

In a similar way, in daily life, the we-care mindset embraces an ongoing practice of *care yoga*—reframing the social dilemmas of everyday life as opportunities to stretch and expand our ideas and experiences of care. Whereas previously the either/or mindset narrowed care into a binary, the we-care mindset greatly widens the scope of possibilities, increasing our psychological flexibility. And in fact, research has shown how greater psychological flexibility is essential for protecting those tasked with a lot of caring, such as psychotherapists, from burnout. It seems especially helpful for navigating moments of tension or conflict between self-care and care for others, reducing emotional dissonance and the exhaustion it brings.[7] Consider how a psychotherapist can learn to see their own boredom and frustration during a session as a possible valid signal about how their client is feeling, leading to a new approach that facilitates a therapeutic breakthrough. Practicing the mental yoga of a we-care mindset, our psychological flexibility allows us to peer through the seemingly solid nature of the walls that divide self from other. We realize that, whenever we choose, we can pass right through them.

Full of Heart

Barb is in her early seventies, settling happily into retirement, when she unexpectedly finds herself stretched thin from offering care in three different directions. To her delight, her daughter and daughter-in-law both got pregnant at the same time and had babies within a month of each other. Although she loves babysitting her grand-babies, she finds it overwhelming to be receiving near-daily requests to care for them. At the same time, Barb's elderly mother began developing dementia and needing both more frequent and intensive care from her. Before long, Barb feels that she has more demands upon her care than ever before, leading to a sense of burnout and resistance to caring, especially during the daily trips to visit her mom.

It's one thing to care for someone once and another altogether to be called into intensive, ongoing care. Yet whether for professional, familial, or other reasons, long-lasting caregiving is a reality for many. A nationwide survey in the United States, conducted between 2015 and 2017, found that among adults forty-five years of age and older, over one in five reported caregiving duties for family or friends over the previous month. One third of such caregivers offered twenty or more hours of care per week—numbers expected to grow due to an increasing older adult population.[8] A common risk of such intensive care is a distinctive sort of fatigue, what we previously clarified in chapter 4 to be a form of *empathic distress fatigue*, rather than *compassion fatigue* as it is commonly misnamed. One key practical implication of this was that cultivating compassion, such as through training in practices like Compassion Compass, could be an ideal long-term remedy for preventing and reducing empathic distress fatigue.

Unfortunately, however, when giving so much care to others, caregiving may contribute to a sense of care depletion—a pervasive feeling that there's no more care to go around, least of all for one's inner self. Without denying the reality of feeling depleted by caregiving, it's important to recognize that seeing care as a limited resource can itself be a barrier that causes more depletion. Indeed, studies show how people who view compassion to be limited can experience a self-fulfilling prophecy—tragically leading to not only more empathic distress fatigue but also less overall caring and lower-quality care.[9] Thus, we again encounter the truth that how we think about our care matters for both the quantity and quality of our care.

Fortunately, the seeds for shifting from a mindset of care scarcity to one of care abundance are already planted in basic elements and practices of we-care. As you grow more familiar with the we-care mindset, you greatly expand your experienced reservoir of care. You stop abandoning yourself or others in ways that artificially restrict its flow, generating more energy to care in both directions. Most critical for caregiving, you stop second-guessing the value and importance of your personal self-care. You can more clearly trace a line between your personal well-being and transformation and what's good for those you care for. More than this, as you grow more adept in blending self-care and other-care, you discover the results are not additive but multiplicative. You realize that you don't have to wait to feel more energized—engaging in acts of we-care, whether primarily for yourself or others, often energizes you in ways that ultimately benefit everyone. This builds your capacity to keep your heart open to suffering, while avoiding different kinds of confused care, such as enabling, conflict avoidance, and people-pleasing. Over time, you might even find yourself in awe of the sheer vastness of your undivided heart—a natural, replenishing wellspring of life-giving care.

Aha!

The following words can all be joined with the same missing word to form a compound word or phrase: *white, lined, blank.* Once you identify the missing word, each resulting compound word or phrase will be familiar to you—in this case, the word is *paper.* Below are a few more to try. See if you can identify the missing word. Solutions can be found at the end of this section.

Chocolate, tin, fortune

Got it? If so, then you likely also experienced a very specific burst of neural activity—a *gamma burst*—as the solution came to mind that I'll soon tell you more about. For now, see if you can subjectively notice a subtle felt sense of this neural burst as you solve this next one:

Light, stick, birthday

Feel anything that might correspond to a burst of neural activation? Okay, okay. Let's try one more:

Quick, spoon, coin

Problems like these have been essential to the scientific study of *insight* because of how their solution frequently arises in a flash of instantaneous realization. Insights are largely defined by this experience—sudden "aha moments" in how we're thinking about a problem or situation. They're often accompanied by a sense of breaking through a mental block or suddenly widening a limited way of perceiving, revealing an entirely new angle, inter-pretation, or solution. Mirroring this rapid mental shift within the brain, researchers have consistently found evidence that the neural correlates of such insights involve a gamma burst—a spurt of high-frequency brainwaves that help to bind together diverse inputs and cognitive processes into an emergent, coherent percep-tion or thought.[10]

Given the ubiquity and automaticity of the either/or mind-set, the potential for we-care often arises further downstream in an aha moment, like a beam of sunlight breaking through the clouds. Insightfulness is therefore another key quality of the we-care mindset. But as fascinating and productive as insights can be, their seemingly sudden, out-of-nowhere nature can make it feel like there's nothing we can do to facilitate more of them. When faced with an either/or dilemma in our care, are we simply left to wait for insights about we-care to arise spontaneously?

Although we consciously experience insight in an instant, careful research in psychology and neuroscience has revealed the role of ample subconscious processing occurring in the moments leading up to an insight. This is why, for example, subliminal cues related to the solution of an insight problem can help someone arrive at the solution more quickly.[11] And while we cannot prime ourselves with precise subliminal cues about how to solve our unique care dilemmas in daily life, such research on the role of subconscious processing in insight shows why there's value in making space for it to occur—especially when we're faced with some kind of social dilemma related to balancing our self-care and care for others. In other words, we can't force an insight to occur, but we can set the conditions for them to occur more often.

Embracing a slower pace and pausing for breaks from active problem-solving lets the subconscious play its role effectively. Rather than being cornered into making a quick choice, the will-ingness to sit with the discomfort of uncertainty for extended periods cultivates what is known as *uncertainty tolerance.* This is important because, as you may recall, lack of deliberation is one of the core drivers of the either/or mindset. And truthfully, a rush to resolve can be appealing, especially when the stakes are high and the outcome is significant to us. However, the method we apply in approaching these decisions deserves as much consideration as the act of caring itself, ensuring that we're mindful in every step of the process. This isn't merely slowing down; you are getting your conscious and subconscious mind to work together as a team. This often saves you significant effort and time in the long run.

(The solutions to three-word problems are *cookie, candle,* and *silver.*)

The Creativity of Caring

My wife, Ellie, works in end-of-life care as a spiritual counselor. She's also a visual artist. Years ago, she noticed how little creative inspiration seemed to go into the interior design and chosen art of the skilled nursing communities she frequents, where many of her patients are living out their final years.

Rather than accepting this humdrum as unchangeable, she decided to do something about it. She partnered with a Whole Foods Market nearby, who generously offered to donate their unsold flowers to her new venture—creating fresh flower arrangements for her hospice patients. As you might imagine, the flowers have been greatly appreciated, adding a touch of vitality to otherwise bland scenery. For instance, one day as she delivered flowers to an elderly woman's room, the woman's daughter was present. As Ellie placed the flowers on the bedside table, the daughter quietly expressed her gratitude, saying, "Thank you. Flowers are a symbol of hope for me." Reflecting on these moments as we-care, Ellie finds that exchanges like these not only enrich her visits but also enliven the quality of her care.

In daily life, acts of kindness and care are often quite simple and ordinary. However, the fullest expression of the we-care mindset in daily life invites us to think more creatively each step of the way. After all, care is fundamentally an act of self-expression. A process of being moved and taking the leap of inspired action. Moreover, true to the spirit of we-care, the creative spark has a way of giving in two directions at once. This isn't to say our we-care needs to be story worthy or ostentatious. In fact, creativity is such an ordinary feature of the we-care mindset that it may go unnoticed. There is a basic artfulness needed to break free from the either/or mindset, notice hidden choices that respect both self-care and care for others, and subsequently express the diverse shades and colors of we-care in a world that often sees only in black and white.

The End of Divided Care

Imagine no longer approaching your care mostly in terms of self-care or care for others. You can enjoy your favorite hobby, navigate a difficult conversation, take a nap, or stay a few extra hours at the office to mentor a junior colleague—all from the same underlying source of care. You no longer feel guilty for choosing yourself when you do, nor do you fear abandoning yourself as you seek to support others. You don't have to think, *This self-care is actually we-care because it's benefiting my care for others too*, or *I'm doing this for them now because they will support me in return in the future.* Instead, you simply express care wherever it is needed, sourcing from your undivided heart. You know that self-care, other-care, and all the spaces between are ways of strengthening the social fabric of your life. All are forms of we-care.

At some point along the path of cultivating the we-care mindset, you come to see that it's okay to let go of divided care entirely. You realize it's possible to maintain the practical utility of speaking and thinking in terms of self-care and care for others without believing it as truth. The different essential elements and roots of we-care intertwine, rising and blooming into a holistic mindset that can support all the diverse expressions of care needed to live your life with wisdom, compassion, and grace. Engaging the world from your whole care system allows you to achieve all the same benefits that divided care once did but in a manner that's more clearly aligned with our social nature and more practical than toggling back and forth.

We-Care Practice 6
FREE-FLOWING CARE

It's in the nature of concepts to "carve" a complex, messy, and uncertain world. Applied to understanding care, even nuanced concepts like paradoxes can fall short of capturing its undivided nature. Of course, there's still plenty of practical utility to be found in working directly with your concepts of care—which is why, for example, the practice of Compassion Compass, presented at the end of chapter 4, focused on directing the flow of your compassion toward self, other(s), and both at once. However, there are times when any concept— even the concept of we-care—can create a barrier to experiencing the innate wisdom of your spontaneous care. It can therefore be helpful to sometimes practice caring beyond concepts altogether, unlearning the habit of guiding and shaping care's flow. Hence the uniquely formless approach of this next we-care practice, called Free-Flowing Care.

PRACTICE INSTRUCTIONS

1. *Spark care.* Bring to mind a *care spark*—another being, memory, image, symbol, word, or phrase that

helps you attune to a sense of inner warmth and care whenever you conjure it. It may be the same as your chosen *compassion spark* from chapter 4, except this time we're going to rely on it to cultivate caring feelings more broadly. As examples, your care spark could be your pet or perhaps a cherished memory of the holidays that naturally warms your heart.

2. *Expand your feelings of care.* Holding your care spark in mind, take some mindful breaths to help you deepen and circulate your natural feelings of affection and care. You may notice qualities such as love, compassion, friendliness, kindness, and connection.

3. *Let your care flow where it wants to.* Care is often guided or directed, such as toward yourself or a loved one. In this step of the practice, the invitation is to loosen the grip, no longer trying to direct the flow of your care but rather seeing where it seems to naturally want to go and offer its supportive sentiment. Maybe it wants to flow toward an anxious thought, an unfelt feeling, an achy joint, someone nearby, or a group of people you read about in the news. From one moment to the next, allow your care to flow as it wants to—care leading itself.

4. *Restore the flow.* Over time, you may notice that your care naturally wants to dwell for a few moments on one thing before moving to the next. This is normal and aligned with the overall aims of this practice. However, sometimes care may get a little stuck on something, dampening the free-flow and disrupting the sense of continuity. If this ever happens, you can

simply pause, take a mindful breath, spark care, and begin again, seeing where else your care may want to flow next.

5. *Care beyond concept.* As we allow care to flow from one thing to another, we may notice even subtler concepts still shaping our care. Maybe your care naturally wants to flow toward you and a loved one at the same time. Maybe it wants to radiate in all directions. Or maybe instead of care radiating out from us, it wants to be felt as an energy field or web that surrounds and envelops you. Who knows, care might even want to flow back and care for itself. Whenever you notice this subtler layer of concepts, you can try finding a balance between allowing them and then releasing, opening again to the possibility of caring beyond concept.

CHAPTER 6

Full-Spectrum We-Care

Connected and Protected

> What the virtuous have done that other
> leaders have not is reconciled the duality
> of human existence.
>
> —JEREMY A. FRIMER ET AL., "Hierarchical
> Integration of Agency and Communion:
> A Study of Influential Moral Figures"

Most days, Marietta loves her job as a social worker. Her daily tasks not only align with her values but also make her feel connected to her wider community. Despite this, she often struggles with feelings of inadequacy and guilt, especially when she cannot participate in important community actions or events. For example, there's a rally planned at the state capitol on the following Saturday for a cause she passionately supports. Unfortunately, she had already committed to spending that day with her family, who not only would be upset if she canceled but would also disagree with her political stance. When she explains to her friends why she can't attend the rally, their response is dismissive. They laugh and suggest she should challenge her parents' views more assertively.

This reaction leaves her feeling isolated and criticized by those she hoped would understand her predicament.

Discovering we-care for oneself, from the inside out, is essential. However, as Marietta's dilemma shows, it's more of a continuous journey of discovery than a destination. As we-care moves from being purely an inner experience into the territory of outer expressions and caring responses, we may be confronted with the reality that—no matter how deep our inner realization of we-care—fully embodying and skillfully enacting it is anything but neat and tidy. We'll revisit Marietta's story later in this chapter to see the specific steps she took to embody and enact we-care. For now, let's draw from her example to underscore this essential point: We-care does not occur in a vacuum. Not only are further skills needed to express and respond from a place of we-care, but much of we-care's transformative power is determined precisely at the intersection of inner and outer—in the process of translating your we-care mindset into meaningful expressions. In social settings where division reigns, choosing we-care means digging deep. We must courageously resist both our own either/or mindset and that of others. At times, one act of we-care may even challenge deep societal divides—collective either/ors present in the mindsets of millions.

Rosa Parks stands as a towering figure in history for her simple yet profound act in 1955, when she boldly refused to give up her seat on a bus—an expression of care that served as a spark for the Civil Rights Movement throughout the 1950s and 1960s. And while the story leading up to Parks's refusal is commonly oversimplified by narratives that overlook her decades-long commitment to civil rights and social justice activism, it's clear that her decision that day was not merely an expression of self-care. However, it was not entirely selfless either—at least not in the strict, divided sense of self-sacrifice that had nothing to do with her personal well-being. Per Parks's own words, "People always say that I didn't give up my seat because I was tired, but that isn't true. . . . No, the only tired I was, was tired of giving in."[1] Thus, as is evident in this quote, Parks's refusal was about asserting her dignity and that of the broader African American community—I see it as a self-directed, courageous expression of we-care.

But while some may find it easy to agree with my claim that Parks's refusal appears to be an expression of we-care, you would be right to be skeptical about this claim, particularly if you know what happens next in Parks's story. She was arrested, lost her job, and faced widespread societal backlash from those who supported segregation. How could the self-care element of we-care have been present given those consequences? It's vital not to downplay the reality that Parks personally suffered as a result of her refusal that day and also to recognize that there was clearly a strong emphasis on other-oriented care in her decision. But then, that's not the end of her story either. Despite these negative impacts, she catalyzed a movement—thirteen months of mass protest—that played a pivotal role in achieving her aim of dismantling segregation, something that benefited all Americans. And of course, she would eventually be widely recognized for her enduring contributions as a highly respected leader, symbol of civil rights, and luminary.

As Parks's story reveals, fully appreciating the depth and impact of we-care in a societal context requires adopting a perspective that looks beyond immediate consequences and accounts for one's values, self-directed goals, and deeper sense of purpose. This includes recognizing the profound and lasting impact that some expressions of we-care can have on the broader social fabric. Bearing this in mind, we can see that—though few people will ever operate on the scope of a Rosa Parks—it's both possible and realistic to find meaning in the overlap between one's personal we-care journey and one's power to have a positive impact on numerous others in our lives, the systems and organizations we are part of, and society more broadly. Awake to this potential for impact, the individual practice of we-care can serve a broader, collective purpose, enriching the lives of loved ones, the communities to which we belong, and even complete strangers.

Balancing Agency and Communion in We-Care

The story of Rosa Parks offers a provocative and inspiring case study of how one person's we-care can radically transform society. It has also been the subject of scientific research on another vital piece of the we-care puzzle. Listed below are three groups of fairly well-known public figures from this research.[2] You may not recognize every name, but based on those you do, I'm guessing it won't shock you to learn there are marked differences in the psychological profiles between them. Before we delve into these differences, however, I want to instead invite you to reflect on what all three groups could possibly have in common. It's a subtle yet fundamental quality of their character that distinguishes them in a similar way from most other people. And it can be discerned both from their well-known actions, like Parks's refusal, and from the ways they spoke about themselves and their lives.

Group A. Adolf Hitler, Jiang Qing, Vladimir Putin
Group B. David Beckham, Marilyn Monroe, Bill Belichick
Group C. Rosa Parks, Mohandas Gandhi, Eleanor Roosevelt

Have you figured it out? The answer relates fundamentally to power, direction, and achievement—what psychologists call *agency*. Agency is a broad psychological dimension that encompasses motives and behaviors needed for effective goal pursuit and influence, including assertiveness, instrumentality, and competence. You can get a feel for who in your social world may be high in agency by contemplating the following: If there were suddenly a societal collapse or world-upending event that required swift and bold actions to survive, who would you want on your "team" to help effectively navigate the dark days ahead?

For personality theorists, agency stands in contrast to *communion,* an opposing term encompassing qualities such as friendliness, warmth, cooperation, and sensitivity. Whereas you might want someone high in agency if the world were falling apart around you, you would likely prefer those high in communion when you are just hanging out and relaxing. Who from your social circle would you want accompanying you for your next weekend plans when you're simply aiming for a good time? Odds are, that person is high in the quality of communion.

To understand agency and communion in a nonreductive way that does justice to their complexity, we'll soon review some other terms for reflecting on their many roles in we-care. Until then, it's best to think of them as broad, flexible signposts our minds rely on to organize our social worlds—describing and sorting people, mindsets, actions, and states of being. Like other binary distinctions in this book, the reality of agency and communion is far from either/or. Even though we can identify people high in one or the other, most everyone is a complex mix of agency and communion, and that's a good thing—too much agency or communion alone can be problematic both personally and socially.[3]

This point brings us back to what the three groups above have in common and likewise what distinguishes them. The individuals in all three groups appear to be high in agency when compared to the average person. To understand what sets them apart, it is essential to consider not only their agency but also their levels of communion. This includes examining the specific roles that these qualities play or played in their lives.

In a scientific study on so-called "moral exemplars," such as those in Group C above, researchers examined their degree of, and practical reliance on, agentic and communal qualities as a lens for distinguishing them.[4] The comparison groups were made up of others like those listed in Groups A and B above and were selected to be similarly famous and influential, but for other reasons. Studying exceptional people in a category, such as influential moral figures, offers researchers a reference point of *positive deviance*, which refers to individuals who deviate from the average person in a positive or constructive way. More frequently, researchers focus on negative deviance. But only through studying moral exemplars like Rosa Parks can we see the higher reaches of what's possible for moral development, revealing valuable insights that could help to move the moral needle for us all.

In the case of this study, a striking pattern of agency and communion was found to differentiate the moral exemplars from the other two groups. Although high agency characterized the short-term goals and actions of both moral exemplars and dictators, differences emerged in their long-term goals. Specifically, moral exemplars (Group C) relied on highly agentic goals and deeds to pursue long-term *communal* aims. In other words, their strategic goal pursuit and wielding of power were instrumental to their ultimate aim of empowering many others. For instance, Rosa Parks asserted her power by disobeying a rule (agency) in order to promote greater equality in society (communion). In clear contrast, actions derived from the short-term agency of Groups A and B were aimed at long-term *agentic* aims. Further distinguishing the two groups, Group A's agentic aims may be seen as tyrannical and morally wrong, while Group B's long-term goals appear more morally ambiguous. Thus, influential moral figures are different not because of their especially high agency *or* communion, but rather in how they integrate them—relying on varied agentic means to pursue a communal goal of a better world for many. It's a profound integration of inner division that also holds the power to transform outer division.

Vulnerability and Strength in the Dance of We-Care

In April 2020, inspired by questions about transforming compassion as an inner experience into skillful care, I had the opportunity to help plan and lead a think tank at Naropa University on the Buddhist concept of *skillful means*. This term derives from Mahayana Buddhism, but in secular contexts I think of it as adept social action that effectively integrates wisdom and compassion.[5] The collaborative effort brought together leading compassion scientists, scholars, and trainers for a days-long dialogue. As you might guess from its timing, we had to move the event online due to the COVID-19 pandemic. But despite us all still getting used to our virtual world, the think tank proved a success, raising a number of fascinating questions and catalyzing more than a dozen original articles for a special issue of a peer-reviewed journal. Most exciting for me personally was the growing sense, both during the meeting and from the ensuing research, that we were homing in on something that could be scientifically studied to unravel the rich complexity of enacting care and compassion within a societal context.

In chapter 1, I introduced three key trade-offs, or dividing lines, in our care that distinguish the Superhero from the Hurt, and in other earlier chapters we've explored two of them in-depth—*self versus others* and *feeling versus action*. Now, to fully understand Parks's refusal as a powerfully effective form of we-care, we have to consider how we-care bridges the final divide. This third dividing line is that of *communion versus agency*, which I earlier called *vulnerability versus strength*. The role of these qualities in we-care is often most pronounced at the intersection of inner and outer, helping to explain a range of skillfulness in how care is expressed in our lives. However, *vulnerability* and *strength* make up just one of three accessible pairs of synonyms for *communion* and *agency*. Next, we'll explore these qualities in relation to we-care through all three pairs of synonyms, starting with *yin versus yang*, then considering *short-term versus long-term*, and finally returning to *vulnerability versus strength*.

Yin versus Yang

As with we-care's approach to self-care and other-care, we can learn to knowingly embrace and participate in a mindful back-and-forth between communal and agentic expressions of our care. But also like balancing care toward oneself and others, there is a critical difference between divided expressions of communion and agency, and actions that combine them as interconnected parts of a greater whole. Ideally, one can wield both agentic and communal actions together, emphasizing one without losing sight of the other. We can illustrate this through comparing two versions of the familiar yin-yang symbol.

In this context, the yin-yang symbol on the left, without the dots, is intended to illustrate divided expressions of communion and agency in which one is being *either* communal *or* agentic. By contrast, the right yin-yang is presented in its more familiar form, including the dots that indicate yin within yang and vice versa. This latter version reflects we-care in which one approaches communion and agency as interconnected. We can build on this metaphor by assigning the black to communion and white to agency—a meaning not too far afield from traditional interpretations of the yin-yang symbol in which black (yin) symbolizes the feminine principle, and white (yang) represents the masculine principle. In fact, femininity and masculinity are another set of terms sometimes used to distinguish the qualities of communion and agency, respectively, within scientific research.[6]

Through this lens, yin care (communal, feminine) tends to be more receptive, relational, and accommodating, whereas yang care (agentic, masculine) is more goal-driven and strategic. For example, a mental health counselor embodying the communal approach might prioritize creating a warm and empathetic atmosphere, encouraging clients to share emotions and experiences at their own pace. By contrast, a counselor who prioritizes the agentic approach might be more focused on setting clear goals for therapy, with structured steps and measurable outcomes to track progress.

Returning to the version on the left, without the dots, care is either yin (communal) or yang (agentic). Even though the two appear to be in some kind of relationship, they are not awake to one another. When the dots are included, however, each quality naturally contains a seed of the other. For example, consider how a counselor who focuses on the yang aspect of goal setting in the early stages of therapy inherently nurtures the yin aspect by fostering a sense of shared purpose, which can deepen the therapeutic alliance. As clients feel more understood and their goals acknowledged, they often grow more open and engaged, revealing a yin essence of care within the structure of yang.

Short-Term versus Long-Term

As noted above, while both moral exemplars and dictators evince highly agentic behavior in the short-term, the longer-term arc of influential moral figures bends toward communion—toward goals that can improve the welfare of vast numbers of people over the long run. This insight is instructive even on a day-to-day basis because it encourages us to look past the short-term deeds of others when assessing their character. This is easier said than done. Research has consistently shown that we have built-in biases, sculpted by evolution, that cause us to favor others' communal expressions of care over their agentic ones. The scientific explanation for this inherent bias is complex, involving the relative advantages of communion and agency for others and one's individual self.[7] What's essential is knowing the bias exists, as it can sometimes lead to misinterpreting agentic expressions of care as selfish or not genuinely care-based.[8]

These scientific perspectives notwithstanding, the notion that agentic acts of care garner more skepticism is not too surprising when we reflect on what it's like to be on the receiving end of them. Communal forms of care, such as empathetic listening or deep affection, often simply feel better when compared to receiving agentic care such as constructive feedback or strategic support. This is partly because agentic care tends to be instrumental—a means to an end. For example, consider someone who, in aiming to aid their friend through a period of unemployment, insists they set a budget to manage their finances. This form of agentic care focuses on practical advice aimed at improving the other's long-term financial stability, but it does not provide immediate emotional comfort or validation. Even if the recipient knows setting a budget is aligned with their long-term well-being, they still have to endure the challenge or discomfort of it all.

Fortunately, the short-term relief offered by communal care can be combined with the strategic compassion of agency. By also offering emotional support, active listening, and validation of their friend's feelings, the giver of advice can soften the austerity of their agentic guidance. For instance, before ever discussing the budget, they might spend time talking about their friend's feelings about unemployment, offering reassurance and understanding. In such a dynamic, both forms of care—communal and agentic—enhance each other, fostering both a deeper connection and a more resilient support system. Ultimately, this holistic approach is a more skillful form of we-care, not only helping navigate the practical challenges but also ensuring that the emotional and relational health of both individuals is nurtured.

Vulnerability versus Strength

It's nearly dawn, and the tick of a clock on the wall of the hospital waiting room echoes loudly in your ears. Your insides feel like a cocktail of hunger, worry, and fatigue—the product of a sleepless night that began shortly after dinner when your partner doubled over in pain, a vivid image you can't seem to shake. Now, with the doctor's update that surgery is imminent, you are bracing for an even longer wait. Despite your weary state, you are determined to stay tethered to this spot, a selfless beacon of strength for your partner.

As the sun rises outside, however, an opportunity for self-care you've been ignoring beckons you again. One of your best friends lives just blocks from the hospital. They'll soon be waking up to start their day, and they have a spare bedroom that could offer a chance to recharge. You know a brief respite could sharpen your support for what lies ahead, once your partner is out of surgery. Moreover, your friend would want to be updated about all that happened and would be eager to help however they could.

Can you soften enough to allow yourself this self-care and receiving of care? Or does your steadfast resolve to remain strong in the waiting room overpower your ability to unstiffen and get some much-needed rest?

Navigating care for ourselves and our loved ones is a dance of strength and vulnerability. Leading a caring life requires listening in many directions at once—to the heart's wishes, the body's needs, the mind's plans—and making adjustments as we go. When we err too far in the direction of strength or agency, we risk losing touch with our own vulnerability and our sensitivity to the needs of others. We might even fail to notice and allow opportunities for self-care that are clearly aligned with nurturing our strength. Conversely, when we lose touch with strength, we may not believe in our capacities to do what is needed, sparking a self-fulfilling prophecy of compromised care.

These three pairings—yin and yang, short-term and long-term, vulnerability and strength—represent just a few facets of communion and agency as researchers understand them. I've highlighted them here because I consider them essential to how communion and agency show up in relation to we-care. Having reflected on each individually, let's now zoom back out to consider them in combination. This broader view can help us to delineate the varied approaches we might take to transforming the we-care mindset as an inner experience into skillful expressions and responses, bridging inner and outer to encompass one's *approach emphasis* to we-care.

Approach Emphasis

		Communion	Agency
We-Care Emphasis	Self-Care	*e.g., resting, tending to one's needs, receiving care*	*e.g., exercise, boundary setting, goal pursuit*
	Other-Care	*e.g., nurturing, deep listening, accommodating*	*e.g., activism, acts of service, strategic support*

The examples presented in this table represent just a few of many possible forms of agentic versus communal we-care, but together they show how both self-care and other-care can be expressed through either approach emphasis. This reveals something crucial to countering one way we-care can be misunderstood in daily life. Due to the built-in biases I mentioned earlier, there's a pervasive tendency for people to think of care as what falls neatly within communion. This greatly limits the scope of possible caring in ways that devalue agentic expressions of care, leading both to less skillful care and more confused forms such as conflict avoidance, enabling, weak boundaries, and people-pleasing. Similarly, on the side of self-care, undervaluing agentic actions can result in less effective care. For example, constantly prioritizing rest over exercise can be detrimental when an adaptive balance, attuned to your evolving needs, is more beneficial for your overall health and sense of vitality.

From a we-care perspective, overcoming the bias against agentic care is critically important for fulfilling our heart's dual wish to care for ourselves and others. After all, embodying and enacting we-care frequently demands consideration of the wider impact of our care over the long-term. This is especially true when we consider the complex realities of trying to practice we-care in social and societal contexts characterized by division, such as what Parks faced that fateful day in 1955. However, it's also clearly evident in everyday care dilemmas, which often require integrating agency and communion as parts of broader *we-care strategies* that can help you to translate undivided inner states into undivided expressions of care.

Four Key We-Care Strategies

Kenji feels caught between a rock and a hard place. He's overwhelmed with a major project at work, with his boss breathing down his neck about a looming deadline that will require a week of late nights at the office. If that weren't bad enough, his best friend, Waylen, is going through a very challenging time personally and emotionally and has reached out for support. He's asked to meet Kenji for dinner or a drink before the week is over. Kenji knows his self-care routines are downright necessary for his mental health when he's this busy. In the past, anytime his self-care suffers, his anxiety spikes, undermining his focus for work. Checking in with himself, Kenji feels that he simply doesn't have the bandwidth to help Waylen without compromising the quality of his work and self-care.

On second thought, Kenji is an adept student of we-care. He spots the either/or mindset in some of his thinking, which he knows is making it seem like he has to choose between binary options: self-care *or* Waylen. Career *or* friendship. This prompts him to slow down and allow care for himself and Waylen to be present in his mind and heart simultaneously. He reflects, *Are there any hidden choices I haven't thought of yet? Is there possibly an ideal both/and solution?* Reflecting in this way, the various qualities of Kenji's we-care mindset come together to reveal four distinct we-care strategies: *sequencing, coupling, blending,* and *unifying.* Let's review each in turn.

Sequencing

Sensing into his own vulnerability, Kenji knows there's bound to be a time when he's as desperate for Waylen's support as Waylen is now. He can clearly see how prioritizing care for Waylen now, no matter how hard, will help him in the future. What's more, after the upcoming deadline at work, his schedule will allow him plenty of time to catch up on his self-care.

The we-care strategy of *sequencing* involves emphasizing one orientation of care at a time, with an expectation that you will emphasize the other in the future in an equal or complementary way.

It's embedded in practices like Forward Self-Care, as presented in chapter 2, in which your self-care gets prioritized with future plans in mind. The both/and thinking underlying sequencing effectively reintegrates the either/or mindset through a temporary emphasis on one orientation of care, without needing to fully divide care internally. If Kenji instead decided to emphasize self-care first, he could prioritize his self-care more strongly during the week, while communicating to Waylen that he will support him more fully after the deadline.

Coupling

Some of the work Kenji needs to accomplish before the deadline naturally lends itself to breaks and pauses, whether it's waiting on a colleague's email response or allowing a computer program to complete its processing. Therefore, as long as Waylen doesn't mind a few interruptions, Kenji can hang out with his laptop nearby and open, alternating easefully between meaningful conversation and short bursts of work tasks to keep the project moving forward.

Coupling can look many different ways, but it always involves some kind of back-and-forth between self-care and other-care. It frequently emerges spontaneously in a conversation, as each person takes their turn to speak and share. However, as in Kenji's situation, coupling sometimes requires more deliberate planning and structure to ensure there's sufficient attention to both sets of needs.

Blending

Kenji realizes he could also more seamlessly blend his meeting with Waylen, combining it with one of his self-care activities. For instance, Waylen could use Kenji's guest pass at the gym, joining him for his workout. This way, they could talk without Kenji having to sacrifice one of the activities that nurtures his mental health— and who knows, a little exercise could be good for Waylen's well-being too.

This sort of *blending* strategy allows for fulfilling self-care and other-care through creative combination. For instance, if you're dreading an upcoming work meeting, you could pick up your favorite beverage to sip on beforehand. Or if you feel resistance to visiting your in-laws, you could bring along that novel you've been dying to read, letting it fill any downtime.

Unifying

As Kenji contemplates further, he has an aha moment. He realizes he's being too rigid about his self-care routine. Rather than helping to keep his anxiety at bay, it seems to have become a contributing factor in this instance. Viewed in this light, he recognizes that giving up some of his self-care time to instead support Waylen could actually be a form of radical self-care. After all, it will help him get his mind off of himself and his work for a little while—the same intention that underlies his self-care during such stressful periods.

Compared with sequencing, coupling, and blending, the we-care strategy of *unifying* takes the integration of self-care and other-care to a whole new level, effectively erasing distinctions between them. It commonly arrives as an insight, leading to a sudden shift in perspective that contains or supports an unforeseen solution. And while Kenji's form of unifying turns what looks like other-care into self-care, unifying can also be experienced the other way around, or in moments where distinguishing self-care from other-care no longer matters at all.

Critically, each of these four strategies would allow Kenji to navigate his dilemma in a way that honors both his need for self-care and his care and commitment to his friend. And while we may favor one strategy or another, in practice, all are needed for the path of we-care. We can conceptualize these strategies as outgrowths of the we-care strengths, or as drawing on the emergent qualities of Kenji's broader we-care mindset, such as creativity and insight. However, the layer of transforming we-care from an inner experience into outer expressions involves something more: to skillfully implement any of these strategies, Kenji would need to integrate communal and agentic approaches.

To help you explore these we-care strategies as they apply more broadly in day-to-day life, the figure below presents a brief description and simple example for each. I've also highlighted how there's an overall increase in the functional integration of self-care and other-care as you move from left to right, such that unifying represents the most integrated form of we-care.

Functional integration ⟶

Strategy	Sequencing	Coupling	Blending	Unifying
Description	One orientation of care (e.g., self-care) now will support the other orientation in the future	Move back and forth between self-care and care for others	Creative or dynamic combination of self-care and other-care	Self-care and care for others become one
Example	Taking a break for self-care today will support higher quality care for others throughout the week	In conversation, each person takes turns speaking and serving as a mindful listener	Combining a meeting with one's mentee with a hike	Graciously receiving a gift that someone eagerly wants to give

Connected and Protected

Returning to Marietta's dilemma from the start of this chapter, we can now see how working toward causes much bigger than ourselves can create multiple layers of tension between our sense of communion and agency. This includes being confronted by others' either/or mindsets about these qualities—such as the dismissive response of Marietta's friends toward her care for her family. Navigating such situations requires drawing on all the different facets of communion and agency—yin and yang, short-term and long-term, vulnerability and strength—to embody and express we-care. Doing so can help us identify pathways forward that keep us feeling connected and protected, rather than feeling forced to divide ourselves one way or the other.

To help her navigate the complex web of her dilemma, Marietta sets some time aside for journaling about it. This helps her clarify what would most honor her sense of we-care, namely feeling harmony or even synergy between standing up for herself and feeling connected to her family, friends, and broader community. She realizes that spending time with her family presents a chance to have a deeper conversation about her work and values, including how it will sometimes result in political activism they disagree with. If things get heated, she plans to point out that she chose to be with them today, despite the pressure of her friends to attend the rally at the capitol. When breaking the news to her friends, she'll start by joking that sure, she'll confront her parents—just as soon as her friends also agree to challenge their partners' often-questionable political views. She'll also be ready with a list of other ways she's supported the rally's cause—ways her friends haven't—just in case they decide to give her more grief. Finally, given the extra push this plan will take her over the next few days, she signs up for her favorite yoga class on Sunday to help her unwind and still be ready for the next workweek.

Marietta's approach is complex, but so is the dilemma she faces. Through skillfully weaving communion and agency and integrating self-care and other-care with feeling and action, she is not shying away from this complexity. This comprehensive strategy offers her a more realistic shot at actually achieving her varied goals. Importantly, the aim here is not perfection. Marietta knows she will likely have to revise her approach, practice acceptance, and seek additional support from others along the way. However, by practicing this sort of full-spectrum we-care—transforming stark contrasts into countless vibrant forms of care—she avoids the deeper layer of stress that often characterizes such situations. Marietta is not second-guessing her multifaceted aims and approach. In fact, she feels somewhat exhilarated by the fullness of it all. The layered complexity of social situations in daily life underscores why effectively engaging in we-care requires a dynamic integration of yin and yang, short-term and long-term thinking, vulnerability and strength—especially when your heart's care extends to societal levels.

We-Care Practice 7
HANDS OF CARE

We previously relied on breathing as an embodied metaphor for experiencing the essential and interconnected roles of self-care and other-care in our lives, as well as for scaffolding the flow of care during Undivided Heart Breathing. In a similar way, this next we-care practice involves grounding our understanding of communion and agency in an embodied metaphor, this time using our hands.[9] Most people have a dominant and a nondominant hand, each playing subtly different roles in their lives, offering a natural metaphor for communion and agency, respectively. Like the role of these qualities in we-care, the hands also commonly help us to transform our caring intentions into skillful expressions of care.

PRACTICE INSTRUCTIONS

1. *Hold your nondominant hand in your dominant hand.* While sitting or standing, rest the back of nondominant hand within the cupped palm and fingers of

your dominant hand, holding them in place in front of your belly. As you position your hands and hold them in front of you, simply notice what it is like to do so. Then, at your own pace, reflect more intentionally on your nondominant hand as a metaphor for the role of communion in we-care, while considering your dominant hand as representing agency. For example, how does it feel to fully rest your nondominant hand in your dominant hand? Could this reflect anything about your how you experience the roles of yin (communion) and yang (agency) in your we-care?

2. *In reverse.* Switch out the roles of your hands, next holding your dominant hand within the open palm and fingers of your nondominant hand, exploring what it's like as a metaphor for communion to support agency. Does the felt sense of holding your hands in this way reveal anything about how your vulnerable (communion) side backs your strength (agency) in daily life?

3. *Back-and-forth.* Switch the roles of each hand back and forth, exploring the varied combinations of sensing and reflecting for as long as you'd like. You might, for example, reflect on which hand position feels more natural and comfortable, sparking similar reflections for your predominant approach to we-care. Additionally, during this phase of the practice, you can try reversing the metaphor, imagining that your nondominant hand now represents agency and your dominant hand, communion. Does this change reflect anything about their roles in your we-care?

4. *Both/and.* Finally, bring your hands together in a mutually supportive position. This can be done in a few ways, such as by interlocking your fingers or by pressing your palms together as if in prayer. What might this mutual support of your hands signal about the interconnectedness of communion and agency in your we-care?

PART III

THE PATH OF WE-CARE

I like to think of ideas as potential energy. They're really wonderful, but nothing will happen until we risk putting them into action.

—Mae Jemison

CHAPTER 7

Circles of Care

Expanding We

> Let your heart be as big as
> your whole experience.
> —JACK KORNFIELD,
>   "Heart As Big As the Sky"[1]

After presenting at the United Nations conference in Bangkok back in 2010—following the events I recounted in chapter 1—I was fortunate to have a whole week before my return flight, trekking around Thailand without an agenda. As my trip drew to a close, I boarded a local flight to Phuket for one last adventure. Phuket is the largest island in Thailand, home to stunning beaches, crystal blue waters, and a giant Big Buddha on the peak of Nakkerd Hill—a wakeful presence that can be seen for miles. Touching down at the airport, I found my way onto a crowded bus that eventually dropped me where I could rent a small motorbike—an odd fit for my hefty traveler's backpack, but it offered me an affordable way to travel the lengthy distance to my budget hotel near the southern tip of the island.

For three days, I zipped around the island solo on my motorbike. On the last day, mere hours before my flight back to Bangkok and then home, all I had left to do was return the motorbike—the turning point in this story where everything started going wrong. Try as I might, I couldn't find the address for where I had first rented it. My copy of the rental contract had seemingly vanished from my backpack, and trying to locate it via the internet left me even more puzzled. Without another plan, and emboldened by the Big Buddha's presence in the distance, I got on my motorbike, hefty pack and all, and started the perilous drive back across the large island, searching for the rental shop via a mental pushpin in my memory alone.

You guessed it: I did not find the pushpin by memory. But what happened next taught me an enduring lesson about the nature of we-care and the critical importance of receiving care from others, even strangers. After over an hour traversing the busy streets, I felt desperate. Not only was I already at risk of missing my plane back to Bangkok and beyond, I could be on the line for thousands of dollars, maybe even accused of trying to steal the motorbike. The only thing in my favor were some vague memories of a bus stop far from the airport, an old man at the top of a hill, and a street lined with motorbikes like mine.

Frantic, confused, and dripping with sweat, I parked my motorbike in front of a shop and stumbled in, much to the shock of the three women and teenage girl inside, who were all busy making flower arrangements.

"*Sawasdee khap*," I croaked the Thai greeting. "I, uh, could use some help."

Their initially blank stares confirmed my English wouldn't help me here. But thanks to my frazzled look and the anxious pitch of my voice, they got what I meant. They dropped what they were doing and started speaking rapidly with each other, peering curiously back at me from time to time. Most memorably, I recall feeling shocked when they slammed the door shut on a teenage boy who had tried to enter the shop. Was helping me leading them to selflessly turn down customers? I hoped not.

"Er, sorry," I said after a frenzied fifteen seconds. "Lemme see if my friend's available." I fetched the burner phone from my backpack—a gift from a Thai friend I'd met at the conference, who insisted I take the phone when I told them about my solo travel plans. I hit dial on their number, the only one stored in it.

"Sawasdee kha," my friend's familiar voice answered, filling me with relief.

"Hey, uh—sawasdee khap," I replied. "You were right about giving me this phone." I explained my situation as carefully as I could before putting the phone on speaker and passing it to one of the women in the shop. Just then, the door behind me swung open again, and the same Thai teenage boy tried to force his way in. Once again, he was pushed back outside by one of the women. This time, however, I noticed him exchange a brief smile with the girl, hinting at the social dynamic that could explain his unwelcome status in the shop.

Unfortunately, even after having my dilemma translated by my friend, I learned that no one knew of any motorbike rental place nearby that matched my description. Now I felt hopeless. I offered thanks many times in Thai and pivoted to exit the shop, finding myself face-to-face with the teenage boy who was again pushing open the shop door. I stepped aside as he dashed in, seemingly unfazed by the disapproving looks of the three older women.

A heated conversation unfolded in Thai until, to my surprise, stern faces turned into laughter. The teenage boy looked to me and gestured excitedly, inviting me to follow him and the girl, who was now standing by him, blushing as she beamed. My friend, still on speaker phone, explained: The boy knew the exact motorbike rental place I'd been searching for and had offered to show me the way. More than that, everyone was laughing because he'd been begging for days to get permission from the girl's mother to take her daughter on a date. Now that he could help me, she had softened and said yes to the date, effective immediately.

Onto my motorbike I went for one last ride, barely keeping up with the blazing speed of a teenage boy showing off to his crush, whose arms were wrapped tightly around him. Eventually, we crested the hill, and I parked my bike where it belonged and promptly pulled out my wallet.

"For your date," I said, holding out a handful of Thai baht. The pair, giddy with happiness, laughed and said something in Thai, pushing my hand away. I smiled and pocketed the cash, knowing what they'd said without needing a translator: Their assistance to me had helped them too. Through accepting their kindness, giving and receiving could blend more seamlessly into each other, completing a circle of care.

The Wisdom in the Roots of Loneliness

The past year had isolated Peyton in ways he never imagined possible. A severe bout of illness had sapped his energy, making it increasingly difficult to maintain old friendships, let alone forge new ones. As months went by, the once-steady stream of supportive messages from friends and family dwindled to a trickle, and some even accused him of abandoning them due to his delayed replies and calls. While Peyton has now recovered from the illness, he finds it hard to shake the profound sense of social unworthiness that had developed, leading him to doubt whether, even now that he's better, he has much to offer his friends. Recently, he received an unexpected invitation to a friend's birthday party—a rare glimmer of hope and excitement. Yet, beneath his initial relief, Peyton wrestles with uncertainty. Can he muster the courage to push against his self-doubts and attend? And if he does, will the friends who had felt abandoned by him be open to reconnecting?

Most people recognize the importance of meaningful relationships to a "good life," an understanding that's consistent with findings from one of the longest longitudinal studies ever conducted in psychology.[2] Despite this recognition, or perhaps partly because of it, a significant number also report experiencing detrimental levels of loneliness—a poignant sense of lack, or a discrepancy between the relationships they have and those they yearn for.[3] The detrimental impacts of loneliness on health are profound and far-reaching, with mortality effects exceeding that of obesity, physical inactivity, or smoking fifteen cigarettes a day.[4] These negative health consequences may be explained by the upstream influences loneliness has on stress hormones, sleep, and infection susceptibility, and they have spurred descriptions of loneliness as an epidemic and global health threat.

But although external barriers to social connection can contribute to feeling lonely, loneliness transcends the physical state of being alone and is defined instead by a subjective feeling of disconnection. There are marked changes in not only the social behavior but also the brains of lonely individuals, with research uncovering structural and functional changes in regions linked to social rejection, self-criticism, fear detection, and dampened social reward.[5] Thus, loneliness represents a significant shift in one's subjective experience and orientation toward social situations, and it also manifests physically in the brain as symptoms similar to those that appear when there is a threat of some kind. This threat-related orientation to one's social life can create a kind of self-fulfilling prophecy that intensifies loneliness over time.

Dr. John Cacioppo was a pioneering researcher on loneliness whose work continues to offer valuable insights into the workings of the lonely mind and brain, as well as its potential for transformation. For me, his scientific legacy and impact is inspiring because of how he brought more attention to the severity of loneliness as an epidemic and worked to identify more effective solutions.[6] These efforts included critically examining a variety of seemingly common-sense approaches to decreasing loneliness that ultimately proved ineffective. However, each was instructive based on its unique point of failure. Integrating these findings, we discover three important hidden lessons—pieces of a map that, when combined with key learnings about we-care, reveal pathways out of this destructive mental state and societal dilemma.

Lesson 1: From Connection, Not For Connection

The first lesson arose from researchers testing whether reversing the deleterious effects of loneliness could occur through increasing the amount of social interaction lonely people had. Unfortunately, this simple approach did not work because, as noted above, loneliness is more about the quality and subjective appraisal of one's social life than one's quantity of friends or frequency of social interaction. This mirrors many other areas of our lives in which we find that solutions that focus solely on changing the externals have limited success. This isn't to say that the structure and form of our social networks make no difference to loneliness. For instance, some populations, such as younger people, Hispanics, and those in rural locations, report experiencing higher rates of loneliness than others.[7] On a personal level, however, it's not hard to see that too much emphasis on how big your social circle is or who's in it can trade off against quality time and authentic connections.

As a vital piece of our tripartite map out from loneliness, this first lesson invites us to care *from* connection rather than *for* connection. When we care from connection, we source from an inner reservoir of affiliative emotion, warmth, and good will. When we extend kindness, it is genuine, aligned with care-based feelings and thoughts that are already present within our hearts and minds. This feels very different from caring for connection, which tends to be more about seeking approval and validation from others, an orientation that can generate all manner of confused forms of care. One may, for example, do a good deed for someone primarily to win them over and avoid being rejected by them. This disingenuous approach to kindness reflects a misalignment between one's inner experience and one's outer behavior, and accordingly, research has found it to be linked to higher anxiety and depression.[8]

I recognize that, upon first encountering this lesson, the idea of caring from an inner source of connection may seem out of touch with the realities of feeling intense loneliness. And indeed, receiving professional support and guidance can be a critical step in reducing loneliness for many reasons, especially when it helps target the maladaptive appraisals that underpin it.[9] Beyond this, however, there are many practical steps one can take to begin caring from connection even in the midst of loneliness. Indeed, many of the lessons and practices we have focused on previously—from healthy self-care to training in compassion and cultivating the we-care mindset—emphasize fostering we-care from within, which can help give rise to more opportunities to care *from* connection. This further underscores why nurturing we-care from within is essential to fully experiencing its benefits.

Lesson 2: Choose Connection, Even When It's Hard

Researchers also explored whether improving the social skills of lonely individuals could help, which leads to our second key lesson. Overall, there's been mixed evidence regarding whether or not social skills training can reduce loneliness, perhaps depending on other factors in one's life. We know for certain though that poor social skills are often an outgrowth of being in a lonely state, rather than the primary driving factor that leads to loneliness. Knowing this is powerful because, if you are experiencing loneliness, you may notice your social skills feel a bit rough around the edges. Rather than believing this is a permanent state, it's important to recognize that it is, in fact, reversible.

We are social creatures. It's our default state, with our brains expecting the presence of others and performing many essential functions better when surrounded by social support. Loneliness, therefore, is an exceptional state from an evolutionary and neurobiological standpoint. When we're hit with a spike in loneliness, our social brains shift into an individually self-focused, threat-related mode. This shift causes disadvantageous changes in social perception and behavior that can, over time, reinforce one's lonely state. As described by Dr. Cacioppo, "When you experience loneliness you focus more and more on yourself, your brain engages in self-preservation. You are not necessarily aware of that happening. . . . You often stop taking empathetic or compassionate positions and therefore you lose social skills."[10]

What's most important here is recognizing how these shifts in sociality decrease one's willingness to enact other-focused care. It's yet another manifestation of the either/or mindset, this time trapping us in an extremely self-focused state. The practical implication is that we can find our way out of loneliness partly through initiating and choosing connection, even when it feels scary or uncomfortable to do so. In a world in which the either/or mindset is rampant, it is not easy to do this. And yet, it is only through being willing to initiate social connection despite feelings of loneliness and self-focus that we can begin to push against the either/or mindset in ourselves and others.

Speaking of the either/or mindset, let's revisit research relying on the prisoner's dilemma game for another angle on this lesson. In chapter 2, we discussed how the tit-for-tat strategy—defecting when others defect and cooperating when others cooperate— ended up winning Axelrod's famous tournament. Since then, however, researchers have discovered a way to subtly modify tit for tat to further augment its outperformance. The idea is to randomly reintroduce cooperation into the tit-for-tat approach, meaning that every so often in the midst of ongoing defections, one occasionally cooperates again.[11] This "generous tit-for-tat" strategy maintains the discernment needed to balance self-care with care for others, while nonetheless relying on one's agency to create openings that may initiate a mutually beneficial dynamic.

This updated tit-for-tat approach is instructive because, in the midst of daily life, we will similarly be confronted with the either/or mindset of others in ways that initially demand a more cautious, defensive mode. When this happens repeatedly, we can come to internalize other people's either/or mindsets until it's our personal default approach. Sadly, as Dr. Cacioppo described, this defensive mode often becomes a kind of self-fulfilling prophecy. Consider the common experience of sending someone a text message to initiate a hangout, only to be "ghosted" with no reply. At times, the lack of response reflects a valid message about the other's availability or interest, with research indicating it can even arise from a misplaced sense of care.[12] However, this behavior is also frequently circumstantial. It's only when we can muster the courage to choose connection and send a kind follow-up text that we can be more certain of what's happening on the other person's side.

Careful research has shown that even though people wish to hear from past friends and report benefiting from unexpected social contact from others, they are personally apprehensive about being the one to reinitiate contact—resulting in less connection all around.[13] Over time, through practicing we-care, we grow more discerning and less fearful of rejection because we know we can offer ourselves care when needed and that we have the tools to build enduring reciprocal relationships with many people over time.

Lesson 3: Prioritize and Cultivate Mutually Beneficial Connections

The final piece of our map is the one most clearly resonant with we-care, as it addresses why one-directional relationships aren't sufficient for decreasing loneliness. It emerged from researchers examining whether offering more social support to lonely individuals—such as through assigning them a mentor—could help.

It turns out that decreasing loneliness requires not only receiving care but also offering it to others. To feel deeply connected, we need to experience what it's like to share our strengths and gifts in impactful ways. This can manifest in simple interactions, such as the gratification that comes from knowing a story we shared has genuinely moved someone or piqued their interest.

We must equally be willing to be impacted by others. In the context of we-care, this means we can graciously receive acts of care that are offered to us. So far throughout this book, I've primarily emphasized the dynamic balancing of self-care and other-care in we-care, with less attention paid to the importance of receiving care from others. Yet many people report discomfort and anxiety when they're on the receiving end of care, something that research indicates can be a barrier of its own to experiencing fulfilling connection.[14] The reasons why receiving care is difficult for some are complex, and there are certainly times when others' offers of care merit a judicious or even cautious approach. However, when the care is genuine and likely to actually support us, denying it could greatly diminish connection. Often, the most caring response to another's offer of care is to kindly receive it.

There are a few more actionable insights we can derive from this lesson and its relationship to our broader focus on circles of care. Firstly, you may remember from earlier chapters that we-care rarely feels like a fifty-fifty split between self-care and other-care; therefore, it's critical not to oversimplify the view that connection requires giving and receiving. Wise discernment is key, but genuine we-care should not feel transactional. When applying this understanding to the topic of reducing loneliness, we can remind ourselves that the give-and-take aspects of connection need not occur in the same moment, nor do they need to unfold on the same timescale. For instance, someone may support their friend through many months of grief, subjectively experiencing we-care in the friendship without receiving much support in return. This is made clearer when we consider a second point, namely that a mutually beneficial connection can entail different types of benefits for each person. The friend offering care may derive meaning and purpose from doing so, experiencing deep connection in moments of shared laughter and tears and feeling honored to be trusted with supporting their friend's healing journey.

Reducing loneliness through give-and-take also sometimes involves accepting care that may not meet one's ideal standards. As research has shown, people's preferences for specific types of care can vary depending on the situation.[15] In some moments, one can simply appreciate general efforts and expressions of care from others, while in others they may hold rigid standards for what constitutes satisfactory care. While of course it's important to communicate and advocate for one's needs and preferences, it's also true that being too fixed about the care one finds acceptable risks creating emotional barriers that can impede the feeling of meaningful connection. Learning to place more value on the underlying efforts behind someone's care—even when it is not exactly what we had envisioned or hoped for—can enhance feelings of connectedness.

Expanding Connection beyond the Baseline

Picture this: You arrive at a party right on time, eagerly anticipating meeting your friends. Suddenly, you receive a text—they are running half an hour late. How might your mindset and emotions at that moment shape what happens next? If you were in high spirits, feeling energetic and connected, you may take this minor setback in stride. But if you were already having a day of feeling low and disconnected, the same news might hit you harder. Could this initial difference in your inner state lead you to react in divergent ways, resulting in very different approaches to how to spend the next half hour? If yes, how might these differences subsequently influence how you feel toward your friends when they arrive?

For most, it's likely easier to imagine that feeling good internally would translate into a more easeful and enjoyable evening—but what accounts for that outcome? To social psychologists and neuroscientists, positive emotions are not simply about reward. They are adaptive states meant to facilitate unique patterns of thinking and behavior that helped our ancestors navigate distinct kinds of challenges—different challenges from those supported by negative emotions. The *broaden-and-build theory* aims to elucidate these unique qualities of positive emotions, describing how they broaden our mindset in ways that promote building new resources and social connections.[16] Thus, if you were already in high spirits at the party, your broadened mindset might foster more openness to initiating a conversation with a stranger, who may later become a new friend and confidant for you. Likewise, when your friends finally arrive, your more resourced and connected state would allow you to shrug off any downsides from their delay and focus on having a good time together, strengthening your bonds throughout the night.

The three lessons reviewed above are pieces of a map not only leading out from loneliness but also guiding us toward a greater depth and breadth of connection, far beyond the baseline. Whether we're seeking deeper intimacy with a romantic partner or hoping to establish a friendship with someone new, it will be similarly helpful to source from a caring place within, to be willing to initiate and choose more connection and to embrace both giving and receiving care. What's different about reducing loneliness versus enhancing connection far beyond it is how well we can draw on all of the various tools in our care tool kit to generate numerous positive feedback loops.

All this said, the degree of connection we can experience with another will always be partly determined by them. Not all of our connections will have what it takes for deep intimacy or profound closeness, and that's okay. As we will soon explore in more detail,

research shows that it's beneficial to have interactions and relationships at various points along a continuum of connection. But
of course, we should prioritize those relationships where we can
experience natural circles of giving and receiving care, rather than
one-sided dynamics.

Circles Ordinary and Strange

Circles are symmetrical and uniform. We-care—not so much. Reciprocal flows of care rarely follow predictable paths. Instead, our
care twists and turns as it inspires and connects. When offered
freely, it might meander alongside someone else for a while before
looping back toward its starting point, benefiting you personally.
Once you start looking around you for circles of care, you are
likely to notice a rich variety of give-and-take "species," each with
its own unique shape and logic. So although the metaphor of a
circle can help to emphasize the mutually beneficial nature of we-
care, I want to also highlight a few other metaphors I've found
useful for noticing more nuanced shapes and patterns of mutual
care and its benefits in everyday life.

To begin with, the metaphor of a *care mirror* can be instructive
for times when our care for one person instantly reflects back
to us an area or need of care for others or ourselves. Consider
how extending your care to a friend who is sick can serve as a
poignant reminder to take extra care of yourself. Or how the tug
at your heart when hearing someone lost a family member in a
tragedy can remind you to express love to your own family members. This reflective nature of care may also happen in reverse,
before doubling back on itself. For instance, when you are caring
for yourself in the midst of pain or distress, try thinking of others
who may be enduring something similar. By increasing awareness of *common humanity*, this sort of contemplation can activate
not only other-focused care but also clarify and bolster care for
your personal well-being.

Another metaphor relates to the potential mutual benefits of sharing positive events and emotions, or what researchers call *capitalization*. Capitalizing on positive events occurs when there's an enhancement of positive feelings and connection for two or more people after one of them shares good news about their life.[17] Imagine, for instance, how it would feel for a close friend to respond enthusiastically when you shared the news of getting a promotion at work. Personally, I find the idea of a *care echo* useful for noticing and appreciating the unique qualities of capitalization in daily life. Scientists have shown that, under the right conditions, an echo can actually appear louder than the original sound. Likewise, when we share our joys with others who resonate with our positive feelings, there's potential for amplifying the well-being of us and them. Might the friend who responded enthusiastically to your promotion then feel more motivated to pursue positive changes in their own career?

It can be fun to imagine all the unique forms our care might take, but I'll share just two more metaphors here: A *care boomerang* prompts reflection on how the outflow of one's care can sometimes extend far beyond oneself before circling back. This metaphor seems especially helpful for reflecting on how care flows within our complex modern society, where the outpouring of care offered in one moment is rarely returned to us in kind right then and there. This is not to say that all our care will circle, mirror, echo, or even boomerang back to us. However, we are more likely to notice these moments when we are willing to look beyond simple, direct forms of reciprocity. Finally, my favorite metaphor is that of a *care spiral* because it captures how the back-and-forth nature of receiving and giving in a close relationship can, over time, widen and deepen the care experienced by both individuals. Contemplating this metaphor reminds me that the circles of care in my life are not merely repetitive or static, but rather they have a direction—upward and outward. Each loop therefore represents not just a return to giving or receiving but an elevation and expansion of care, which grows more profound and encompassing with each cycle.

Distinct Yet Overlapping Selves

In individualistic societies, there is a strong emphasis on being a whole self. Yet, there is also significant messaging around others making us whole—especially romantic partners. From a we-care standpoint, informed by the psychology and neuroscience of self-hood, wholeness is more nuanced; it is something we must heal into, move toward, and cultivate throughout all of our different relationships with others. This may sound abstract, so let's compare and contrast different illustrations of how people might depict themselves in a social context, drawing on and adapting a few models my colleagues and I developed for understanding compassion.[18] We'll start with a model that clearly distinguishes the individual self and other as whole circles unto themselves and illustrates the flow of self-care and other-care as one-directional arrows.

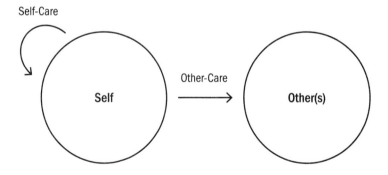

Self-Care

Self

Other-Care

Other(s)

This way of depicting care may be how care is typically viewed in individualistic societies. I think it's also a pretty good visual representation of care as experienced by someone in the either/or mindset. There's a clear distinction between self and other, and the pathway of care always flows clearly in just one direction.

Compare this with the next model in which self and other are overlapping circles with circular arrows at their intersection.

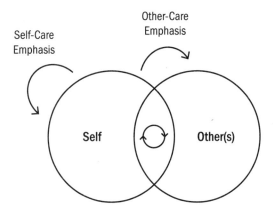

Notice how this second model effectively integrates the first, while adding some unique features that better align with the interconnected view of we-care. The model maintains the potential wholeness of each individual while acknowledging the potential for overlap between people. Based on this overlap, it's easier to see how self-care and other-care are interconnected emphases because now self-care is partly caring for the other and vice versa. Finally, in the overlapping portion, I've added a set of arrows forming a circle— illustrating the potential for emphasizing integrated experiences of care. Despite the various improvements of this second model, if we truly want to represent the expansive potential of we-care for enhancing our feelings of connection, it is not yet complete.

An Expanding We

Imagine someone dared you to strike up a conversation with a random stranger this week, and more specifically a stranger who is wearing a watch. Does this challenge excite you, terrify you, or evoke feelings somewhere in between? How might you go about sparking conversation with a total stranger? And how do you imagine your mission would turn out in the end? Do you expect this stranger to feel bothered? Might they simply ignore you? Even if you got to talking, would you and this person have anything in common?

If you're introverted like me, I realize this dare, even just within your imagination, might feel overwhelming. But if you can bear with this exercise for just a moment longer, I'd like for you to imagine one last thing: Switching roles in your mind's eye, picture yourself as the stranger wearing a watch, who happens to be approached in a free moment by a random passerby. Maybe they smile and say, "Hi there, I really like your watch. Do you mind telling me where you got it?" Hearing this, would you welcome the opening into a social interaction or feel cautious and suspicious? Can you picture the interaction potentially unfolding well, leaving you in a better state than how it all started?

In a study on speaking with strangers, participants were dared in similar ways to strike up conversations not once, but daily for a week.[19] Based on prior work, the researchers anticipated the participants would be far from enthused about initiating conversations with strangers. They therefore cleverly turned the endeavor into a scavenger hunt, incentivizing participants through a points system to approach the strangers, with each interaction they completed increasing their chances of winning a prize. They compared this experimental group with a control condition that was tasked only with mindfully observing a stranger each day.

The results were striking: Compared to the control group, those tasked with speaking to strangers developed a more positive attitude toward doing so, became less fearful of rejection, and grew more confident in their conversational skills. Together with other studies on the topic, it revealed how speaking with strangers is a skill that we can improve on, not unlike picking up a new hobby. These findings offer further support and another angle on the three lessons for decreasing loneliness discussed earlier; they are also uniquely important because they highlight how minimal social interactions, not just close relationships, are an important driver of personal and social well-being.[20] In other words, our innate sociality means we likely require not only deep intimacy but also a diverse range of social interactions, including minimal ones.

Zooming out, studies like this are just one of many examples within contemporary psychology and neuroscience revealing the significant gap between people's expectations of initiating social connection, and what it is actually like.[21] This finding challenges a widespread misperception of how people tend to view others, leading them to artificially shrink their circles of care and thereby miss out on opportunities for connection in everyday life. Recognizing this, the practice of we-care invites us to interface with the world from a bigger view of our interconnectedness, one in which care ripples from our hearts to close others, acquaintances, strangers, and beyond. To illustrate this, we can build upon our earlier model, adding more circles to depict the overlap between oneself and others at various psychological distances.

Ideally, the *we* in our we-care need not be tightly bound to a select set of family and friends, or neighbors and country. It can instead be something flexible and wise. Something that expands to encompass other people, even strangers and those we find difficult, when doing so can foster our own and others' well-being. Of course, this needs to be carried out with mindful discernment, awake to both short-term and long-term consequences. Crucially, however, the science on speaking with strangers indicates how much we tend to underestimate the potential benefits of engaging our social lives in this way. When we can extend our we-care practice toward others beyond our inner circle, our sense of connection vastly expands, revealing yet more opportunities for experiencing circles of care and transforming us from passive participants in our social lives into active creators of a growing network of mutually beneficial relationships.

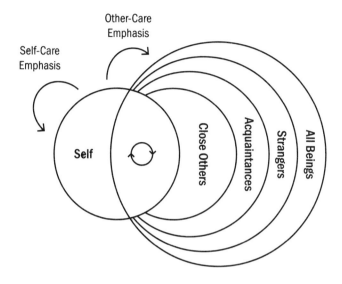

In that spirit, it's worth mentioning how readily you can begin to apply this aspect of we-care for yourself, perhaps even right here and now. If you happen to be reading this in a public setting, like a library or café—or the next time you visit a public place—I dare you to strike up a conversation with a stranger who's wearing a watch. You can even blame it on me, if you'd like, saying something like, "Hi there, sorry to interrupt. I hope you don't mind me asking, but I'm currently reading a book that dared me to chat with someone new. Your watch caught my eye. Do you mind sharing a bit about how you chose that particular watch?" Before you slam the book shut on me, remember: if the science is right, both you and they will likely enjoy completing this dare more than you think.

We-Care Practice 8
CIRCULAR CARE

One key takeaway from our exploration of the science of loneliness and connection is the crucial importance of offering care to others and being able to receive care from others. Receiving care may sound like a passive and self-caring process—hardly something that needs to be cultivated through intentional practice. But skillfully receiving care from others can be as nuanced as offering it, requiring a dynamic balancing of all the elements that I consider essential for healthy we-care—self-care and other-care, feeling and action, communion and agency.

Viewed through the either/or mindset, receiving care may feel selfishly indulgent and intimidatingly vulnerable. Conversely, when the care offered to us is not actually supporting our well-being, it can be hard not to forsake our needs and preferences. Through the more balanced approach of we-care, we can see how it is natural to hold both ourselves and others in mind as we receive. We can accept and appreciate the care being offered, while also asking for things that might improve it. And although the emphasis of receiving care is most often on self-care, we-care helps us stay connected to our care for others. We can relax in the knowledge that deeply receiving others' care can benefit not only us but also the person offering it and many others too. The next practice of Circular Care is therefore designed to offer you a chance to train in receiving care as a form of we-care.

PRACTICE INSTRUCTIONS

1. *Identify an opportunity for receiving care.* You can engage in this practice spontaneously by waiting for an offer of care, such as a loved one offering to cook

you dinner after a long work day. Alternatively, you can plan for it, choosing an ideal form of receiving care for you, such as a session with your therapist or a massage.

2. *Set a we-care intention.* At the outset of receiving care, set an intention for it to nourish you in ways that can eventually benefit others too. This intention need not be about directly benefiting the person who's offering you care; however, it may support your sense of we-care to express your gratitude to them in a way that's not transactional.

3. *Receive care as we-care.* As you receive this care from someone, try to stay in touch with your own care for yourself and others. This might include kindly requesting changes that could further enhance its benefits for you. As always, it's okay to ask for what you need while still accepting that the care you receive may not be exactly as you'd wished. Ideally, this sense of we-care allows you to receive even more deeply, recognizing it as another expression of your undivided heart.

4. *Revisit your we-care intention.* As the period of simply receiving care comes to a close, revisit your intention for it to benefit both you and others. Take a moment to reflect: Can deeply receiving care like this help you feel more resourced to offer care to others, whether through direct reciprocity or paying it forward? If so, allow this contemplation to expand your awareness of the essential interconnectedness of receiving and giving—the circular nature of your care.

CHAPTER 8

Care-Based Boundaries

Energy Vampires, Dictators, and Psychopaths—Oh My!

> When you say "yes" to others, make sure
> you are not saying "no" to yourself.
> —PAULO COELHO[1]

Discovering that Elizabeth Gilbert had reshared my social media post about energy vampires was a wake-up call. Best known as the author of *Eat, Pray, Love*, Gilbert had reposted one of my brief writings from my Instagram account, @mindfulboundaries—an online community I founded in 2019 to share creative ideas and reflections at the intersections of mindfulness, we-care, and healthy boundaries. It wasn't just that her one million followers might now encounter and read something I wrote. It was how much she and they appeared to resonate with its central message, with the post eventually receiving 30,000 likes, 650 comments, and countless reshares. It read, "Each time you set a good boundary, an energy vampire loses a fang."

As I watched the number of likes, comments, and reshares climb that day, I took in the potential for ideas related to we-care to have a widespread impact on society—a topic we'll explore in the next and final chapter. But beyond this broader lesson, the high engagement with the post confirmed a key insight: many people relate to the need for healthy boundaries that can protect them from others who have significant care blind spots. Another, subtler implication—as I intended the post—is that setting boundaries might also catalyze change in others by illuminating their blind spots for them, thus disrupting their harmful relational patterns.

As we'll explore, this potential for the dual impact of boundaries is not solely about so-called *energy vampires*—a popular yet oversimplified concept to describe people who frequently leave us feeling drained of energy. In everyday social life, terms such as *setting boundaries* and *healthy boundaries* highlight behaviors that are needed across all of our interactions and relationships but especially in moments of conflict and stress, when our we-care gets put to the test. Framed in this way, you might think of boundaries as an advanced we-care topic and practice. However, we've actually been exploring what it takes to cultivate them throughout the entirety of this book. All the key lessons and practices of we-care nurture the soil from which healthy boundaries can naturally emerge.

Now, by focusing on boundaries more directly throughout this chapter, you will learn about what boundaries are and how to embrace them as opportunities for deepening and expanding your practice of we-care. We'll focus specifically on how to set boundaries from a place of care, drawing on many of the same tools and perspectives reviewed in earlier chapters. Approached in this way, healthy boundaries entail acknowledging and addressing the care blind spots of others, while not losing sight of possible blind spots of your own. Ultimately, care-based boundaries have the power to protect you from others' care blind spots while also promoting a broader awareness of them, thereby reducing their potential to cause harm to you and others.

Punishing Dictators

There is no certain science of energy vampires. They are carica-
tures, after all, seeming to loom wherever someone claims them
to be. For instance, on the comedy horror television series, *What
We Do in the Shadows,* the character Colin Robinson is an energy vampire. He preys on coworkers at his office job, or what he
calls his "hunting ground," simply through talking to them about
boring topics or subtly annoying them by loudly sharpening his
pencil.[2] In real life, energy vampires are often considered a more
serious threat, such as in this characterization by performance
coach Dan Go, "I believe vampires are real. The ones in real life
won't suck your blood but they will suck your energy."[3] There are
even entire books written about the threat of energy vampires to
one's health and well-being, such as *Dodging Energy Vampires* by
Dr. Christiane Northrup, who describes them as, "People who are
nearly devoid of empathy, compassion, caring, and the willingness
or even capacity to change."[4]

Surveying all the varied ways the term gets used, it is clear to
me that energy vampires are also shapeshifters, fitting the profiles
of diverse traits and relational dynamics. Then there's the potential
for harmful dehumanization that could result from anyone taking
the idea of an energy vampire too seriously. Fortunately, social
scientists have developed a number of more precise concepts and
methods for gaining insight into the draining social dynamics
that underlie at least some of what's meant by *energy vampire* in
popular discourse. In this chapter, we'll explore two such under-
standings from social science to set the stage for a more detailed
introduction to care-based boundaries. The first relies on game
theory and decision-making games, similar to what we previously
explored with the prisoner's dilemma. In this context, it's a social
trial called the dictator game that's proved especially informative.

Picture arriving at the prestigious Max Planck Institute to participate in a study. You are guided to a modern computer lab and

given instructions that prepare you for what's next: Based on luck of the draw, you've been selected to be a sort of judge, and it will be up to you to decide the fate of two other participants. Watching them play a game, you will come to see that one is a selfish "dictator" whom you witness wielding their power over another player, using their superior status in the game to take advantage economically. But according to the game's rules, and unbeknownst to these players, you are actually the one with the final say—you've been granted the ultimate power to reward or punish each player to the degree you see fit. Having witnessed the selfish behavior of the dictator, will you wield your power to penalize them to the fullest extent—taking all their earnings while offering more to the victim? Or might you redistribute the earnings equally between the two players, aiming to teach the dictator a lesson about fairness?

So went one of three variants of the dictator game played by participants in an innovative study on human ethics and social responsibility.[5] Crucially, there was another feature to this study: Half the participants were advanced meditation practitioners who had completed at least three years of full-time meditation retreat during which they had engaged in countless hours of practice to cultivate care and compassion. The goal was to compare their responses to a control group of nonmeditators, examining whether long-term training of one's care system toward greater compassion could influence complex decisions about justice and fairness. Most intriguing was the question of whether such compassion training would lower their willingness to enforce justice, assessed through the decision to punish unfair and self-interested actions during the game.

The findings revealed an intriguing pattern of differences and similarities in social behaviors exhibited by those with a history of compassion training and those without. The compassion practitioners gave larger donations to the victims of injustice than did the control group, but they enacted equal levels of punishment for the dictator. They also increased how much they punished the dictator based on how unfairly that person behaved, in a similar fashion to the control group. Thus, compassion training had clearly not erased their willingness to enforce justice.

The study included another clever way to test the two groups, examining their emotions as they played the game. In comparing them, they discovered that the compassion practitioners felt significantly less angry as they witnessed the injustice unfold and made their decisions, despite still deciding to punish the dictators to an equal degree.

When I consider all these findings, I think the researchers uncovered a profound yet nuanced insight into the transformative power of compassion to shape complex social behavior. But before sharing my own views, here's how the researchers themselves summarized their findings: "The fact that [long-term compassion practitioners] punished in the relative absence of anger suggests that training in compassion can lead from sanctioning as a function of vengeful and retributive motives (i.e., punishment to punish the transgressor) to sanctioning in order to restore justice and equity (i.e., to solve the problem). . . . That justice can still be done without negative emotions such as anger highlights potential health benefits of compassion training as a buffer to antagonistic social situations."[6]

The sort of compassion described here resonates with my perspective on care-based boundaries. It does not yield to harmful actors but rather helps to wield one's power to stand up for principles such as fairness and justice, while also protecting oneself from the toxic stress that often accompanies social conflict and dilemmas.

I'm not advocating for limiting one's views of power, fairness, and justice to simplistic ideas about reward and punishment, as was intentionally done for this study. Rather, what I see as compelling about these findings is that they reinforce the value of drawing on all the tools of one's care system when confronted by social challenges—simultaneously moving beyond the binaries of self and others, feeling and action, communion and agency. You can thereby advocate for yourself and others all together, with a restorative outlook focused on social harmony and the greater good. And you can do this from an empowered place, without closing your heart due to excessive feelings of anger or getting pulled into the exhausting dynamics of other people's care blind spots and dramas.

From Dark Psychology to Care Blind Spots

Another key scientific approach to the study of undesirable social behaviors involves personality psychology, which focuses on identifying the distinctive *dark traits* of those likely to provoke harm or engage in antisocial actions. A number of dark traits have been proposed over the years, but four in particular have received the most attention: narcissism, psychopathy, Machiavellianism, and sadism.[7] Even when limiting focus to these four traits, it's important to emphasize their breadth and diversity, as each one is known to vary by intensity, overlap with other traits, and exhibit a range of behavioral expressions. This point is essential because labeling anything *dark* risks misunderstanding it or possibly worsening relations between people who might otherwise find common ground. For instance, these days, people seem quick to label others with whom they're having difficulty or whom they simply dislike as *narcissists* or *psychopaths*.

We can avoid these and other pitfalls of relying on sweeping labels by focusing more on specific mental and social behaviors— the *care blind spots*—that appear common to the four traits above. For example, if you're having difficulty with your boss at work, instead of going straight to, "He always prioritizes his own needs; he's such a narcissist," you might try something like, "My boss seems to have a chronic care blind spot of repeatedly putting his needs ahead of others at work." This shifts the focus away from broad labels toward key problematic intentions and behaviors that instigate and maintain destructive social dynamics and imbalanced relationships.

As I'm sure is clear from our earlier exploration of care blind spots, they are something we all share, even though they vary greatly in intensity and potential harm. So, while I do not mean to imply all care blind spots are the same, recognizing our personal blind spots can help us avoid the all-too-easy trap of dehumanizing individuals with more pronounced blind spots than our own.

In chapter 2, we reviewed the close relationship between care blind spots and the either/or mindset. Research on dark traits suggests the role of either/or thinking is similarly at play in more extreme care blind spots.[8] Knowing that, you might be tempted to think that simply pointing out others' either/or thinking would be sufficient to address them, but that's often not the case. Consider, for instance, that individuals higher in psychopathy are likely to exhibit cognitive and emotional biases favoring selfishness, short-term gains, and risk-taking, all of which can make it more challenging to overcome an either/or mindset.[9] Furthermore, some people actually derive pleasure from causing pain and suffering to others.[10] For these individuals, naming how their behavior negatively affects you may not produce the intended effects.

At the other extreme of the either/or mindset, people can have deeply ingrained blind spots in self-care, leading to symptoms such as personal self-sabotage, self-destructive behaviors, or many other kinds of self-harm. As different as these self-care blind spots are from those of other-care, they can be similarly devastating in their impacts. Further exacerbating the harms they produce is the reality that, no matter how much care is offered to remediate such blind spots, there can still be times when another person's self-harm completely undermines and nullifies all your efforts to help them. Put simply, when others will not or cannot prioritize their own needs and well-being, even the most skillful attempts to care for them may fail.

Though it can be uncomfortable to acknowledge that major care blind spots exist, especially in loved ones or people, such as colleagues with whom we must have regular contact, healthy boundaries require a clear-eyed recognition that they do. This includes acknowledging the unique challenges that they pose to our practice of we-care, such as their potential to cause immense suffering and their relative insensitivity to efforts aimed at changing them.

The following two high-level summaries of relevant research can be helpful to support the establishment of care-based boundaries in the face of such challenges. First, consider this observation by social neuroscientist Dr. Abigail Marsh: "Extreme deficits in care emerge early in life and may reflect developmental abnormalities in the neurocircuitry that underlies the care system."[11] This underscores why dealing with extreme care blind spots may require a different approach than dealing with subtler ones. Additionally, Daniel Goleman, author of *Social Intelligence*, has written about the far-reaching negative health impacts of harmful social interactions, highlighting why it is critical that we take steps to protect ourselves from these harms: "Nourishing relationships have a beneficial impact on our health, while toxic ones can act like slow poison in our bodies."[12] Thus, while I'm a firm believer that all care blind spots can be remediated to some degree, we must also be mindful not to minimize the harms they cause many people throughout society, including those who have them.[13] Severe care blind spots often signal deeper personal and societal issues and therefore should not be the sole responsibility of those who are adversely affected by them. For anyone grappling with significant care blind spots, whether in others or yourself, I strongly advise seeking professional guidance to help you navigate these challenges.

What Are Boundaries Anyway?

When Frances Klein, a teacher and poet from Alaska, boarded a flight and arrived at her seat in early 2024, she found that a woman was already seated in it. Frances quickly relayed that this was, in fact, her assigned seat. However, the woman sitting in it refused to move, responding that she was "holding a boundary."[14] As mundane as this encounter may seem, it received a lot of attention online, with commenters highlighting the seated woman's misuse of the term *boundary*. But then, was it truly an incorrect use of the term? And if so, what would the right use of "holding a boundary" be? To fully answer these questions, we would first need to agree on what, exactly, a boundary is.

Over my years of studying boundaries, I have noticed that the term is rarely defined. When it is, the definitions often rely on metaphor or lack the level of precision required for scientific assessment of them. This lack of conceptual clarity is not just an academic problem—it informs many strategies by which people aim to set and maintain boundaries in their daily lives. This leads to situations like Frances faced on the plane as well as other, more severe problems.

For over a decade since first encountering this problem, I've aimed to refine my understanding of boundaries from a variety of perspectives, focusing especially on developing the conceptual clarity needed to define and study them scientifically. But before sharing my definition, I want to clarify which uses of the term I'm aiming to describe, since it can be used in numerous ways—from physical boundaries to social role boundaries to informational boundaries or even boundaries of the mind. Further complicating things, there is often conceptual overlap between these different types of boundaries, such that substituting one for the other works in some instances but not in others. For our purposes, the most relevant boundaries are interpersonal, relating to how people treat each other and pursue goals within relationships and social interactions.

Examining boundaries scientifically for a decade has led me to a number of insights I do not see well-represented elsewhere, so my approach to this topic likely differs from others you've encountered. Boundaries *can* be clearly defined—not through inventing a whole new scientific theory but through adapting existing terms and frameworks from related areas of research. Additionally, as I've grown clearer on what, exactly, boundaries are, I've realized that clarifying their definition actually broadens their relevance such that boundaries as I understand them now span more types of behaviors than what's commonly understood. Viewed in this way, boundaries pertain not only to trying moments but also to the everyday choices and adjustments by which people seek to make their social lives more supportive. This understanding has practical significance: When you limit your idea of boundaries to only certain types of actions, you limit the scope of potential options when you find yourself needing to set a boundary. Conversely, when your view of boundaries is broader and more flexible, you have a wider range of options to draw from in any given situation.

Given this background, let's now turn to a definition of boundaries consistent with my scientific perspective:

> *Boundaries*: A wide variety of deliberate actions, both internal and external, aimed at modifying social situations or relationships to better align with one's needs, goals, and values.

The first thing to note is that this definition specifies that boundaries can be internal or external actions, thus encompassing mental behaviors like decision-making about one's preferences within a relationship, as well as outer actions like communicating these preferences. It also emphasizes the active role boundaries play in creating and maintaining a personal and social environment that effectively integrates one's intentions and principles, thereby promoting well-being. From this perspective, *setting a boundary* describes the onset of a deliberate action, or set of actions, aimed at shifting a social situation closer toward one's ideal. And whereas many definitions of boundaries emphasize their defensive or protective role, this approach highlights how they can also be proactive and constructive, increasing the likelihood of experiencing social interactions that are genuinely supportive. This broader perspective recognizes that boundaries are a fundamental aspect of all social dynamics, not just moments of conflict or significant challenge. Examples of this more subtle boundary setting include asking one's date to stop talking about an ex-partner in order to minimize emotional discomfort, interrupting a coworker's long tangent in a meeting to refocus on the agenda, or setting a "phone-free" rule during family meals to encourage presence and connection.

Defined in this way, there can also be quite a range in how effective and healthy one's boundaries are. In fact, there's an interesting we-care twist embedded in my definition above: Although boundaries are aimed at supporting one's *own* needs, goals, and values, it is possible for these to be integrated with the needs, goals, and values of others—to varying degrees. Across diverse social situations, this potential for integration is foundational to how I distinguish *healthy boundaries*.

Naturally Arising Healthy Boundaries

Common approaches to cultivating healthy boundaries rely on reviewing examples, memorizing scripts, or drawing inspiration from metaphor. While these "outside-in" approaches can be helpful, they are a far cry from the full transformation needed to set and maintain healthy boundaries in daily life. Bearing this in mind, the central lesson of this chapter is this: You can cultivate healthy boundaries *from the inside out.*

My research and that of others indicates that the same key ideas, lessons, and practices involved in cultivating we-care can naturally give rise to healthy boundaries.[15] This is because the essential ingredients of healthy boundaries are the same as those needed for full-spectrum we-care; namely the experience of interconnected care that integrates not only self-care and other-care but also feeling and action as well as communion and agency.

How do healthy, care-based boundaries emerge naturally from we-care? When you commit to both self-care and care for others as essential and interconnected aspects of your approach to situations, you avoid the extremes of abandoning yourself or others. Therefore, in times where there is some kind of inner conflict or tension between self-care and other-care, there's less risk you will collapse your care entirely in one direction or another. This ensures that your responses to people or situations integrate your needs, goals, and values with those of others to at least a minimum degree, providing an undivided foundation from which you can further self-advocate as needed. Moreover, because you are not dismissing your care for others, you sidestep all sorts of ineffective approaches to boundaries, improving the chances that others will respect the boundaries you set and maybe even feel appreciative of them at times.

It may seem hard to believe, but boundaries rooted in we-care can accomplish everything that's been promised by divided, either/ or approaches to boundaries—things like safeguarding you from people with major blind spots, securing the respect of others, empowering your authentic self, and reducing your vulnerability to manipulation. However, depending on what you've heard about boundaries in the past, this care-based approach may require first unlearning a few things. Let's therefore bust a few myths about boundaries as a way of reviewing what's unique about the healthy boundaries that arise from full-spectrum we-care.

Myth 1: Healthy Boundaries Equal Self-Care

Boundaries are often framed as self-care, but from a we-care perspective, this is an oversimplification. While it's true that many boundaries place strong emphasis on self-care and fierce self-advocacy, experiencing boundaries arising from we-care means that you are not thinking solely about yourself as an individual. Care-based boundaries are grounded in a bigger view of care where, most ideally, everyone gets to feel empowered, connected, and protected—even when there's clear disagreement or conflict. Healthy boundaries arise naturally from this bigger view because you can more readily perceive the possibility of a better relationship, community, or society. Thus, care-based boundaries can help you communicate and advocate for your needs and goals as an undivided expression of your care for many.

Why have boundaries commonly been framed only as forms of self-care? Over the years of teaching and fielding questions about boundaries, I've noticed that people who are strongly drawn to cultivating them tend to focus initially on one or more *very* challenging people in their lives. These are usually those others who have moderate to severe care blind spots and with whom one may even feel concerned about physical and psychological safety. As difficult as these situations are, there could be one silver lining in having dealt with them: they can wake one up to the value of healthy boundaries more broadly. However, it's crucial to recognize that the kind of fiercely self-caring boundaries needed to address some of the most difficult people we've encountered can lead to boundaries that are miscalibrated for other relationships. Healthy boundaries look radically different across different people and social dynamics. Additionally, over time, the path of healthy boundaries should ideally shape one's social life to lessen the necessity of setting fierce boundaries.

Even when fierce boundaries aren't needed, the journey of setting and maintaining boundaries still requires a lot of trust in the value of we-care. This includes trust that you're not being selfish, despite the old storylines in your head or the finger-pointing of others. Perhaps even connecting with a sense of trust as you experience waves of guilt or shame, forcing you to remember the bigger picture again and again. At times, you might need to trust in the greater good of letting go of someone you once held dear. But as tough as the different trials of establishing boundaries can be, this trust eventually transforms into confidence. One healthy boundary at a time, you see the majority of your relationships steadily improving, and you find yourself increasingly surrounded by those who resonate with your personal sense of we-care. This further strengthens your capacity to enact we-care, deepen connection, and embody wisdom throughout all of your relationships.

Myth 2: Healthy Boundaries Produce Disconnection

Overcoming this next myth can result in a profound inner shift in how you think about boundaries. When you start experiencing boundaries as acts of care that deepen connection, you become more inclined to set and maintain them in all your relationships. Conversely, the discourse around boundaries often emphasizes creating distance and erecting walls between people. Zooming out just a little to take in more context, one can see that healthy boundaries are instead declarations of the kinds of connection you value. In setting a healthy boundary, you are not producing more disconnection, even within those most challenging situations in which your aim is to reduce or end social contact with someone. Typically, your boundaries are responses to a sense of disconnection that is already shaping a social interaction or relationship, representing the first conscious step toward experiencing more connection. This does not necessarily mean you're seeking deeper connection with the person you set a boundary with. Often, healthy boundaries will be about first deepening your connection with your inner self. Ultimately, however, setting care-based boundaries leads to a life filled with more satisfying connections of many kinds.

Myth 3: Healthy Boundaries Excuse Disrespect

A core assumption of the care-based approach is that everyone has care blind spots, even those we trust the most. Viewed in this way, cultivating healthy boundaries is both about addressing the harmful patterns we see as well as being prepared for what is not yet seen. There's another, subtler implication of this acknowledgment: by clearly recognizing the ubiquity of care blind spots, encountering them in others tends to feel less personal and therefore less painful. After all, severe care blind spots arise from longstanding biases or limits of someone's awareness, often shaped by generations of trauma and harm if not millennia of evolution. Thus, we do not need to be so all-or-nothing about them, because we recognize that we are fundamentally working with people's confusion and confused behaviors—not their most essential and conscious self. This makes it so we can say no to someone's care blind spots while embracing the person more broadly. And we can demand others take responsibility for their blind spots without reducing them to their worst moments.

Setting boundaries from this perspective further strengthens their transformative potential for us and others because they not only protect us as needed but also honor and encourage the positive, wakeful qualities of others. By contrast, divided approaches to setting boundaries, such as suggesting people "burn bridges" along the way, embed a layer of disrespect in their implementation.

My sense is that those who advocate for this kind of boundary setting generally mean well and are focused primarily on the most egregious instances of care blind spots. However, it's not only possible to set equally strong and effective boundaries without disrespect, it is wiser and more effective to do so.

I'm not suggesting that an ideal approach to boundaries lacks emotion and passion, nor are care-based boundaries about conflict avoidance. I'm also not saying things won't get messy from time to time. But as the author Adam Grant highlights, "Respect is a social responsibility. Treating it as optional reveals a lack of concern for others."[16] In other words, disrespect is a clear signal that someone is operating from an either/or mindset. On any path of healing and transformation, we must remain mindful not to become that which we are pushing against.

Myth 4: Apologies Are Disempowering

A prevailing narrative in discussions about boundaries asserts that one should never apologize for self-care and self-advocacy. Like most myths, this one contains a bit of truth. Some people report apologizing in moments where it is not needed, subtly undermining their self-care and the boundaries they set. This sort of disempowering apology may stem from feelings of guilt or anxiety, leading one to mistakenly believe that others are upset with them, even when they're clearly not. Excessive apologizing might also occur due to learned habits or care blind spots that were modeled and reinforced by others, alongside societal or cultural expectations.[17] This truth aside, what makes the idea a myth is that there are plenty of times when adding an apology to the sequence of setting a boundary can be a highly effective antidote to some of its unwanted side effects—things like awkwardness, inconvenience, and confusion. In other words, one is not apologizing for the boundary itself but rather for any unintended friction it may create for the other person or the relationship.

Does this mean apologizing is a necessary component of every healthy boundary? Absolutely not. And as noted, there's a risk of overapologizing. But when an apology feels like another expression of your we-care, it may help you set effective boundaries that avoid needless conflict and drama.

Myth 5: Healthy Boundaries Require Bold Actions

When you decide it's time to set a boundary with someone, it might be tempting to imagine doing something daring or flashy, picturing the look of shock on their face. In actual practice, however, healthy boundaries span a range from bold and public to subtle and private. What's key is knowing what kind of boundary will be most skillful to address the context you are in.

Many situations are best served by a simple inner shift or *mental boundary*, which entails changing how you are thinking about a person or relationship. Imagine finding yourself at a social gathering where your ex-partner is also present, clearly acting out in an attempt to provoke your jealousy. The most effective boundary in this situation might be to consciously disengage from their actions. You could choose to focus on other guests, immerse yourself in different conversations, and internally affirm that their behavior further validates your decision to not be with them. It may also be helpful to remind yourself that their hurtful behavior likely stems from their own unresolved issues and suffering—a mental reframe that's frequently true and helps depersonalize others' unkindness.

When weighing what sort of boundary to set, another significant factor is the risk of escalating unnecessary conflict or getting more entangled in someone else's care blind spots or other confusions. This may partly explain the success reported by those who've implemented a boundary strategy called *gray rocking,* in which one intentionally responds in neutral and dull ways to someone demanding attention or trying to get under one's skin.[18] This approach requires a high degree of emotion regulation and cool-headed equanimity, but it's said to reduce unwanted social contact with that person over time and in a manner that safe-guards against backlash or subtle reinforcement of their unwanted attention- and reaction-seeking behaviors.

Whatever approach you choose in a given situation, it's helpful to remember that, more often than not, when you feel like burning a bridge, it is wiser to simply leave it be and venture further down-stream, where more supportive bridges and relationships await.

Mindful Boundaries: Creating Space for We-Care

When you realize there's a need for a boundary arising from we-care, it may feel difficult to discern whether you are carefully adapting to the needs of others or caving to them. True balance is a moving target, as each social situation interacts with your inner experience, necessitating a tailored approach. For these and other reasons, an inherent challenge of setting care-based boundaries is to first get crystal clear about your needs, goals, and values in rela-tion to each specific scenario. I call this more mindful approach to social situations *context-integrative*—a term that represents a nuanced approach to social behavior, a few steps beyond *context-sensitive*. To be context-integrative, you are not only sensitive to who and what is present but also taking in a holistic feel for the situation, making sense of it in relation to your goals, and rely-ing on your we-care tool kit to bridge the demands of inner and outer.

Depending on the situation, many skills and behaviors may be needed to fully realize this mindful, context-integrative approach. That said, the foundation of being context-integrative with one's boundaries is often rather simple—it's just taking more space and time to reflect. Because of this, the first layer of healthy boundaries you will often need in tricky situations involves actions that help you create more space between a social dilemma and your full response to it. This could look like taking a break from a heated conflict to go on a walk, waiting a day or longer to respond to a charged text or email, or simply pausing to collect your thoughts before responding. Of course, it's important to ensure that these boundaries are not used as a way to avoid establishing other, more essential boundaries. Instead, the aim is to give yourself the chance to feel both your self-care and other-care together, including any tension or potential for integration that exists between them. You therefore bridge your feelings and actions to clarify your approach to the specific context you're in, helping you to set truly context-integrative boundaries.

Drawing the We-Care Line

Jiya is struggling with yet another sleepless night. But unlike previous times when her roommate Meredith's noisy antics kept her awake, the apartment is silent. Tonight, Jiya's restlessness is due to her own spiraling thoughts about a recent argument she had with Meredith, during which Jiya tried to set a boundary that was not well-received. Now she's at a crossroads, contemplating whether to renew her lease and continue living with Meredith, who is also a longtime friend, or to move on, considering Meredith's recent pattern of excessive drinking and bringing home strangers that wake Jiya up and cause uneasy situations. Worst of all, Jiya has been noticing the effects of these disturbances on the rest of her life. Lately, she's not been feeling like herself, which has been reflected in comments from several friends and colleagues.

At a distance, it may seem obvious what Jiya should do, but when it's your own longstanding relationship on the line, especially when that relationship used to be much better, it is often much harder to gain clarity at such crossroads. There are so many factors, it can be hard to identify the most essential things to help you cut through the noise. Should Jiya try talking to Meredith again, clarifying her request for Meredith to not bring strangers home on weeknights? Is it possible Meredith did not understand what Jiya meant, and that's why she responded by calling her "selfish"? And what about all the times Meredith helped Jiya in the past? Perhaps, Jiya wonders, she should be more forgiving due to their history of mutual support.

Frankly, we cannot know what the best course of action for Jiya will be without standing in her shoes. Yet there is one more line of questioning that can help her to get clear: Will continuing to live with Meredith compromise her capacity to care for her other friends and loved ones? This question is purposefully aimed at Jiya's other-focused care beyond how she cares for Meredith and is thus consistent with the we-care strength of an *adaptable we*, as introduced in chapter 3. Of course, Jiya should likewise weigh the impact of her decision on her own well-being. Somewhat para-doxically, however, she may need to first expand her care to others beyond Meredith to better understand her own self-care and we-care. In a similar way, she might find it valuable to reflect on what she might say to a friend or loved one in her situation.

If you are ever faced with a dilemma like Jiya's, contemplating in these ways may help you to get honest with yourself about whether one person or relationship is draining you of all the energy that's meant to care for many people, including yourself. Even if it's clear you're feeling drained, reflecting on and acknowledging the impacts of your situation on others you care about is valuable. After all, care-based boundaries both rely on and ensure your ability to offer effective support to yourself and many others—not just one person.

If it is not wise or preferred, for any reason, to completely end a relationship with someone, know that you can first try dialing down your energy investment without saying goodbye forever. When evaluating this, it can be helpful to reflect, *Am I putting in all the work to improve this relationship without any reciprocated efforts or signs of progress?*

After her latest sleepless night, as much as Jiya wants to act decisively, she intentionally slows down and takes a few days to contemplate her approach, focusing on its broader impacts for those she loves and for herself. She realizes that living with Meredith through this turmoil has been costing her more than she initially realized. Most importantly for her, she sees that it has been making it hard to offer support to her other friends and family members in moments of need. To respect her longstanding friendship with Meredith, Jiya decides she is willing to have one last conversation. She calmly explains that, due to the impact on not just herself but all her other friendships and obligations, she will not be renewing the lease—unless Meredith can promise to stop partying on weeknights, effective immediately.

Again, Meredith does not take Jiya's boundary well, doubling down on claims that Jiya is acting selfishly. Consequently, Jiya reduces her contact with Meredith until the lease ends, finds a new place to live, and eventually moves out. It isn't easy, especially during moments when she lets herself feel the loss of the friendship she once had with Meredith. Yet Jiya never strongly doubts her decision, and she soon notices an improvement in her capacity to care for herself and many others.

A few months later, Jiya receives a text from Meredith. She reveals that she has recently stopped drinking and asks if Jiya might be open to meeting for coffee sometime. Jiya agrees.

The Courage in Care-Based Boundaries

Beyond the personal benefits of boundaries, my social media post about energy vampires highlighted their potential to effect change in other people—perhaps even those with moderate to severe care blind spots. Although I believe this to be true over the long run, in actual practice, even the most skillful boundaries rarely produce immediate gratification. Initially, as old patterns break down, boundaries often lead to negative reactions in others, such as defensiveness, anger, anxiety, stonewalling, guilt, shame, and conflict. Why does this happen, and can care-based boundaries help?

Let's start by reviewing three causes of others' reactivity to boundaries. The first is that, when someone is operating from within the either/or mindset, someone else's self-advocacy may appear as a threat. This is based on the false premise that one person's gain is necessarily another's loss. Viewed through the divided mind, another person's boundary feels inconvenient at best, and at worst, like an all-or-nothing battle between needs or a struggle for limited resources.

A second vital reason is that boundaries often emphasize agency over communion, leading to assertive and influential actions. As we discussed in chapter 6, humans are wired to perceive agentic actions in biased ways, as motivated primarily by individual self-interest. This bias can shape others' perceptions of our boundaries even when we are acting with care and mindfully communicating our care-based intentions.

Third and finally, at the most basic level, healthy boundaries disrupt habitual patterns of interacting and behaving, thus inviting people to reflect upon and even change their ways. The more people resist change generally, the more resistance is likely to shape their reactions to the boundaries others set.

Thus, although the long arc of healthy boundaries bends toward less social friction, it can sometimes create more conflict and interpersonal challenge over the short- to medium-term. This is true even when we approach them from a we-care perspective and set healthy boundaries that clearly hold the potential for mutual benefits. Because of this, the path of setting healthy boundaries takes both courage and patience. You are disrupting the relational habits of at least two people at once—yourself and those you set the boundary with—and so must be willing to endure pushback and be misunderstood. You must also embrace the challenge of outright conflict when it arises, ready to draw on all the tools in your we-care tool kit to guide it in a constructive direction. At times, when the harms are too great or another person refuses to change, you may even have to let go of a connection altogether. When faced with difficulties like these, it's essential to remember that negative consequences are usually temporary, while the positive effects of care-based boundaries endure.

Even though a care-based approach to boundaries does not instantly free you of all the challenges involved in setting them, you can still anticipate a number of distinct benefits by adopting this approach. One clear outcome is that because you are being mindful of the effects of your boundaries on others, the negative reactivity and backdraft you encounter should be less overall. A care-based approach also helps you avoid ineffective strategies that come from closing your heart, like putting up walls instead of setting boundaries or retracting a boundary out of guilt. As time goes on, you will grow increasingly adept at setting effective boundaries without all the second-guessing or self-criticism that's a symptom of more divided approaches. In these and other ways, you are cultivating a deeper boundary of no longer allowing the either/or mindsets and divisive behaviors of others to cause you to divide your own mind and heart. As you experience the lightness of being this can bring, you can embrace the path of mindful, care-based boundaries even more fully. Although situations will vary, you will increasingly realize that every healthy boundary you set has the power to set both you and others on a course toward greater social connection and personal freedom.

We-Care Practice 9
CARE CLEARING

There are times when your caring system has been so active, tending to so many, that you come to experience an indescribable muddle of tenderness. Even with impeccable we-care and boundaries, you may still feel uncertain about everything you have absorbed or given away. The following practice of Care Clearing is designed with such moments in mind, though it can also be practiced proactively to support and strengthen your care-based boundaries more broadly. It works by disentangling the different strands of we-care, releasing what needs to be released and reconnecting you with anything essential you lost touch with. Thus, it facilitates the emergence of healthy boundaries from within.

PRACTICE INSTRUCTIONS

1. *Mindful breathing.* Take a few moments to breathe naturally, simply noticing what it is like to inhale and exhale with mindful awareness.

2. *Exhale what is not yours to carry.* Gently invite more of your attention to each outbreath as it occurs, pairing it with an intention to release anything extra you may be holding in your body or mind that does not belong to you. The general idea here is that each person is only meant to carry so much at a time, so it's supportive to let go of any problems, tensions, or burdens that aren't meant for you. Letting go in this way is not about leaving a burden behind that others must now shoulder but rather aligning your inner experience with what will be best for everyone. You can silently express this intention with a phrase such as, *With this outbreath, I release what is not mine to carry, for the benefit of all, including myself. May this energy go where it is most needed and beneficial.* If it helps with your mindful release, visualize white light softly rippling from your heart in ever-widening circles, gently clearing the space within and around you. Stay with this stage of the practice for however long you find it supportive.

3. *Inhale to reconnect with your vitality.* Focus more awareness on each inbreath, joining it with an intention to reconnect with and reclaim any personal vitality you have lost touch with. For this step, the view is that everyone you care for benefits more when you are fully resourced and attuned with all of your natural energy. A supportive intention you can repeat silently is, *On this inbreath, I reconnect with all my vital energy. Anything I lost touch with, I call back to me for the benefit of all, including myself.* If visualization supports your practice, you can imagine nourishing energy gently returning to and enhancing the shimmer of your heart with each inbreath.

4. *Return to the outbreath.* Take a few more mindful breaths and return to noticing the exhale, releasing any tension or problems that are not yours to shoulder. If you'd like, you can again visualize circles of light traveling from your heart, gently clearing the space within and around you.

5. *Set an intention for healthy boundaries.* Drop any sense of effort or visualization and breathe naturally, feeling the innate clarity of your heart. You may sense it as an inner warmth in your chest or visualize its steady glow. As you attune to this innate clarity, set one last intention that your breath will continue to foster care-based boundaries throughout daily life. You can silently state this intention: *May my natural breath continuously nourish and energize my healthy boundaries.*

CHAPTER 9

Personal Meets Global

We-Care in a Divided World

> You cannot get through a single day
> without having an impact on the world
> around you. What you do makes a
> difference, and you have to decide what
> kind of difference you want to make.
> —JANE GOODALL

When Amber first hears about the humanitarian crisis in Sudan, her heart sinks for the millions of people displaced or fleeing the country due to violent conflict. She isn't sure why it affects her so much, compared to other crises, but she immediately feels as though it's her personal mission to find a way to help. Yet as she begins researching ways to help effectively, she becomes overwhelmed by grief and heartbreak. The crisis is unimaginably vast, affecting so many. Then again, Amber finds it hard to look away: the more she learns, the more she feels both grateful for her life in the United States and guilty for how good it is in comparison. Scouring the web and watching the news, she notices how little attention Sudan gets compared to other crises. Talking to family and friends only deepens her frustration. She is frequently met with indifference or whataboutism, with some questioning her level of care and appearing more concerned for her mental health than for the countless Sudanese victims. This only adds to her inner turmoil, causing near-sleepless nights and impacting her energy for work and relationships. Despite her initial determination, Amber's deep conviction starts to waver: *How could she, from halfway around the world, ever hope to have a positive impact?*

To truly realize the transformative power of we-care—both individually and collectively—we must continue to confront its barriers head-on. The either/or mindset is a pervasive and formidable counterforce to we-care, stoking division within and between human beings from ancient times up to the present. On a personal level, we can see signs of this inner division anytime we completely abandon our personal needs to care for those of others, dehumanize someone we're in conflict with, experience inner conflict after setting a firm boundary, or feel resentful at another's happiness, perceiving it as a threat to our own. Collectively, the either/or mindset sows deep divisions throughout society, driving polarization, loathing, and even violence between groups and entire nation-states. As the Buddhist teacher Pema Chödrön insightfully notes, "War and peace start in the hearts of individuals."[1]

Then there are the intersections where personal meets collective, like in Amber's desire to help the people of Sudan. These intersections can amplify the either/or mindset, leading to *compassion collapse* or *care bypassing*—two contrasting ideas I'll introduce more fully later in this chapter, before revisiting Amber's dilemma in light of them. In modern times, this amplifying effect seems most evident in the polarized landscape of social media discourse and online interactions, a space where factors such as physical separation and anonymity empower it to manifest openly, unchecked, and in ways that actively solicit reward. Consider the following four *dark laws of online engagement,* put forward by Dr. Jay Van Bavel, a social neuroscientist who studies communication and behavior on the internet. The laws summarize numerous research findings on what predicts greater content engagement and virality:

1. Negativity bias drives headline clicks.

2. Extreme opinions drive in-group sharing.

3. Out-group animosity drives engagement.

4. "Moral-emotional" language goes viral.[2]

Each of these laws intersects with the either/or mindset in different ways, but the middle two are particularly relevant for understanding its mass appeal and prized status in the online world. Together, they show how the either/or mindset is a key determinant of content engagement, including whether and how something goes viral. Weighing the evidence that's informed this summary leaves little doubt that the modern amplification of divided modes of thinking both reflects and contributes to the weakened social fabric and pervasive disconnection of our times. And unfortunately, the deleterious impacts of this division do not end there. Research has shown that the subjective experience of disconnection, namely loneliness, is itself contagious.[3] Thus, the either/or mindset ripples out in widening waves of harm, from the inner division it reinforces in those who wield it to how it's received and rewarded by others to the contagious nature of disconnection itself. Against this societal backdrop, we've witnessed the continuous rise of self-care—a ubiquitous concept originally intended as an antidote to imbalanced care but that can be misused by the either/or mindset to activate and justify divided care.

Yet despite its visibility and influence in driving online virality, compelling evidence suggests the either/or mindset may be weaker than it seems. A study conducted on the social media posts of American senators found that, although divisive messaging received greater online engagement such as likes and reshares, this engagement only reflected the views of an especially vocal minority with extreme views, representing just 6 to 7 percent of Americans.[4] Thus, online engagement and virality can create the appearance of widespread endorsement of divisive perspectives, rather than reflecting the majority of the public who instead prefer constructive, collaborative solutions. This disconnect between people's online engagement and their private views is a fascinating and growing area of research. What's important for our discussion is its implications for weighing the relative strength of the either/or mindset throughout society. If most people hold less divided views than what is typically amplified online, it might explain how the spirit of we-care occasionally breaks through. When it does, acts of care can capture public attention and go viral.

Suspended Coffee and the Three Layers of Contagious Care

Finding my place in line at the Humble House Cafe in Golden, Colorado, I surveyed a clothespin string board populated with dozens of notes marked "Pay It Forward"—each describing a possible customer who might claim its cash value. Many described people struggling in specific ways, such as "Someone who just lost their mom," "A veteran who has gone through mental/physical trauma," or "A person struggling with an addiction." However, not all were intended for a suffering stranger. My personal favorite was penned in the messy handwriting of a small child, "For a kid who loves a cat." The line shuffled forward, and I'd not yet found a note that seemed destined for me. Nearing the counter, my ears caught a lyric of the song being played throughout the café:

"Every action has a ripple effect."[5] It reminded me that I wasn't there on a mission to receive a stranger's kindness but instead to add to the board—a personal experiment of what it's like to participate in the practice of *suspended coffee,* in which one purchases a coffee for a stranger to enjoy in the future. I conveyed my order for a coffee, as well as one Pay It Forward note. Informed by my experience scanning the board, I sat down and wrote a description I expected could resonate widely with future customers: "For someone cultivating self-care so they can better care for others."

Although Humble House is not your everyday coffee shop, my experience there isn't entirely unique. The tradition of suspended coffee, or *caffè sospeso,* may go back more than a century in Italy, with a more recent revival in 2011. The practice has since gone viral around the globe via the internet, with an estimated fifteen million suspended coffees purchased across thirty-four countries as of 2015.[6]

It's intriguing to imagine what might happen if a major company like Starbucks decided to adopt the practice worldwide. This also raises an interesting question: What is it about buying a cup of coffee for someone else that makes it such a widely appreciated and positively infectious act of care? Could it be that the act of buying coffee for someone else is often accompanied by enjoying a warm cup oneself and is therefore readily experienced as we-care?

Suspended coffee offers a fascinating case study on what makes an act of care go viral. But rather than focusing on the specific factors that contribute to virality per se, I want to instead use it as an entry point to reflect on the interconnection embedded in and rippling out from most all of our caring acts. From this standpoint, something rising to the extent of virality is simply a more pronounced and visible example of events that commonly occur but often go unnoticed.

We can deepen our appreciation for this contagious nature of care by exploring its scientific underpinnings, reviewing the evidence and underlying mechanisms of care contagion in the three interrelated layers described in the sections below. Each layer is significant for both everyday acts of care and more widespread, viral instances, demonstrating the intersections between personal and collective care. By growing more aware of the cascading effects of your care and contemplating the interactions between these layers, you'll find lessons that empower you to embrace the full impacts of your we-care.

Spreading Seeds of Care: The Informational and Motivational Layer

"That's right—shrimp!" my friend confirmed enthusiastically before expounding on the neglected plight of billions of tiny crustaceans around the globe. Strange as it sounded, I couldn't deny he was right: I had never deeply considered the maltreatment of shrimp. Each new facet of his argument pushed back against my indifference until eventually I found myself genuinely moved by my friend's impassioned plea, enough to commit to making a donation to the Shrimp Welfare Project—an organization dedicated to improving the lives of shrimp.

The first layer of care contagion is so basic that it can be easily overlooked. When someone else cares deeply for something, it can move us to care for that thing too—even something as quixotic as shrimp. This informational and motivational route of care contagion is significant because, as research shows, we are all motivated empathizers.[7] We approach or avoid the experience of caring based on factors such as anticipated costs of caring or how favorably it may be perceived by others. Thus, when someone communicates and expresses their care, and especially when they act on it, they reveal to us what they deem worthy of caring for. Intuitively, we recognize they have had to overcome mental and emotional barriers to caring in this way, and so we ourselves may experience more openness to exploring it.

We can also feel more motivated by the potential to strengthen our connection with another person, a potent pathway of social transmission deeply ingrained in our social wiring. This transmission of care can happen with or without words and is a strong enough driver that people employ all manner of persuasive tactics to enhance its power. This informational and motivational layer of care even carries the potential to achieve virality through celebrity endorsements or mainstream entertainment like music and documentaries. These mediums intentionally elevate causes with powerful devices such as evocative storytelling and high-impact visuals. Interestingly, however, this initial layer of transmitting who and what we care for is also plagued by many different mental and emotional biases, as well as by intense competition for attention.

Regarding biases, consider the phenomenon of *compassion collapse*—the counterintuitive tendency for people to experience and express *less* compassion when there are *more* sufferers.[8] For example, studies have shown that donations can be higher to aid a single identifiable victim than for large groups suffering from the same plight. On the one hand, this idea underscores the limitations of our motivated empathy, exposing one of many moral "bugs" that can bias our care when we rely primarily on our innate empathy as our guiding compass. On the other, it speaks to the tremendous power one person can wield when they choose to not back down from compassion for mass suffering, assuming they can do so effectively without forsaking themselves in the process.

Regarding competition and rivalry, I'm consistently struck that well-intentioned campaigns to promote care can backfire when they become too assertive with their messaging. There can also be a tendency to judge what others care about, even when it's clearly aligned with one's own broader values. For example, some might have felt disappointment when they learned I donated to support shrimp welfare, believing other causes were more deserving of that money. In extreme cases, differences in commitment levels to certain causes can weaken or even completely end relationships. Here, I believe it's critical to remember the interconnected nature of diverse forms of suffering, such that one person's care for something can indirectly support our care for something else, and vice versa. Ideally, instead of experiencing tension between who and what we care for, we could openly discuss the merits of different care actions while still celebrating each other's idiosyncratic set of concerns. Even better, this process could deepen our commitment to the causes we care about and further broaden our scope of care.

Acts of Care Catch On: The Behavioral Layer

Imagine you are playing an online video game with a precious in-game resource represented by a digital candle. You're told that you are free to offer this candle to a fellow anonymous player nearby—not as a tool for enhancing your in-game status but as a means of unlocking deeper levels of interaction with them. Such was the focus of a study conducted in 2022 in which researchers examined the altruistic behaviors of nearly one million players in *Sky: Children of the Light*, an award-winning video game.[9] The study focused on *Sky* partly because its popularity enabled such a large-scale investigation but also because the game's unique design allowed them to isolate variables related to the social contagion of care. Consistent with studies conducted in many other contexts, they found that care-based behaviors—whether directly experienced or simply observed—can inspire more individuals to extend care to others.[10]

Shifting our focus from where care is directed to its execution, we uncover a second layer of care contagion: the social transmission of generosity and kindness. Reflecting on the role of emotion in this process is useful, as researchers have identified specific emotional states that significantly drive the behavioral contagion of care. The first and most direct pathway involves the emotions of *warm glow* and *gratitude*, positive states commonly experienced on the giving and receiving ends of care, respectively. Frequently, these positive emotions facilitate back-and-forth reciprocity between people; however, under the right conditions, they can also prompt a pay-it-forward response or even set off a chain reaction of prosocial behavior.[11] This is known as *upstream reciprocity*, which refers to when a person who receives social support at one moment is inspired to perform an act of kindness toward a different individual who was not part of the initial exchange.

A second, less direct effect can occur through witnessing the caring acts of others. The key emotional driver for this pathway is *elevation*—a state of upliftment that follows after observing another person carry out an act of care, especially one that's extraordinary.[12] Consider what it might feel like to witness a police officer approach a shoeless man on the street, who's simply there asking for change in the freezing cold of winter. The officer then pulls out a new pair of socks and boots, gifts them to the man, and helps him put them on. Now imagine this heartwarming moment was caught on camera and posted to the internet, greatly expanding its potential to inspire many more acts of care. This is exactly what happened when a photo captured police officer Lawrence DePrimo giving boots to a man after seeing his blistered, bare feet and deciding to help.[13]

Many of the drivers and mechanisms underlying the behavioral contagion of care are unique to other-oriented care. However, research indicates that healthy self-care behaviors can also be socially contagious. As one example, careful research has demonstrated that physical exercise can be transmitted throughout social networks.[14] To study this, researchers relied on fitness tracker data to study the physical activity of over one million runners around the globe, finding that the likelihood of a person running on any given day increased based on their friends' running habits. This spread of healthy self-care may be driven partly by social comparison, another important social route of transmission that may help to explain the contagion of more enduring outcomes, such as obesity and happiness.[15] Thus, while there are various distinct routes through which other-care and self-care spread, this behavioral layer of contagion encompasses them all and is crucial for understanding the long-term impacts of care contagion.

Mending the Social Fabric: The Long-Term Outcomes Layer

The first two layers of care contagion demonstrate something profound about the natural interconnectedness of our care. However, research on this topic has also shown how fragile and transient these social contagion effects can be. For instance, pay-it-forward generosity or elevation-based altruism can fade rapidly within a network, and it's significantly weaker when individuals are not personally inclined toward prosociality.[16] Thus, despite strong evidence for the first two layers of care contagion, skepticism about its relevance in modern life is understandable. Perhaps it seems like an inconsequential quirk of our legacy as a social species, similar to contagious yawning. However, evidence points to a third layer of care contagion that reveals its lasting impacts and helps to quantify its reach.

Much of this evidence emerged from the Framingham Heart Study, an extraordinary longitudinal study on residents of the town of Framingham, Massachusetts, which has provided valuable insights beyond its central focus on cardiovascular disease. Most relevant to care contagion, social scientists have used its data to examine the spread of complex psychological states, such as loneliness and happiness, finding evidence that they, too, are socially contagious. Moreover, this research has revealed their spread within networks of up to three degrees of influence.[17] In simple terms, this means the mental state of not only a close friend but even the friend of a friend of a friend can impact your own mental state—measurably shifting how you perceive yourself and your social world.

This third layer underscores the profound collective impact of care contagion, showing that the benefits of both self-care and other-care can ripple beyond the individual, mending and protecting the broader social fabric in enduring ways. Yet these effects are so remarkable that they might seem hard to believe. For me, it has been helpful to reflect on how exactly these reparative and protective effects of care contagion occur. To do so, we can draw on the insights of Dr. John Cacioppo, whose pioneering research on loneliness was first reviewed in chapter 7. Consider his following illustration of how loneliness spreads:

> It is actually stunningly simple as a mechanism. In one study we looked at people's connections, every three to four years. This process happens over time. Let's say that you and I are neighbours. I have become lonely for some reason and you are my friend. As a suddenly lonely person I am now more likely to deal with you cautiously, defensively, as a potential threat to me [because you might leave and add to my pain], and you recognise that so we are going to have more negative social reactions. And over three or four years we are more likely to stop being friends. So that is one less confidant for both of us. . . .
>
> And it doesn't end there. Because you interact less well with me as a neighbour, when you go to work we can see you are more likely to interact negatively with someone else. And so it goes on.[18]

Now, let's embed deliberate acts of care into this scenario to better grasp how the effects of care contagion could shift the outcomes toward greater connection for many. You and I are neighbors. You recently committed to practicing we-care throughout your life. Thus, you begin to not only enact more self-care but also to say hello to me and other neighbors, check in, and even occasionally lend a hand. The warm glow and gratitude generated by these brief interactions positively influences my impression of you, leading me to reciprocate. Through this process, we develop a stronger bond and become a support system for each other in both good and challenging times.

As part of your self-care routine, you often load your mountain bike onto your car. One day, this sparks a conversation that inspires me to dust off my old road bike from the garage and start riding again, which in turn motivates you to start road biking too. These mutual benefits do not end with us but ripple outward: our emotions and approaches evolve across many more interactions at home, work, and beyond. As time goes on, we experience a richer network of mutually supportive and meaningful connections. When community action is needed, organizing and catalyzing collective change becomes easier.

Care Multiplier: Owning Your Impact

Even when we get specific, breaking care contagion down into distinct layers and underlying mechanisms, it can still feel abstract and theoretical. I find this to be true even after diving deeply into the evidence base. Therefore, I believe it's important to slow down enough to contemplate what it all means for you personally. Toward this end, it's possible to use some very basic math to make reflecting on these findings more concrete and meaningful. Specifically, the steps below will guide you through a simplified method for calculating how many people three degrees of influence represents for you, producing an estimate that you can rely on to glimpse the relevance of care contagion in daily life. You'll also have a chance to draw on this estimate to enhance your experience within our final we-care practice, Beaming We-Care, presented at the end of this chapter.

1. *Count your first-degree connections.* Write down the number of people you commonly interact with directly—friends, family, colleagues, neighbors, or anyone else fitting this description. This number can vary significantly from one person to the next, so don't worry if your estimate is much higher or lower than my example below. You can also be more or less conservative in this step based on factors that alter the likelihood of contagion, such as how close by a connection lives. For this approach, I invite you to count any individual with whom you have mutual recognition, direct communication (whether in-person or digital), and relatively frequent contact—meaning that it's unsurprising when you interact with them. For instance, my current neighbor, whom I chat with about once per week, would count for me. However, my former neighbor would not because even though I occasionally see her around town, it's now rare and surprising when it happens.

   Example: You have 10 first-degree connections: 3 close in-person friends + 3 close coworkers + 2 close family members + 1 close friend in another state + 1 close neighbor.

2. *Estimate second- and third-degree connections.* The goal of this next step is to estimate how many first-degree connections, on average, your other connections have, starting with the people you counted in Step 1. As noted, this number varies widely between people, so unless there is something unique that might impact your network's average, it is probably best to rely on

an estimate derived from other publications on this topic, which is about 15.[19] Alternatively, you might choose to use your number if you think it could more accurately reflect others in your network. Later on, I'll also introduce the option to adjust your estimates for the potential overlap of individuals across these social circles.

Example: Using my recommended average, you estimate 15 second-degree connections and 15 third-degree connections.

3. *Calculate your total network size.* Follow these simple instructions to crunch the numbers:

   a. Record your number of first-degree connections (the final number from Step 1 above).
      Example: 10

   b. Multiply your number of first-degree connections (Step 1) by the number of your second-degree connections (Step 2).
      Example: 10 x 15 = 150

   c. Multiply the answer from letter b above by your number of third-degree connections (Step 2).
      Example: 150 x 15 = 2,250

   d. Add the results from a, b, and c to get your estimated total network size.
      Example: 10 + 150 + 2,250 = 2,410

Starting with just 10 first-degree connections, this method shows that you are part of a network of 2,410 individuals who can both influence you and be influenced by you through various routes of social and care contagion.[20] Thus, your acts of self-care and care for others have the potential to ripple out and impact many people, likely including people you've never met.

Similarly, this reveals that your feelings and actions are likely to be influenced by a wide network of people, even if you don't realize it. Reflecting deeply on this, with the specificity of this approach, can further enhance your appreciation for your social nature and strengthen your commitment to practicing we-care for the benefit of many.

The Paradox of Care Bypassing

Through the lens of we-care, you can see how enacting healthy self-care is an act of caring for others too. Care contagion takes this a few literal degrees further, helping you grasp the broader ripple effects of all your care. In this light, many of us are likely underestimating the full impact of our care, a limiting view that might also lead to misjudging who and what needs our care most. This may be especially true when someone is grappling with how best to engage with issues as big as international conflict or a humanitarian crisis. In such situations, the either/or mindset can interact with underestimating the ripple effects of care, leading to feelings of hopelessness, guilt, shame, and aggression. People in such a bind may even come to believe the direct tasks of caring for themselves and others in their social circles are unimportant and boring. Rather than rising into the complexity of we-care, one falls into *care bypassing*—a condition in which one's care for a broader social or societal issue causes one to overlook more essential acts of care for themselves and others.

Don't get me wrong; sacrificing personal comforts and putting in the work to stand up for principles like justice, compassion, and nonviolence are often natural outgrowths of we-care. However, when someone falls into care bypassing, this sacrifice gets taken to an extreme. The net consequence is no longer serving them or the greater good they are aiming for. While all divided expressions of self-care or other-care entail a measure of bypassing one's care for others or one's personal self, what I mean by care bypassing per se is when this process extends to broader social causes or even global crises. Thus, care bypassing is another face of pathological altruism, a divided expression of other-focused care that causes harm to oneself and commonly others too. It's like the mirror image of compassion collapse, mentioned earlier, where one's compassionate concern for others diminishes as the number of sufferers increases—explaining why people may sometimes care less for major crises. In care bypassing, the pressure of caring on a mass scale instead intensifies self-sacrifice and undermines caring for the more immediate people and needs of one's life.

Care contagion should make us take the perils of care bypassing even more seriously, as we risk sacrificing what power we do have to make an impact for something that—while often vitally important in its own right—is less within our sphere of influence. There's an important paradox here. On one side, we need to be honest with ourselves about how much we can truly effect change on a more collective scale. Conversely, the implications of we-care and care contagion reveal that our everyday acts of care have a much bigger impact than we typically realize.

We-care offers a path to resolve this paradox. It's not one or the other, no matter how much the either/or mindset tells you differently. Through practicing we-care, it becomes easier to discern a realistic path for enacting radical care for many others—both locally and globally—while avoiding the traps of compassion collapse and care bypassing. Awake to the collective impact of all your care, you sidestep these and other extremes. And since you're more aware of a wider network of interconnected care surrounding you, you may also feel less alone in all your efforts to create a better world. This awareness further buffers you from divided approaches, allowing you to engage wholeheartedly in societal and global change efforts while tending to your personal wellbeing, your responsibilities, and those around you. Ideally, you discover synergies in your care at multiple levels—from self-care to community care to global care—enabling transformative actions and collective impacts that would otherwise remain out of reach.

Embracing Your Role in We-Care's Rise

Having reflected on care contagion, compassion collapse, and care bypassing, let's now revisit Amber's dilemma to see how we-care could support her in moving forward with her goal of helping the people of Sudan. After three sleepless nights, Amber realizes she is falling into a familiar pattern. Her empathy and collective care are overshadowing her own self-care and other responsibilities. Guided by we-care, she gives herself space to feel and reflect. Instead of relying on friends and family that had been unsympathetic, she reaches out to an old friend from college who she thinks could resonate with her mission. The phone call that follows helps Amber clarify her role in relation to the crisis, set realistic expectations, and emphasize the importance of self-care. After a few restorative days, she returns to her goal of finding an effective way to help. She contacts organizations within her city that are already supporting refugees, making connections and ultimately identifying a personally resonant, yet clearly needed, path to support Sudanese refugees. Weeks later, she updates her supportive friend who, entirely unprompted, sends a donation for this new initiative. Encouraged by this, Amber revisits the topic with other friends and family, light-heartedly acknowledging her initial intensity and sharing her newfound clarity. Moved by her wise compassion, many others decide to contribute, eventually sparking even more donations from her extended network.

The science of care contagion and its implications add layers of meaning to your personal practice of we-care. It shows that every act of care, when approached as we-care, has the power to ripple through our communities, impacting far more people than we directly connect with. In recognizing this, you are invited to embrace an even greater path of purpose for your care, one in which your own personal healing and transformation co-arises with that of others and the wider world. This collective journey embeds a deeply felt connection into all acts of care, imbuing them with a sense of shared destiny that goes beyond the visible impacts of your actions, akin to nurturing a shared garden whose full bloom you can feel but may never see.

I suspect most readers of this book already practice and advocate for kindness, self-care, and compassion. But whether through learning about the emerging science on interconnected care or savoring the direct experience of your undivided heart, you can come to appreciate how we-care unites diverse concepts about caring. Practicing and advocating for we-care can uplift the distinct value of both self-care and other-care—alongside their interconnectedness and potential synergies—thereby fostering a world of more conscious and effective care. This spread of we-care need not always be by name, because your acts of we-care alone can also transmit its view, form, and benefits to many others. This turns your journey of transforming inner division into one that synchronously contributes to the healing and transformation of outer division.

Self-care rose to mainstream popularity. We-care includes and transcends self-care—offering a more natural, complete, and beneficial way to care for both yourself and others. With your help, we-care can rise.

We-Care Practice 10
BEAMING WE-CARE

> In this final we-care practice of Beaming We-Care, I invite you to recognize and appreciate the full impact of your we-care on many other people, known and unknown.

The practice builds from and integrates a number of earlier practices, especially Undivided Heart Breathing (chapter 3) and Compassion Compass (chapter 4). Additionally, it draws on key ideas from throughout this chapter about care contagion and the estimated size of your broader social network. Once you become familiar with what it's like to beam we-care through the form of this practice, you can take this experience with you wherever you go, adapting it to radiate your heartfelt wishes to anyone present.

PRACTICE INSTRUCTIONS

1. *Get comfortable.* You can engage in this practice while sitting, lying down, standing, or even walking. Whatever you choose, it's best to strike a balance between feeling relaxed and wakeful.

2. *Breathe in self-care, breathe out other-care.* Breathe in and out mindfully, gathering your awareness around your heart. On each inbreath, breathe in care for your inner self. On the outbreath, imagine your care radiating out to others in all directions. Continue in this way for a short while, synchronizing feelings of self-care and care for others with the inbreath and outbreath, respectively.

3. *Practice Undivided Heart Breathing.* Drop the focus on self-care or other-care, resting instead in a feeling of undivided care within and around your heart. You might experience this as a unified feeling of warmth and affection or visualize it as a field of light or energy. To deepen and strengthen this felt sense of unification, you can explore placing both of your hands over your heart.

4. *Visualize your broader social network.* Imagine three concentric circles of people surrounding you, representing your first-, second-, and third-degree connections. The first circle consists of your closest connections, the second is made up of their close connections, and finally the third circle of individuals— the largest group—represents your third-degree connections. If you calculated your network size earlier in this chapter, you may be able to imagine this network with some specificity. However, there's no need to see everyone or have a precise count of individuals. Perhaps you discern a specific face here and there, helping to ground and deepen your sense of care. But if you're finding it difficult to imagine this or prefer not to, you can also simply feel or otherwise sense the presence of these connections.

5. *Beam we-care.* Return your focus to breathing and attuning to a felt sense of undivided care. From this centered place, feel your heart beaming kind wishes and supportive intentions for yourself, everyone in your network, and those beyond so that all may experience the benefits of we-care. If you find it helpful, you can silently repeat an inner wish as you practice, such as *May we all experience heartfelt care and well-being.* Optionally, you can reintegrate the feeling of self-care on the inbreath and other-care on the outbreath to emphasize your we-care. You might also imagine the spread of we-care as light flowing from your heart in widening circles, benefiting each layer in turn before rippling back to support you too. Continue beaming we-care for as long as you'd like.

Notes

INTRODUCTION

1. C. Daniel Batson et al., "Is Empathic Emotion a Source of Altruistic Motivation?" *Journal of Personality and Social Psychology* 40, no. 2 (1981): 290–302.
2. C. Daniel Batson, David A. Lishner, and Eric L. Stocks, "The Empathy-Altruism Hypothesis," in *The Oxford Handbook of Prosocial Behavior*, ed. D. A. Schroeder and W. G. Graziano (Oxford: Oxford University Press, 2014).
3. Samuel G. B. Johnson, Jiewen Zhang, and Frank C. Keil, "Win–Win Denial: The Psychological Underpinnings of Zero-Sum Thinking," *Journal of Experimental Psychology: General* 151, no. 2 (2022): 455.

CHAPTER 1. THE SUPERHERO AND THE HURT

1. Amit Kumar and Nicholas Epley, "Undersociality Is Unwise," *Journal of Consumer Psychology* 33, no. 1 (2023): 199–212.
2. Jeffrey D. Green, Jeni L. Burnette, and Jody L. Davis, "Third-Party Forgiveness: (Not) Forgiving Your Close Other's Betrayer," *Personality and Social Psychology Bulletin* 34, no. 3 (2008): 407–18.
3. Andrew L. Thomson and Jason T. Siegel, "Elevation: A Review of Scholarship on a Moral and Other-Praising Emotion," *The Journal of Positive Psychology* 12, no. 6 (2017): 628–38.
4. Elaine Hatfield, John T. Cacioppo, and Richard L. Rapson, "Emotional Contagion," *Current Directions in Psychological Science* 2, no. 3 (1993): 96–100.
5. Andreas Olsson, Katherine I. Nearing, and Elizabeth A. Phelps, "Learning Fears by Observing Others: The Neural Systems of Social Fear Transmission," *Social Cognitive and Affective Neuroscience* 2, no. 1 (2007): 3–11.

6. Yi-Ren Wang et al., "A Meta-Analysis on the Crossover of Workplace Traumatic Stress Symptoms between Partners," *Journal of Applied Psychology* 108, no. 7 (2023): 1157–89.

7. Razia S. Sahi et al., "You Changed My Mind: Immediate and Enduring Impacts of Social Emotion Regulation," *Emotion* (2023). Advance online publication.

8. Nicholas A. Christakis and James H. Fowler, "Social Contagion Theory: Examining Dynamic Social Networks and Human Behavior," *Statistics in Medicine* 32, no. 4 (2013): 556–77.

9. C. Nathan DeWall, Richard S. Pond, Jr., and Timothy Deckman, "Acetaminophen Dulls Psychological Pain," in *Social Pain: Neuropsychological and Health Implications of Loss and Exclusion*, ed. G. MacDonald and L. A. Jensen-Campbell (Washington, DC: American Psychological Association, 2011), 123–40; G. M. Slavich et al., "Alleviating Social Pain: A Double-Blind, Randomized, Placebo-Controlled Trial of Forgiveness and Acetaminophen," *Annals of Behavioral Medicine* 53, no. 12 (2019): 1045–54.

10. Chong Shao et al., "Increased Interpersonal Brain Synchronization in Romantic Couples Is Associated with Higher Honesty: An fNIRS Hyperscanning Study," *Brain Sciences* 13, no. 5 (2023): 833; Q. Liu et al., "Inter-Brain Neural Mechanism and Influencing Factors Underlying Different Cooperative Behaviors: A Hyperscanning Study," *Brain Structure and Function* 229, no. 1 (2023): 1–21.

11. Linoy Schwartz et al., "Generation WhatsApp: Inter-Brain Synchrony during Face-to-Face and Texting Communication," *Scientific Reports* 14, no. 1 (2024): 2672.

12. Jeff Truesdell, "'Hero' Ind. Man Who Saved 5 Kids from Burning House: 'I Knew What I Was Risking . . . But Every Second Counted,'" *People*, July 20, 2022, https://people.com/human-interest/nick-bostic-speaks-out-after-rescuing-5-kids-from-burning-house/.

13. Abigail A. Marsh et al., "Neural and Cognitive Characteristics of Extraordinary Altruists," *Proceedings of the National Academy of Sciences* 111, no. 42 (2014): 15036–41.

14. Lynn E. O'Connor et al., "Empathy-Based Pathogenic Guilt, Pathological Altruism, and Psychopathology," in *Pathological Altruism*, ed. B. Oakley et al. (Oxford: Oxford University Press, 2012).

15. C. Daniel Batson, "These Things Called Empathy," in *The Social Neuroscience of Empathy*, ed. J. Decety and W. Ickes (Cambridge, MA: MIT Press, 2009).

16. Simón Guendelman et al., "Regulating Negative Emotions of Others Reduces Own Stress: Neurobiological Correlates and the Role of Individual Differences in Empathy," *Neuroimage* 254, no. 119134 (2022).

17. Siyang Luo et al., "Brain Structural and Functional Substrates of Personal Distress in Empathy," *Frontiers in Behavioral Neuroscience* 12, no. 99 (2018).

18. Tania Singer and Olga M. Klimecki, "Empathy and Compassion," *Current Biology* 24, no. 18 (2014): R875–78.

19. Jo-Ann Tsang and Stephen R. Martin, "Four Experiments on the Relational Dynamics and Prosocial Consequences of Gratitude," *The Journal of Positive Psychology* 14, no. 2 (2019): 188–205; S. B. Algoe and B. M. Way, "Evidence for a Role of the Oxytocin System, Indexed by Genetic Variation in CD38, in the Social Bonding Effects of Expressed Gratitude," *Social Cognitive and Affective Neuroscience* 9, no. 12 (2014): 1855–61.

20. Daisuke Hori et al., "Prefrontal Activation while Listening to a Letter of Gratitude Read Aloud by a Coworker Face-to-Face: A NIRS Study," *Plos One* 15, no. 9 (2020): e0238715; Glen R. Fox et al., "Neural Correlates of Gratitude," *Frontiers in Psychology* 1491 (2015); Jet U. Buenconsejo, Frank D. Fincham, and Jesus Alfonso D. Datu, "The Perks of Being Grateful to Partners: Expressing Gratitude in Relationships Predicts Relational Self-Efficacy and Life Satisfaction during the COVID-19 Pandemic," *Applied Psychology: Health and Well-Being* 15, no. 4 (2023).

CHAPTER 2. HALF-HEARTED

1. Robert Axelrod and W. D. Hamilton, "The Evolution of Cooperation," *Science* 211, no. 4489 (1981): 1390–96.

2. Some readers may find it useful to reimagine that they were the sole player in the tournament who planned to donate the $5,000 prize. Thus, even if the prize was not personally motivating, one might still want to win—in this case, to benefit others.

3. Ej Dickson, X, April 7, 2023, https://x.com/ejdickson/status/164439853 0339979264?s=20.

4. Audre Lorde, *A Burst of Light* (Ithaca, NY: Firebrand Books, 1988).

5. "Pawnee Rangers," *Parks and Recreation*, 2011, as quoted on IMDb, https://www.imdb.com/title/tt2041051/characters/nm2106637.

6. Ryan W. Carlson et al., "Psychological Selfishness," *Perspectives on Psychological Science* 17, no. 5 (2022): 1359–80.

7. Barbara Oakley et al., ed., *Pathological Altruism* (Oxford: Oxford University Press, 2011).

8. Chunliang Feng, Yue-Jia Luo, and Frank Krueger, "Neural Signatures of Fairness-Related Normative Decision Making in the Ultimatum Game: A Coordinate-Based Meta-Analysis," *Human Brain Mapping* 36, no. 2 (2015): 591–602; Alexander Soutschek, Marian Sauter, and

Torsten Schubert, "The Importance of the Lateral Prefrontal Cortex for Strategic Decision Making in the Prisoner's Dilemma," *Cognitive, Affective, & Behavioral Neuroscience* 15 (2015): 854–60; James K. Rilling and Alan G. Sanfey, "The Neuroscience of Social Decision-Making," *Annual Review of Psychology* 62 (2011): 23–48.

9. Shotaro Numano, Chris Frith, and Masahiko Haruno, "Selfish Behavior Requires Top-Down Control of Prosocial Motivation," bioRxiv, 2024, https://doi.org/10.1101/2024.01.04.574159.

10. Mirre Stallen and Alan G. Sanfey, "The Cooperative Brain," *Neuroscientist* 19, no. 3 (2013): 292–303.

11. Shai Davidai and Stephanie J. Tepper, "The Psychology of Zero-Sum Beliefs," *Nature Reviews Psychology* (2023), advance online publication; M. Fisher and F. C. Keil, "The Binary Bias: A Systematic Distortion in the Integration of Information," *Psychological Science* 29, no. 11 (2018): 1846–58.

12. Carlson et al., "Psychological Selfishness," 1359–80.

13. Scott Barry Kaufman and Emanuel Jauk, "Healthy Selfishness and Pathological Altruism: Measuring Two Paradoxical Forms of Selfishness," *Frontiers in Psychology* 11 (2020): 1006.

14. Lynn E. O'Connor et al., "Empathy-Based Pathogenic Guilt, Pathological Altruism, and Psychopathology," in *Pathological Altruism*, ed. B. Oakley et al. (Oxford: Oxford University Press, 2012).

15. Lucius Annaeus Seneca and James S. Romm, trans., *How to Keep Your Cool: An Ancient Guide to Anger Management* (Princeton, NJ: Princeton University Press, 2019).

16. Kaufman and Jauk, "Healthy Selfishness," 1006.

CHAPTER 3. AN UNDIVIDED HEART

1. Thich Nhat Hanh, "The Insight of Interbeing," Garrison Institute, August 2, 2017, www.garrisoninstitute.org/insight-of-interbeing/.

2. Thich Nhat Hanh, "Insight of Interbeing."

3. Edward N. Lorenz, "Predictability: Does the Flap of a Butterfly's Wings in Brazil Set Off a Tornado in Texas?" (lecture, American Association for the Advancement of Science, 139th meeting, December 1972).

4. Richard A. Geist, "Connectedness, Permeable Boundaries, and the Development of the Self: Therapeutic Implications," *International Journal of Psychoanalytic Self Psychology* 3, no. 2 (2008): 129–52.

5. Matthew Fisher and Frank C. Keil, "The Binary Bias: A Systematic Distortion in the Integration of Information," *Psychological Science* 29, no. 11 (2018): 1846–58.

6. Jamil Zaki and Kevin Ochsner, "You, Me, and My Brain: Self and Other Representations in Social Cognitive Neuroscience," *Social Neuroscience: Toward Understanding the Underpinnings of the Social Mind* 26 (2011): 48.

7. James A. Coan, Hillary S. Schaefer, and Richard J. Davidson, "Lending a Hand: Social Regulation of the Neural Response to Threat," *Psychological Science* 17, no. 12 (2006): 1032–39.

8. Lane Beckes and James A. Coan, "Social Baseline Theory: The Role of Social Proximity in Emotion and Economy of Action," *Social and Personality Psychology Compass* 5, no. 12 (2011): 976–88.

9. Jared R. Curhan et al., "Silence Is Golden: Extended Silence, Deliberative Mindset, and Value Creation in Negotiation," *Journal of Applied Psychology* 107, no. 1 (2022): 78.

10. Paul Gilbert et al., "Fears of Compassion: Development of Three Self-Report Measures," *Psychology and Psychotherapy: Theory, Research and Practice* 84, no. 3 (2011): 239–55.

11. Thich Nhat Hanh, *How to Fight* (Berkeley: Parallax Press, 2017), 73.

CHAPTER 4. THE EMPATHY-COMPASSION GAP

1. Fyodor Dostoevsky, *Winter Notes on Summer Impressions*, trans. David Patterson (Evanston: Northwestern University Press, 1997).

2. D. M. Wegner et al., "Paradoxical Effects of Thought Suppression," *Journal of Personality and Social Psychology* 53, no. 1 (1987): 5–13.

3. Alexander R. Daros, Jeffrey D. Wardell, and Lena C. Quilty, "Multilevel Associations of Emotion Regulation Strategy Use during Psychotherapy for Depression: A Longitudinal Study," *Journal of Affective Disorders* (2023). Advance online publication.

4. Tori D. Wager et al., "A Bayesian Model of Category-Specific Emotional Brain Responses," *PLoS Computational Biology* 11, no. 4 (2015): e1004066.

5. Kristen A. Lindquist, "Emotions Emerge from More Basic Psychological Ingredients: A Modern Psychological Constructionist Model," *Emotion Review* 5, no. 4 (2013): 356–68; Lisa Feldman Barrett, *How Emotions Are Made: The Secret Life of the Brain* (New York: Houghton Mifflin Harcourt, 2017).

6. Jamil Zaki, "Empathy: A Motivated Account," *Psychological Bulletin* 140, no. 6 (2014): 1608–47.

7. Robert P. Spunt and Matthew D. Lieberman, "The Busy Social Brain: Evidence for Automaticity and Control in the Neural Systems Supporting Social Cognition and Action Understanding," *Psychological Science* 24, no. 1 (2013): 80–86.

8. Jordan T. Quaglia, "One Compassion, Many Means: A Big Two Analysis of Compassionate Behavior," *Mindfulness* 14, no. 10 (2023): 2430–42.

9. Olga M. Klimecki et al., "Differential Pattern of Functional Brain Plasticity after Compassion and Empathy Training," *Social Cognitive and Affective Neuroscience* 9, no. 6 (2014): 873–79.

10. Yair Dor-Ziderman et al., "Synchrony with Distress in Affective Empathy and Compassion," *Psychophysiology* 58, no. 10 (2021): e13889;

T. Singer and O. M. Klimecki, "Empathy and Compassion," *Current Biology* 24, no. 18 (2014): R875–78; David B. Yaden et al., "Characterizing Empathy and Compassion Using Computational Linguistic Analysis," *Emotion* (2023), advance online publication.

11. G. Chierchia and T. Singer, "The Neuroscience of Compassion and Empathy and Their Link to Prosocial Motivation and Behavior," in *Decision Neuroscience: An Integrative Perspective*, ed. Jean-Claude Dreher and Léon Tremblay (Cambridge, MA: Academic Press, 2017): 247–57.

12. Sara H. Konrath, Edward H. O'Brien, and Courtney Hsing, "Changes in Dispositional Empathy in American College Students over Time: A Meta-Analysis," *Personality and Social Psychology Review* 15, no. 2 (2011): 180–98.

13. Jeremy Hogeveen, Michael Inzlicht, and Sukhvinder S. Obhi, "Power Changes How the Brain Responds to Others," *Journal of Experimental Psychology: General* 143, no. 2 (2014): 755.

14. Greg J. Depow et al., "The Compassion Advantage: Leaders Who Care Outperform Leaders Who Share Followers' Emotions" (2023), retrieved from https://psyarxiv.com/md2g8.

15. Izzy Gainsburg and Julia Lee Cunningham, "Compassion Fatigue as a Self-Fulfilling Prophecy: Believing Compassion Is Limited Increases Fatigue and Decreases Compassion," *Psychological Science* 34, no. 11 (2023).

16. Olga Klimecki and Tania Singer, "Empathic Distress Fatigue Rather Than Compassion Fatigue? Integrating Findings from Empathy Research in Psychology and Social Neuroscience," *Pathological Altruism* 5 (2012): 368–83.

17. Maria Di Bello, Cristina Ottaviani, and Nicola Petrocchi, "Compassion Is Not a Benzo: Distinctive Associations of Heart Rate Variability with Its Empathic and Action Components," *Frontiers in Neuroscience* 15 (2021).

18. Marcus Aurelius, *Meditations* (London: Penguin, 2006).

19. Jack Levin, Arnold Arluke, and Leslie Irvine, "Are People More Disturbed by Dog or Human Suffering? Influence of Victim's Species and Age," *Society & Animals* 25, no. 1 (2017): 1–16.

20. Jack Kornfield, *Buddha's Little Instruction Book* (New York: Bantam, 2018).

21. G. Kolata, "When Doctors Use a Chatbot to Improve Their Bedside Manner," *New York Times*, June 12, 2023, www.nytimes.com/2023/06/12/health/doctors-chatgpt-artificial-intelligence.html.

CHAPTER 5. THE END OF DIVIDED CARE

1. Gabriel reviewed this story and agreed to have his name shared.

2. S. Katherine Nelson et al., "Do Unto Others or Treat Yourself? The Effects of Prosocial and Self-Focused Behavior on Psychological Flourishing," *Emotion* 16, no. 6 (2016): 850.

3. David R. Cregg and Jennifer S. Cheavens, "Healing through Helping: An Experimental Investigation of Kindness, Social Activities, and Reappraisal as Well-Being Interventions," *The Journal of Positive Psychology* 18, no. 6 (2023): 924–41.

4. Lara B. Aknin, Elizabeth W. Dunn, and Ashley V. Whillans, "The Emotional Rewards of Prosocial Spending Are Robust and Replicable in Large Samples," *Current Directions in Psychological Science* 31, no. 6 (2022): 536–45.

5. Dalai Lama XIV and Howard C. Cutler, *The Art of Happiness: A Handbook for Living* (New York: Riverhead Books, 2018).

6. Amit Kumar and Nicholas Epley, "A Little Good Goes an Unexpectedly Long Way: Underestimating the Positive Impact of Kindness on Recipients," *Journal of Experimental Psychology: General* 152, no. 1 (2023): 236.

7. James J. Clarke et al., "Emotional Labor and Emotional Exhaustion in Psychologists: Preliminary Evidence for the Protective Role of Self-Compassion and Psychological Flexibility," *Journal of Contextual Behavioral Science* 31 (2024).

8. "Caregiving for Family and Friends—A Public Health Issue," Centers for Disease Control and Prevention, 2020, www.cdc.gov/aging /caregiving/pdf/caregiver-brief-508.pdf.

9. Izzy Gainsburg and Julia Lee Cunningham, "Compassion Fatigue as a Self-Fulfilling Prophecy: Believing Compassion Is Limited Increases Fatigue and Decreases Compassion," *Psychological Science* 34, no. 11 (2023).

10. John Kounios and Mark Beeman, "The Cognitive Neuroscience of Insight," *Annual Review of Psychology* 65 (2014): 71–93.

11. Edward M. Bowden and Mark Jung-Beeman, "Aha! Insight Experience Correlates with Solution Activation in the Right Hemisphere," *Psychonomic Bulletin & Review* 10, no. 3 (2003): 730–37.

CHAPTER 6. FULL-SPECTRUM WE-CARE

1. James A. Banks, "Transforming the Mainstream Curriculum," *Educational Leadership* 51 (1994): 4–8.

2. Jeremy A. Frimer et al., "Hierarchical Integration of Agency and Communion: A Study of Influential Moral Figures," *Journal of Personality* 80, no. 4 (2012): 1117–45.

3. Vicki S. Helgeson and Heidi L. Fritz, "Unmitigated Agency and Unmitigated Communion: Distinctions from Agency and Communion," *Journal of Research in Personality* 33, no. 2 (1999): 131–58.

4. Frimer et al., "Hierarchical Integration," 1117–45.

5. Jordan T. Quaglia and Judith Simmer-Brown, "Compassion and Skillful Means: Diverse Views, Novel Insights, and Extended Applications for Compassion Science and Training," *Mindfulness* 14, no. 10 (2023): 2293–98.

6. Ashley E. Martin and Michael L. Slepian, "The Primacy of Gender: Gendered Cognition Underlies the Big Two Dimensions of Social Cognition," *Perspectives on Psychological Science* 16, no. 6 (2021): 1143–58.

7. Andrea E. Abele and Bogdan Wojciszke, "Communal and Agentic Content in Social Cognition: A Dual Perspective Model," in *Advances in Experimental Social Psychology*, ed. Mark P. Zanna and James M. Olson, vol. 50 (Cambridge, MA: Academic Press, 2014): 195–255.

8. Andrea E. Abele and Bogdan Wojciszke, "Agency and Communion from the Perspective of Self Versus Others," *Journal of Personality and Social Psychology* 93, no. 5 (2007): 751.

9. If needed or preferred, this practice can be readily adapted, such as through standing and shifting weight from one leg to another or through the closing and opening of each eye.

CHAPTER 7. CIRCLES OF CARE

1. Jack Kornfield, "Heart As Big As the Sky," May 22, 2024, in *Heart Wisdom*, produced by Be Here Now Network, podcast, https://jackkornfield.com/heart-wisdom-ep-239-heart-as-big-as-the-sky/.

2. Robert Waldinger and Marc Schulz, *The Good Life: Lessons from the World's Longest Study on Happiness* (New York: Penguin Random House, 2023).

3. "Cigna's U.S. Loneliness Index: Survey of 20,000 Americans Examining Behaviors Driving Loneliness in the United States," Cigna, 2018, www.multivu.com/players/English/8294451-cigna-us-loneliness-survey/.

4. Julianne Holt-Lunstad et al., "Loneliness and Social Isolation as Risk Factors for Mortality: A Meta-Analytic Review," *Perspectives on Psychological Science* 10, no. 2 (2015): 227–37.

5. Jeffrey A. Lam et al., "Neurobiology of Loneliness: A Systematic Review," *Neuropsychopharmacology* 46, no. 11 (2021): 1873–87; R. Nathan Spreng et al., "The Default Network of the Human Brain Is Associated with Perceived Social Isolation," *Nature Communications* 11, no. 1 (2020): 6393.

6. Stephanie Cacioppo et al., "Loneliness: Clinical Import and Interventions," *Perspectives on Psychological Science* 10, no. 2 (2015): 238–49; Tim Adams, "John Cacioppo: 'Loneliness Is like an Iceberg—It Goes Deeper Than We Can See,'" *Guardian*, 2016,

www.theguardian.com/science/2016/feb/28/loneliness-is-like-an
-iceberg-john-cacioppo-social-neuroscience-interview.

7. "Cigna's U.S. Loneliness Index."

8. Francisca Catarino et al., "Compassion Motivations: Distinguishing
Submissive Compassion from Genuine Compassion and Its Association with Shame, Submissive Behavior, Depression, Anxiety,
and Stress," *Journal of Social and Clinical Psychology* 33, no. 5 (2014):
399–412.

9. Nisha Hickin et al., "The Effectiveness of Psychological Interventions
for Loneliness: A Systematic Review and Meta-Analysis," *Clinical
Psychology Review* 88 (2021).

10. Tim Adams, "John Cacioppo: 'Loneliness Is like an Iceberg—It Goes
Deeper Than We Can See,'" *Guardian*, 2016, www.theguardian.com
/science/2016/feb/28/loneliness-is-like-an-iceberg-john-cacioppo
-social-neuroscience-interview.

11. Martin A. Nowak and Karl Sigmund, "Tit for Tat in Heterogeneous
Populations," *Nature* 355 (1992): 250–53.

12. YeJin Park and Nadav Klein, "Ghosting: Social Rejection without Explanation, but Not without Care," *Journal of Experimental Psychology:
General* (2024).

13. Lara B. Aknin and Gillian M. Sandstrom, "People Are Surprisingly
Hesitant to Reach Out to Old Friends," *Communications Psychology* 2,
no. 34 (2024).

14. Paul Gilbert et al., "Fears of Compassion: Development of Three Self-
Report Measures," *Psychology and Psychotherapy: Theory, Research
and Practice* 84, no. 3 (2011): 239–55.

15. Jamil Zaki and W. Craig Williams, "Interpersonal Emotion Regulation," *Emotion* 13, no. 5 (2013): 803.

16. Barbara L. Fredrickson et al., "Open Hearts Build Lives: Positive
Emotions, Induced through Loving-Kindness Meditation, Build
Consequential Personal Resources," *Journal of Personality and Social
Psychology* 95, no. 5 (2008): 1045.

17. Collie W. Conoley et al., "Celebrating the Accomplishments of Others:
Mutual Benefits of Capitalization," *The Counseling Psychologist* 43, no.
5 (2015): 734–51.

18. Jordan T. Quaglia et al., "Dualism and Beyond: A Unified Framework
for Self- and Other-Oriented Compassion (unpublished manuscript
2024).

19. Gillian M. Sandstrom, Erica J. Boothby, and Gus Cooney, "Talking to
Strangers: A Week-Long Intervention Reduces Psychological Barriers
to Social Connection," *Journal of Experimental Social Psychology* 102
(2022).

20. Paul A. M. Van Lange and Simon Columbus, "Vitamin S: Why Is Social Contact, Even with Strangers, So Important to Well-Being?" *Current Directions in Psychological Science* 30, no. 3 (2021): 267–73.

21. Amit Kumar and Nicholas Epley, "Undersociality Is Unwise," *Journal of Consumer Psychology* 33, no. 1 (2023): 199–212.

CHAPTER 8. CARE-BASED BOUNDARIES

1. Paulo Coelho (@paulocoelho), "When you say 'yes' to others, make sure you are not saying 'no' to yourself," X, March 5, 2014, https://x.com/paulocoelho/status/441268849871454208?lang=en.

2. Hanna Saab, "What We Do in the Shadows: The 15 Funniest Colin Robinson Quotes," Screen Rant, updated August 3, 2022, https://screenrant.com/what-we-do-in-the-shadows-best-funniest-colin-robinson-lines/.

3. Dan Go, X, February 19, 2023, https://x.com/FitFounder/status/1627343805618823168.

4. Christiane Northrup, *Dodging Energy Vampires: An Empath's Guide to Evading Relationships That Drain You and Restoring Your Health and Power* (Carlsbad, CA: Hay House, 2018), 2.

5. Cade McCall et al., "Compassion Meditators Show Less Anger, Less Punishment, and More Compensation of Victims in Response to Fairness Violations," *Frontiers in Behavioral Neuroscience* 8 (2014): 424.

6. McCall et al., "Compassion Meditators," 424.

7. Delroy Paulhus, "Toward a Taxonomy of Dark Personalities," *Current Directions in Psychological Science* 23, no. 6 (2014): 421–26; Sander Thomaes et al., "The Dark Personality and Psychopathology: Toward a Brighter Future," *Journal of Abnormal Psychology* 126, no. 7 (2017): 835.

8. Peter K. Jonason et al., "Seeing the World in Black or White: The Dark Triad Traits and Dichotomous Thinking," *Personality and Individual Differences* 120 (2018): 102–6.

9. Peter K. Jonason, Bryan Koenig, and Jeremy Tost, "Living a Fast Life: The Dark Triad and Life History Theory," *Human Nature* 21 (2010): 428–42; Laura C. Crysel, Benjamin S. Crosier, and Gregory D. Webster, "The Dark Triad and Risk Behavior," *Personality and Individual Differences* 54, no. 1 (2013): 35–40.

10. Claudia Sassenrath et al., "I Like It Because It Hurts You: On the Association of Everyday Sadism, Sadistic Pleasure, and Victim Blaming," *Journal of Personality and Social Psychology* 126, no. 1 (2023): 105–27.

11. Abigail A. Marsh, "The Caring Continuum: Evolved Hormonal and Proximal Mechanisms Explain Prosocial and Antisocial Extremes," *Annual Review of Psychology* 70 (2019): 347–71.

12. Daniel Goleman, *Social Intelligence* (New York: Random House, 2007).

13. Kelci C. Davis, Nicholas Kavish, and Jaime L. Anderson, "The Personal Cost of Psychopathy: Impacts of Triarchic Psychopathy Traits on Impairment, Internalizing, and Life Satisfaction," *Personality and Individual Differences* 219 (2024): 1–8.

14. Frances Klein, "Therapy speak in this day and age is really wild, because why did this woman just tell me she's 'asserting her needs and holding a boundary' when I told her she's in my assigned seat on the plane?" X, January 15, 2024, https://x.com/fklein907/status/17470384 27525333353.

15. Jordan T. Quaglia, Clarissa Cigrand, and Hannah Sallmann, "Caring for You, Me, and Us: The Lived Experience of Compassion in Counselors," *Psychotherapy* 59, no. 3 (2022): 321; J. T. Quaglia, "One Compassion, Many Means: A Big Two Analysis of Compassionate Behavior," *Mindfulness* 14, no. 10 (2023): 2430–42.

16. Adam Grant, X, March 7, 2024, https://x.com/AdamMGrant/status/17 65757469840572761.

17. Deborah Tannen, "The Power of Talk: Who Gets Heard and Why," *Harvard Business Review* 73 (1995): 138–48.

18. Madeline Holcombe, "How Being a 'Gray Rock' Can Protect You against Narcissists," Mindfulness, updated August 7, 2023, www.cnn .com/2023/08/04/health/gray-rocking-narcissism-wellness/index.html.

CHAPTER 9. PERSONAL MEETS GLOBAL

1. Pema Chödrön, *Practicing Peace in Times of War* (Boulder: Shambhala Publications, 2007), 15.

2. Jay Van Bavel, X, April 10, 2024, https://x.com/jayvanbavel/status/1778 131449176117563.

3. John T. Cacioppo, James H. Fowler, and Nicholas A. Christakis, "Alone in the Crowd: The Structure and Spread of Loneliness in a Large Social Network," *Journal of Personality and Social Psychology* 97, no. 6 (2009): 977.

4. Gordon Heltzel and Kristin Laurin, "Why Twitter Sometimes Rewards What Most People Disapprove of: The Case of Cross-Party Political Relations," PsyArXiv Preprints, 2024, https://osf.io/f3p4s/.

5. John-Robert Rimel, "Good Days'll Come" Spotify, track 4 on John-Robert, *Garden Snake*, Nice Life Recording Company, 2023.

6. Lauren Razavi, "Movement to Pay It Forward with a Cup of Coffee Spills into U.S.," NPR, December 17, 2015, www.npr.org/sections /thesalt/2015/12/17/460001377/movement-to-pay-it-forward-with-a -cup-of-coffee-spills-into-u-s.

7. Jamil Zaki, "Empathy: A Motivated Account," *Psychological Bulletin* 140, no. 6 (2014): 1608.

8. C. Daryl Cameron, "Compassion Collapse: Why We Are Numb to Numbers," in *The Oxford Handbook of Compassion Science*, ed. Emma Seppala et al. (Oxford: Oxford University Press, 2017).

9. Alexander J. Bisberg et al., "The Gift That Keeps on Giving: Generosity Is Contagious in Multiplayer Online Games," *Proceedings of the ACM on Human-Computer Interaction* 6, no. CSCW2 (2022): 1–22.

10. James H. Fowler and Nicholas A. Christakis, "Cooperative Behavior Cascades in Human Social Networks," *Proceedings of the National Academy of Sciences* 107, no. 12 (2010): 5334–38; Joris M. Schröder et al., "The Social Contagion of Prosocial Behaviour: How Neighbourhood Blood Donations Influence Individual Donation Behaviour," *Health & Place* 83 (2023); H. Jung et al., "Prosocial Modeling: A Meta-Analytic Review and Synthesis," *Psychological Bulletin* 146, no. 8 (2020): 635.

11. Martin A. Nowak and Sébastien Roch, "Upstream Reciprocity and the Evolution of Gratitude," *Proceedings of the Royal Society: Biological Sciences* 274, no. 1610 (2007): 605–10.

12. Jonathan Haidt, "The Positive Emotion of Elevation," *Prevention & Treatment* 3 no. 1 (2000).

13. "NYPD Officer's Act of Kindness Goes Viral on Facebook and Reddit," ABC News, November, 29, 2012, https://abcnews.go.com/US/nypd-officers-act-kindness-viral-facebook-reddit/story?id=17838519.

14. Sinan Aral and Christos Nicolaides, "Exercise Contagion in a Global Social Network," *Nature Communications* 8, no. 1 (2017).

15. Nicholas A. Christakis and James H. Fowler, "The Spread of Obesity in a Large Social Network over 32 Years," *New England Journal of Medicine* 357, no. 4 (2007): 370–79; James H. Fowler and Nicholas A. Christakis, "Dynamic Spread of Happiness in a Large Social Network: Longitudinal Analysis over 20 Years in the Framingham Heart Study," *British Medical Journal* 338 (2009): 1–13.

16. Yutaka Horita et al., "Transient Nature of Cooperation by Pay-It-Forward Reciprocity," *Scientific Reports* 6, no. 1 (2016); Adam Maxwell Sparks, Daniel M. T. Fessler, and Colin Holbrook, "Elevation, an Emotion for Prosocial Contagion, Is Experienced More Strongly by Those with Greater Expectations of the Cooperativeness of Others," *PloS One* 14, no. 12 (2019).

17. Cacioppo, Fowler, and Christakis, "Alone in the Crowd," 977; Fowler and Christakis, "Dynamic Spread of Happiness," 1–13.

18. Tim Adams, "John Cacioppo: 'Loneliness Is like an Iceberg—It Goes Deeper Than We Can See,'" *Guardian*, 2016, www.theguardian.com/science/2016/feb/28/loneliness-is-like-an-iceberg-john-cacioppo-social-neuroscience-interview.

19. Fowler and Christakis, "Dynamic Spread of Happiness," 1–13; Nicholas A. Christakis and James H. Fowler, *Connected: The Surprising Power of*

Our Social Networks and How They Shape Our Lives (New York: Little, Brown Spark, 2009).

20. This simple method does not account for the likely overlap in connections between people in the network. To do so, simply adjust your second- and third-degree estimates by a certain percentage you think could reflect this overlap (e.g., to account for a 20 percent overlap, use the average of 12 instead of 15).

Index